The Social Politics of FEPC

The Social Politics of FEPC

A STUDY IN REFORM PRESSURE

MOVEMENTS *by* Louis Coleridge Kesselman

THE UNIVERSITY OF NORTH CAROLINA PRESS

1948
CHAPEL HILL

To Jenny

Preface

THE CENTRAL PROBLEM OF THE AMERICAN POLIT-
ical system has always been the same: how to implement popular
control over the making of public policy. Our history can be
interpreted as a struggle to make the theory of democratic government a reality. Significant victories have been won with the broadening of the suffrage and the development of the political party as an
instrument for popular control of government. Yet, as time passes, it
becomes more and more apparent that we are still far from having
attained a system in which the will of the people is translated quickly
and accurately into government policy.

Our tradition of a two party system has the great merit of assuring
majority control of government. On the other hand, in their eagerness
to win as many adherents as circumstances will permit, the large
amorphous parties follow broad general programs, rarely giving precise representation to their supporters. Increasingly this broad type
of representation has become out of joint with our infinitely complex
modern social order made up of many special groups having distinc-
tive interests which they desire to have safeguarded and advanced
by government.

It is this situation which has given rise to the vast number of pressure groups operating on all levels of our political life. Indeed, we
have reached the point where some observers despair for the unity and
survival of our system under the impact of the demands of powerful
pressure groups, each seeking selfish objectives not always compatible
with the public interest. Through both scholarly studies and muck-
raking journalism we have become familiar with the organizations and
operations of many of the major economic interest groups. These
analyses have thrown some rays of light on how public policy comes
into being.

This study, however, does not deal with one of the giant pressure
groups upon whose decisions the fate of parties and policies rests.

• vii •

Rather, it seeks to examine one of the many humanitarian movements which have sought to influence public policy toward the amelioration of conditions regarded by them as being contrary to Christian and democratic doctrine. These reform movements have been exceedingly valuable to our political system for their refreshing idealism and for the constructive criticisms which they have directed against inequities in this country.

The fact remains that with the exception of a notable few, such as the Anti-Saloon League, the great majority of reform movements find that challenging the existing order of affairs is an undertaking calling for more resources than they can muster. Hundreds, if not thousands, of well-intentioned pressure groups have been formed, have played their brief role, and have quietly disbanded without having achieved their objectives. No one can properly assert that their energies have been wasted for social change is often the result of the accumulation of pressures from a wide variety of forces over a considerable period of time. Even so, it would be of value to have more precise information on why so many reform groups fall short of their objectives in order that better use of their energies might be made to bring about desired changes in our system. The purpose of this study is to analyze one such as yet unsuccessful movement to indicate both its strengths and its weaknesses.

The movement for a permanent national Fair Employment Practice Commission to deal with discriminatory practices in employment is a rewarding subject for study. Its sudden origin, its spectacular role on the congressional scene, its methods of operation, and its objectives make it one of the important reform pressure movements of recent years. Students of interracial relations, social action, the labor movement, civil libertarian activities, and of many other important phases of our community life will find the FEPC movement worth serious consideration because it cuts across all of these areas. While this is primarily a study of the National Council for a Permanent FEPC which spearheaded the movement, appropriate attention has been directed to many other groups and individuals who sought to persuade Congress to enact permanent FEPC legislation.

To assist the reader in following the analysis a brief chronology of the legislative progress of the movement would be helpful at the outset. On June 25, 1941, President Roosevelt issued Executive Order No. 8802, declaring discrimination in defense industries to be a violation of public policy and establishing a five-man Committee on Fair Employment Practice to "receive and investigate complaints of discrimination" and to take "appropriate steps to redress valid grievances."[1] Failure of the Committee to deal adequately with problems of wartime discrimination in employment led to two related movements by proponents of fair treatment for minority groups. The first was the attempt to strengthen the temporary President's Committee which succeeded in obtaining Executive Order No. 9346, extending and fortifying the Committee's jurisdiction and enforcement powers.[2] The second, with which this study is chiefly concerned, was the movement to make the Committee a permanent statutory administrative agency with authority to issue orders enforceable in the courts.

On the congressional scene at least one FEPC bill was introduced in the House in 1942.[3] A concerted drive for enactment of permanent FEPC legislation got underway with the establishment of the National Council for a Permanent FEPC in the latter part of 1943. Under its aegis three identical bills were introduced in the House on January 17 and 18, 1944, proposing a Fair Employment Practice Commission patterned after the National Labor Relations Board.[4] These bills were referred to the House Labor Committee from which the Scanlon bill was finally reported favorably on December 4, 1944, but the Rules Committee failed to report it out. An attempt to bring the bill to the House floor by a discharge petition failed to secure sufficient signatures before the end of the 78th Congress. In the Senate an FEPC bill introduced by Senator Dennis Chavez (Dem. N.M.), on behalf of himself and five other senators, suffered a similar fate.[5] The bill was reported out by the Committee on Education and Labor on September

---

1. *Federal Register* Doc. 41-4544, 6 *Fed. Reg.* (Part 4) 3109 (1941). The Committee was enlarged to six members by Executive Order 8823 on July 18, 1941, and to seven members by Order 9111 on March 25, 1942.
2. *Federal Register* Doc. 43-8651, 8 *Fed. Reg.* (Part 5) 7183 (1943), amended by Executive Order 9446 on December 20, 1945.
3. H.R. 7412, 77th Congress, 2d Session (1942), introduced by Rep. Vito Marcantonio (A.L.P.—N.Y.).
4. H.R. 3986 by Rep. Thomas E. Scanlon (Dem. Pa.); H.R. 4004 by Rep. William L. Dawson (Dem. Ill.); and H.R. 4005 by Rep. Charles M. LaFollette (Rep. Ind.).
5. S. 2048. The Chavez Bill was identical with the Scanlon Bill in the House.

20, 1944, but its sponsors were unsuccessful in their efforts to bring the bill to the floor in the dying days of the 78th Congress.

Within a month following the opening of the first session of the 79th Congress on January 3, 1945, thirteen FEPC bills were introduced in the House and one, Senate Bill No. 101, in the upper chamber under the sponsorship of six senators representing both major parties.[6] On February 20 the House Labor Committee reported H.R. 2232, a committee bill. From this date, until the end of the Congress some twenty-two months later, FEPC supporters in the House battled vainly to secure a rule from the Rules Committee to permit the bill to come to the floor for debate and a vote. Discharge Petition No. 4, inaugurated to discharge the bill from the Rules Committee, obtained fewer than 190 of the requisite 218 signatures. Last ditch efforts to secure passage of the bill in the House through use of the Calendar Wednesday rule also proved unsuccessful.[7]

The Senate bill suffered a similar fate. Reported out favorably by the Senate Committee on Education and Labor on May 24, 1945, by a vote of 12 to 6, the bill was not brought to the floor in 1945. When the second session of the 79th Congress opened, a sudden move by Senator Chavez and other FEPC supporters to obtain Senate consideration of S. 101 touched off a twenty-three day filibuster led by southern Democrats which was finally terminated by an agreement to vote on a cloture petition to limit debate. The vote on cloture was defeated by a vote of 48 to 36, 8 fewer than the requisite two-thirds. The bill was restored to the calendar where it died with the 79th Congress.

This study is not concerned, except incidentally, with the highly involved parliamentary situations faced by FEPC legislation in the period under consideration. It is the writer's belief that, in order to

---

6. See House Committee on Labor, Report 187, 79th Congress, 1st Session (1945), for an account of the House bills.

7. According to House Rule XXIV, 7, adopted in 1909, Wednesdays are set aside for the consideration of committee reports otherwise requiring a rule from the Rules Committee. Committees are called up in a specified order; if one brings up a bill at this time, debate and final vote must be completed on the same day or the bill returns to the committee. It is difficult to employ this rule successfully in securing passage of a controversial bill because of the time element. In recent years use of the rule has declined because of the desire of House leadership to use the day for what it considers to be more pressing legislation.

determine the basic reasons for the movement's failure at the time of writing, attention should be centered largely upon the forces which sought to persuade Congress to enact the desired legislation, rather than upon parliamentary maneuvers.

For purposes of analysis this study has been divided into three parts. The first four chapters will examine the general problem of discrimination in employment, early efforts to deal with the problem, and the objectives, organization, leadership, and finances of the National Council for a Permanent FEPC. Part II deals with the factor of social cohesion: probing the infinite difficulties involved in bringing together greatly diverse minorities, race relations, civil libertarian, church, labor, and women's organizations for the purpose of exerting maximum pressure upon Congress. This section will also deal with problems of an ideological character and, to some extent, with the opposition. Finally, Part III explores the field of communication to determine which avenues for persuasion are open today to reform pressure groups of this variety. It is not intended that this study should be regarded as all-inclusive on the subject of reform pressure groups; it is meant merely to indicate the problems which confronted one group and, in turn, it may be helpful in understanding others.

In the preparation of this study only slight recourse could be had to books and secondary materials, except for the Negro press which gave the best public coverage to the pressure campaign. Some use was made of standard studies of pressure groups such as Peter Odegard's *Pressure Politics* (1928), E. P. Herring's *Group Representation Before Congress* (1929), Belle Zeller's *Pressure Politics in New York* (1937), Dayton D. McKean's *Pressures on the Legislature of New Jersey* (1938), and T.N.E.C. Monograph No. 26, *Economic Power and Political Pressure* (1941), by Donald C. Blaisdell, for purposes of comparison. For the most part the material was gathered from the files of the National Council for a Permanent FEPC in Washington, D.C. and through interviews and correspondence.

The writer wishes to express his debt to Mrs. Anna Arnold Hedgeman and her co-workers at the National Council's headquarters for making this study possible by opening the files of the organization to him and by patiently answering the multitude of questions which he raised in connection with the group's work. To his former colleague,

Professor E. Allen Helms of the Ohio State University, the author is deeply indebted for the inspiration and insights into political processes which almost ten years of association as student and then colleague and friend have given him. He owes more than he can here express to Professors Henry R. Spencer and Alma Herbst of the Ohio State University for their guidance and for their constructive criticism of the manuscript. To Professors Francis R. Aumann, Frederic W. Heimberger, Meredith P. Gilpatrick, Harvey Walker, and Carl H. MacFadden, the author is also grateful for suggestions arising out of reading all or parts of the manuscript. Also deserving thanks are Joseph R. Miller and the University of Louisville for making this book possible. Finally, to his wife and children, who have tolerated lengthy fits of absence of mind and body, acknowledgement is due. Wherever possible, the information contained in this study has been checked for accuracy and relevance. For all remaining inaccuracies the writer assumes complete personal responsibility.

Table of Contents

PART II - THE FACTOR OF SOCIAL COHESION

PART III - THE FACTOR OF COMMUNICATION

Tables

PART I

Discrimination In Employment

CHAPTER **1** *The Stakes*

- THE SETTING • "TO ARMS!"—NATIONAL DE-
FENSE • "GOVERNMENT OF THE PEOPLE" • FIRST
STIRRINGS • THE CITADEL CAPITULATES • PRESI-
DENT'S COMMITTEE UNDER 8802 • ILL-FATED
8802 • PRESSURE FOR A STRONGER PRESIDENT'S
COMMITTEE • PRESIDENT'S COMMITTEE UN-
DER 9346 • WARTIME FEPC KILLED

THE ADMINISTRATION LEADERS IN WASHINGTON will never give the Negro justice until they see masses—ten, twenty, fifty thousand Negroes on the White House Lawn."[1] The speaker was A. Philip Randolph, international President of the Brotherhood of Sleeping Car Porters and a prominent Negro leader; the time was May 1941, in the midst of American defense preparations.

Behind this statement lay months of agitation by Negro, inter-racial, Jewish, church, civil libertarian, and other organizations for government action to eliminate employment discrimination in defense industry. The Negro's perennial economic depression had shown little sign of abating despite mass defense job openings and wide public appeals for workers. The Negro was unwanted in industry; the deeply-rooted prejudice against his full assimilation in the Ameri-can economy remained unshaken. Other minority groups, notably aliens, Jews, and Spanish-speaking Americans, also met with discrimi-nation in hiring, training, and up-grading, but in terms of numbers and general economic distress, this was largely a Negro problem.[2]

---

1. Roi Ottley, "Negro Morale," *New Republic*, 105 (November 10, 1941), 614.
2. According to the 1940 census there were approximately 5 million aliens, 3 million Latin Americans, and 4½ million persons of Jewish ancestry. National origin minorities totaled some 21 million persons. The 13 million Negroes constituted approxi-mately 96 per cent of all non-white workers, the remainder included persons of Japanese, Chinese, Filipino, and Indian origin.

• 3 •

THE SETTING

Economic discrimination was by no means a novel experience for the Negro. Following the Reconstruction Era the Negro was denied an opportunity to share in the South's industrial awakening because of the resentment of white workers against the competition of free Negro labor. The increasingly rigid lines of racial segregation limited Negroes to the least desirable jobs, if industrial employment was available at all. Though the Negro in the South had dominated leading crafts at the close of the Civil War by a five to one margin, by 1890 this ratio had been more than reversed.[3] In the North, where the Negro fared slightly better, progress was slow and wavering.

The position of the Negro in industry before World War II was the product of tradition, economic fluctuations, and changes in methods of production. Thus jobs became known as "white" or "Negro" occupations because of tradition although the tradition, in turn, usually stemmed from the character of the job. Hot, heavy, dirty, poorly-paid occupations were regarded as "Negro jobs" while those which were clean, light, and well-paid were considered to be "white jobs." Technological changes resulted in the transfer of some jobs from the undesirable to the desirable category in the railroad and other industries. Technological developments also altered employer-worker relationships and the social prestige of occupations. However, the Negro rarely benefitted from any of these changes.

Statistics reveal that in occupations where Negroes have been numerous and which have become "preferred" the Negro has lost ground in this century. In seven building trades the proportion of Negroes declined in 1940 from 4.3 in 1910 to 3.8 per cent in the country as a whole and from 26.3 to 15.2 per cent in the South.[4] The proportion of Negro locomotive firemen dropped from 6.8 in 1910 to 5.0 per cent of the total number of firemen in 1940 and from 41.6 to 29.5 per cent in the South in the same period.[5] In the railroad industry the

3. Abram L. Harris and Sterling D. Spero, "Negro Problem," *Encyclopaedia of the Social Sciences*, XI, 339. See also L. J. Greene and C. G. Woodson, *The Negro Wage Earner*.
4. Herbert R. Northrup, *Organized Labor and the Negro*, Table I, pp. 18-19.
5. *Ibid.*, Table IIa, p. 53.

number of Negro railway trainmen fell off from 4.1 per cent of the total in 1910 to 2.5 in 1940 and from 29.8 to 15.1 per cent in the South.[6]

It has become axiomatic that Negroes lose ground faster than other groups in periods of depression and gain more slowly in boom periods. As could be expected the Negro lagged behind in recovering from the last depression. In April 1941 Negroes constituted 16.3 per cent of all WPA workers and only 10.2 per cent of the total population.[7] Only 59 per cent of all colored males, 14 years of age and over, were registered in urban areas as employed in 1940, while the corresponding proportion for urban white males was 68 per cent.[8]

In a few industries, such as basic steel, meat packing, machinery, and automobiles, the Negro gained ground during and after World War I. In light manufacturing and most new industries resistance to Negro employment was great. In 1940 Negroes constituted only 3.1 per cent of all cotton textile workers. The 1940 census reported that only 240, or 0.2 per cent of the 102,740 employees of the "aircraft and parts" industry, were Negroes and that most of these were janitors or outside laborers.[9] Altogether, on the eve of the war effort, 65.4 per cent of all employed Negroes were engaged in domestic service, the service industry, and unskilled farm and industrial labor while only 21.5 per cent of the employed whites earned their livelihood in these occupations.[10]

"TO ARMS!"—NATIONAL DEFENSE

The United States began the transition to a war economy in 1940 when the peacetime draft was instituted and industry stepped up production to meet the demands of the national defense program. For most white Americans this marked the beginning of full employment with adequate wages. As the production pace quickened, industry and government staged national drives to induce workers to take

6. *Ibid.*, Table IIb, p. 53.
7. Richard Sterner, *The Negro's Share*, Table 97, p. 240.
8. *Ibid.*, Table 18, p. 45.
9. Northrup, *op. cit.*, p. 205.
10. Adapted from the *American Year Book*, 1944, p. 572; computed from the Sixteenth Census of the United States, 1940: *Population*, Vol. II (Part I) and from a special report, *Population Characteristics of the Nonwhite Population by Race*, 1940.

TABLE I*

EMPLOYMENT—14 YEARS OLD AND OVER—1940—BY RACE

Employment Status	All Classes %	White	Negro
In Labor Force	52.2	51.6	58.2
Employed (except public emergency work)	47.7	44.3	48.4
At work	43.6	43.2	47.6
With a job but not at work	1.1	1.1	.8
On public emergency work	2.5	2.4	3.4
Seeking work	5.0	4.9	6.4
Experienced workers	4.3	4.1	5.7
New workers	.8	.8	.7
Not in Labor Force	47.8	48.4	41.8
Engaged in own housework	28.6	29.3	21.9
In school	8.9	9.0	8.1
Unable to work	5.2	5.1	6.5
In institutions	1.2	1.1	1.8
Others and not reported	3.9	3.9	3.6

*Statistical Abstract of the United States, 1944-45, p. 126.

TABLE II**

PERCENTAGE OF EMPLOYED PERSONS, 14 YEARS OLD AND OVER, IN MAJOR OCCUPATIONAL GROUPS, 1940

	Total Empl. Excluding Emerg. Wk.	Prof. Wkrs.	Semi-Prof.	Farmers & Fm. Mgrs.	Props., Mgrs. & Off. Wkrs.	Clerical, Sales., etc.	Craftsmen, Foremen, etc.
Total	45,166,083	6.4	1.0	11.5	8.4	16.8	11.3
White	40,495,089	6.9	1.1	11.1	9.2	18.5	12.3
Non-white	4,670,994	2.5	0.2	15.1	1.4	2.0	3.0

	Opera-tives etc.	Domestic Service	Service Workers	Farm Lab. Wage Wkrs.	Farm Lab. Unpaid (Family)	Laborers (excl. Farm)
Total	18.4	4.7	7.7	4.3	2.6	6.8
White	19.3	2.7	7.2	3.5	2.1	6.0
Non-white	10.5	21.9	11.8	11.1	6.6	14.0

**American Year Book, 1944.

defense jobs. Shortages in skilled workers led to emergency training programs. Authorities warned that labor shortages would prevent the realization of production goals and a great public controversy raged over a universal conscription act as a possible solution for the labor problem. Yet, in the face of this, discrimination against Negroes, aliens, Jews, and first generation Americans continued. For these groups the depression had not ended.

In the early defense period some attempts were made to determine how many Negroes could be absorbed in defense industry. The State Commission on the Condition of the Urban Colored Population of Illinois sent a questionnaire to Illinois defense plants and received 146 replies: 95, or two-thirds, reported no Negroes employed; in the 51 plants utilizing colored workers, Negroes comprised only 3.6 per cent of the total working force of which 70 per cent were unskilled workers.[11] A Bureau of Employment Security study in September 1941 revealed that Negroes would not be considered for 51 per cent of the openings anticipated in a selected group of defense plants.[12] In the field of vocational training, Social Security Board figures for the six months from August 1940 to January 1941 showed that of 89,529 applicants accepted for vocational training throughout the country, 2,434 were non-white. Of the 15,455 total placements, 50 were non-white.[13]

Efforts to gain entrance for Negroes into two aircraft companies in 1941 elicited the following replies:

We do not believe it advisable to include colored people in our regular working force. We may at a later date be in a position to add some colored people in minor capacities such as porters and cleaners. (Vultee of Nashville)

We will receive applications from both white and colored workers. However, the Negro will be considered only as janitors and in other similar capacities. . . . It is against the company policy to employ them as mechanics or aircraft workers. . . . There will be some jobs as janitors for Negroes. Regardless of their training as aircraft workers, we will not employ them. . . . (North American Aviation, Inc.)[14]

A Social Security Board pamphlet issued in September 1941 asserted:

---

11. Charles S. Johnson and associates, *To Stem This Tide*, p. 10.

12. Bureau of Employment Security, Social Security Board, *Labor Supply and Demand in Selected Defense Occupations Through the Period May-November 1941*, September 1941.

13. Quoted by *Information Service*, publication of the Federal Council of the Churches of Christ in America, June 14, 1941, p. 1.

14. Quoted by Reverend Aron S. Gilmartin, Chairman, National Executive Board, Workers Defense League and official representative of the American Unitarian Association, *Hearings Before a Subcommittee of the Committee on Education and Labor, United States Senate, on S. 2048*, August 30, 31 and September 6, 7 and 8, 1944, p. 103.

In many of the most important industries associated with national defense, particularly aircraft, tank and armament manufacturing, shell loading, machine tools and shop, in which acute shortages of skilled and semi-skilled labor have developed, there is little evidence that employers are hiring Negroes.[15]

The pamphlet went on to point out that of 8,769 skilled and semi-skilled jobs filled in the aircraft industry from January to March 1941, only 13 went to non-white workers. In the same period fewer than 500 non-white placements were made in the metal trades despite the fact that 60,000 were hired.

The urgency of the national defense crisis did produce some attacks upon the rigidity of the color line by some newspapers, even in border and southern states. In April 1942, the *Baltimore Evening Sun* editorialized:

We are not here concerned with the long-range social consequences which might result from the removal of some of these barriers [against the use of Negroes for skilled work]. We are thinking simply of the ironic situation Baltimore finds itself in right now: on the one hand a desperate shortage of skilled and semi-skilled workmen for our war industries, and on the other hand the existence of a large reservoir of labor which is rarely considered when there is need for skilled rather than unskilled workmen. It seems to us that in this emergency a dispassionate and objective examination of the situation of the Negro in Baltimore's industries is called for.[16]

Far more commonly opinions of the opposite sentiment were voiced, especially in the South. Colonel Kendall Weisiger, War Production Board consultant, summed up the arguments most frequently heard against full utilization of the Negro in industry during the 1942 President's Committee on Fair Employment Practice hearings in Birmingham:

With particular respect to the utilization of the services of colored men in industry, it is said that he is unskilled, that he is not literate, that he has venereal diseases, that he cannot learn skilled trades, that he is unstable as an employee. It is said, on the other hand, that the community might object to the employment of Negroes and whites on the same enterprise, that the employees already on the payroll might resent and rebel and leave the

---

15. Quoted by Earl Brown, "American Negroes and the War," *Harper's Magazine*, 184 (April 1942), 552.
16. Quoted by "The Negro's War," *Fortune*, XXV (June 1942), 80.

plant, that the collective bargaining agencies might not accept, on an equal basis of treatment in industry, the services of the colored men.

The blame for under-utilization of Negroes in industry could not be assigned to management alone. Labor unions, especially American Federation of Labor affiliates and the Railroad Brotherhoods, went out of their way to safeguard "lily-white" trade unionism by excluding Negroes from membership or by relegating them to segregated auxiliary status. National, state, and local governments, too, were averse to anti-discrimination programs, even when the war gave them extensive authority over training and employment reference services.[17] Discrimination was common in government agencies themselves; 25 per cent of the cases handled by the President's Committee through 1945 involved agencies of the national government. In short, a pattern of discrimination had developed over a period of years which colored every thread of our social fabric. It took the crisis of an impending war to bring the situation to a head.

"GOVERNMENT OF THE PEOPLE"

National government planning in the early defense period did not overlook the Negro labor supply as a production factor, but the machinery and techniques adopted to facilitate such integration proved inadequate. In July 1940 the National Defense Advisory Commission, the first coordinating defense agency of the World

---

17. A number of states since 1920 have prohibited discrimination in civil service, publicly-owned utilities, work relief projects and public works, schools, and trade unions. Also, before the war the Roosevelt administration was responsible for placing anti-discrimination clauses in several laws pertaining to federal employment. Such major programs as the Work Projects Administration, the National Youth Administration, and the Civilian Conservation Corps were safeguarded in this manner. In at least two other cases, the federal administrators of the United States Housing Authority and the Public Works Administration interpreted their broad congressional mandate to reduce unemployment to mean that their agencies should prohibit discrimination in the employment of labor on building projects. Except for several notable exceptions, the sketchiness of jurisdiction and the absence of adequate enforcement criteria and procedures limited the effectiveness of government anti-discrimination measures in the period before World War II. See W. J. Trent, Jr., "Federal Sanctions Directed Against Racial Discrimination," *Phylon*, III (Second Quarter, 1942), 171-82; Robert C. Weaver, *Negro Labor*, Chapter I; and the following articles by Weaver: "An Experiment in Negro Labor," *Opportunity*, 14 (October, 1936) 295-98; "Racial Policy in Public Housing," *Phylon*, I, (Second Quarter, 1940); and others in *Crisis* and *Opportunity* magazines.

War II period, selected Dr. Robert C. Weaver to head its Labor
Division's efforts to bring the Negro into the defense program. On
August 31, 1940, the Commission issued instructions to defense contractors that "workers should not be discriminated against because
of age, sex, race, or color." Instructions without implementation became pious wishes. Weaver points out that "management paid only
slight attention to any of the federal policies for labor supply; it
paid even less attention to statements that minorities *should not* be
discriminated against on defense work."[18] Later the Labor Division
secured the agreement of the CIO and AFL to assume responsibility
for removing barriers against Negro workers in defense industries.
Again the agreement was less than fully effective because the negotiating agency lacked enforcement powers.

The NDAC proving inadequate on many counts, the Office of
Production Management was established in 1941. To facilitate minority employment the Negro Employment and Training and the
Minority Groups branches were created in the Labor Division of
OPM. Pressure on the new over-all defense agency from Negroes
and the liberal press resulted in a letter from Co-Director Sidney
Hillman to holders of defense contracts asking for full utilization of
competent Negroes. A few contract holders heeded the appeal and
began to expand their use of Negroes; most continued to follow their
more familiar course of discrimination.

This was also a period of government training programs for defense industry. Millions of dollars were spent to give workers pre-
employment, refresher, and supplementary training courses. The
most important was the Vocational Educational National Defense
Training Program (VEND) under the direction of the United
States Office of Education. Despite the anti-bias clause in the National
Defense Training Act of 1940, discrimination was rife in the administration of this program. Weaver, intimately associated with
the government's efforts to integrate Negroes, says of the training
programs:

This discrimination was in reality a projection of past practices. Most
vocational education officials at the national, state, and local levels were

18. Weaver, *loc. cit.* Chapter IX contains a summary of government efforts in
this period.

not prepared to champion new policies relative to minority groups' training. There were many factors underlying the attitudes and actions of these officials. They had become accustomed to training a limited number of persons for an economy which offered only a few jobs to potential trainees. They were closely allied with management and union officials who opposed the training of Negroes for mechanical operations. They reflected community attitudes, and, in fact, often mirrored the most reactionary sentiments in their efforts to please the right people. Most of them accepted and championed the color occupational caste system.[19]

Regional variations were present. In the South training programs were virtually closed to the Negro. Not even the mounting pressure for more workers in war industries brought about a relaxation of administrative prohibitions against the training of Negroes for skilled occupations down to the end of the war.[20] The situation in northern cities in the early part of the war was better than in the South but not encouragingly so. Only a few Negroes were being trained in welding, machine shop, and aircraft occupations—where the need was the greatest. It was not until the summer of 1942, following repeated protests by local and national citizens' groups, that the northern training picture improved.

The United States Employment Service suffered, like the United States Office of Education, from pre-war procedures and attitudes. According to Weaver:

The defense program was initiated after a long period of depression. During that depression, the Employment Service had become extremely conscious of soliciting employers' business, and it never dared alienate its customers. It had, in addition, developed a fetish for reporting a large volume of placements, and its budget requests were often evaluated on the basis of its placement figures. Most of its Negro placements were in common laboring work and in domestic service. Seldom did it place a skilled Negro, save in a few building trades; as a result, few skilled Negroes registered with it. It was natural, though unfortunate, that USES would continue in wartime to seek the favor of employers. This attitude was reenforced by the fact that during the earlier phases of the war effort, management was free to seek its workers on the labor market, and most

19. *Ibid.*, p. 44; see all of Chapter IV on the training program.
20. In 1942, a survey indicated that the South with approximately 80 per cent of the Negro population was training only about 20 per cent of the Negroes being prepared for defense work and that even these were not given equal treatment with white trainees in the South.

of the larger plants called on the Employment Service only for workers in occupations in which there was a scarcity of labor.[21]

Local USES officials ignored orders coming from the Washington office; skilled Negro workers were encouraged to register for unskilled jobs on the theory that they could not be placed in the higher skills; "white" specifications were accepted without challenge; white workers were imported while qualified Negroes were locally available. These and other abuses were commonplace in the employment services.

FIRST STIRRINGS

Scattered protests appeared early against discrimination in national defense industries. The Hampton Institute Conference on the Participation of the Negro in National Defense, held in November 1940, urged the cooperation of government, industry, labor, and the public in eliminating discrimination in training for defense industry, placement by the public employment service, and education of employers on the "availability, capability and needs of skilled and unskilled Negro labor."[22] President Newbold Morris, of the Council of Freedom of New York City, told the conference: "We are not asking any favors for any class or group. We are only seeking a fair and equal opportunity for the Negroes of America to give their best to America when she is threatened by a world conflict."[23]

At Fordham University a Negro speaker stated that the Negro was being forced into "artificial proletarianism" because of lack of economic opportunities.[24] From the South the chairman of the Georgia State Central Planning Commission called for racial opportunity "in proportion to population" to train for defense jobs.[25] In time, some organizations born of the period, such as the Committee on Negro Americans in Defense Industries, the Conference Against Race Discrimination in the War Effort, the Council for Democracy, and the Coordinating Committee of Jewish Organizations Dealing with Employment Discrimination in War Industry added their voices to the

21. Weaver, *op. cit.*, p. 145.
22. *Findings and Principal Addresses*, pp. 12-14.
23. *New York Times*, November 26, 1940.
24. George Streator before the Catholic Interracial Council, *ibid.*, August 8, 1940.
25. *Ibid.*, August 4, 1940.

opposition to discrimination. It was not long before organized groups of many descriptions seized hold of the issue and raised it to national prominence.

THE CITADEL CAPITULATES

Tensions continued to mount. The wide use of democratic symbols by the government in an effort to unify the population and to wage psychological warfare upon the Axis nations helped to sharpen the contrast between ideals and realities. Negroes became increasingly agitated over their lot; some observers even despaired of their loyalty in the event of war. While succeeding events proved that their loyalty was unimpeachable, their deepening bitterness was ample cause for concern.

After a number of false starts, the first direct action step was taken when Philip Randolph called a conference of top Negro leaders in February 1941, to discuss ways and means for securing a more equitable share of the new jobs rapidly opening up.[26] Out of this conference emerged the March on Washington Movement which captured the imagination of the Negro people and played a leading role in the establishment of the President's Committee on Fair Employment Practice. The MOWM embodied Randolph's theories of "mass non-violent direct action" which was, in reality, an interpolation of the picket line of labor for the attainment of political objectives. The general plan was to stage large mass meetings in major cities in the hope of forcing national action on the elimination of discrimination in the armed services, government, war industries, and labor unions. In the event of the government's failure to respond, a giant march on the nation's capital was contemplated—hence the name of the movement.[27]

At first, public authorities paid little attention to MOWM groups which were staging local meetings and organizing Negro communities. But Randolph refused to be ignored and when the national government failed to act to ameliorate the Negro's economic distress, he

---

26. Those attending included Walter White, Secretary, NAACP; Dr. Channing Tobias, Senior Secretary of the National Council of the YMCA; Mary McLeod Bethune, President of the National Council of Negro Women; Dr. George E. Haynes, Executive Secretary of the Federal Council of the Churches of Christ in America; and Lester Granger, Executive Secretary of the National Urban League.

27. The MOWM is discussed in greater detail in Chapter V, *infra.*

called for a national march of Negroes on Washington to take place on July 1, 1941. Whether he was capable of producing such a march is debatable. Certainly problems of transportation, feeding, and housing made the call, wittingly or not, a gambling bluff. Even so President Roosevelt, recognizing the need for internal unity and fearing possible international reaction to the proposed march in a period of delicate foreign relations, took steps to head off the demonstration.

On June 12 the President addressed a letter to the co-chairmen of the OPM in which he added his weight to the campaign to break down discrimination by defense contractors and labor unions. The President said, in part:

Our government cannot countenance continued discrimination against American citizens in defense production. Industry must take the initiative in opening the doors of employment to all loyal and qualified workers regardless of race, creed, color, or national origin. American workers, both organized and unorganized, must be prepared to welcome the general and much-needed employment of fellow workers of all racial and nationality groups in defense industries.

Though this was an admirable expression of sentiment, it remained merely words. No promise of implementation was made. The March on Washington was not called off.

This failing, the President designated New York's Mayor Fiorello H. LaGuardia, then also head of the Office of Civilian Defense, to confer with the MOWM leaders. LaGuardia and other government leaders who were recognized friends of Negro progress met with Randolph and his associates and sought to persuade them to call off the march. In exchange for cancellation of the demonstration, LaGuardia was authorized by the President to offer a draft of a proposed executive order banning discrimination in defense industry. After some argument over the inclusion of government agencies in the coverage of the order, telephone conferences between Randolph and White resulted in approval of the draft, with amendments, and cancellation of the march.[28] In the final analysis, the executive order was not freely given by the President but was rather "a compromise be-

---

28. Discussions of these conferences which are not entirely in agreement are found in: Earl Brown, "American Negroes and the War," *Harper's Magazine*, 184 (April 1942), pp. 545-52; Will Maslow, "FEPC—A Case History in Parliamentary Maneuver," *University of Chicago Law Review*, 13 (June 1946), 409, n. 4; and Rayford W. Logan, *What the Negro Wants*, p. 16.

tween hard-boiled pressure groups."[29] On June 25, 1941, Executive Order No. 8802 was issued, marking the beginning rather than the end of the struggle for government protection of minority employment rights.

PRESIDENT'S COMMITTEE UNDER 8802

The introductory language of Executive Order 8802 started out promisingly:

Whereas it is the policy of the United States to encourage full participation in the national defense program by all citizens of the United States, regardless of race, creed, color, or national origin, in the firm belief that the democratic way of life within the Nation can be defended successfully only with the help and support of all groups within its borders.

It then proceeded to establish a Committee on Fair Employment Practice in the Office of Production Management which, however, did not quite live up to the preamble quoted above.

To effectuate the order a Committee of five members and a chairman was appointed in July by the President to serve on a part-time volunteer basis.[30] No provision for a real field staff was made. The Committee was obliged to delegate investigation of cases to the Negro Employment and Minority Groups branches of OPM and to depend upon correspondence to do its work. According to the executive order the Committee was "to receive and investigate complaints of discrimination in violation of the provisions of this order" and to take "appropriate steps" to redress valid grievances, "as well as to recommend further measures to the government and the President necessary to carry out the order." Its jurisdiction was limited to industries under government contract and to government agencies concerned with vocational and training programs.[31]

---

29. "The Negro's War," *Fortune*, XXV (June 1942), 80.

30. The first Committee was made up of: Mark Ethridge, publisher of the *Louisville Courier Journal*, Chairman; Philip Murray, President of the CIO; William Green, AFL President; David Sarnoff, President of RCA; Milton P. Webster, Vice-president, BSCP; and Earl B. Dickerson, Negro attorney and member of the Chicago City Council.

31. The legality of the Committee rested upon two presidential prerogatives: 1) his power as administrative head of the executive branch of the national government and 2) his power as commander-in-chief to take action to assure adequate supplies for the military forces.

The substance of the Committee's work was to engage in informal negotiations with the parties covered by the order to secure voluntary compliance with the non-discrimination principle and to hold hearings in areas where widespread discrimination was reported. When employment bias was found, orders were issued instructing the party charged to take specific steps to comply with the President's order. But the Committee was severely limited in its power to bring sanctions to bear if the offending party refused to comply with the "cease and desist" order. Judicial enforcement was not available to the committee; it could, at best, call upon national war contracting and regulatory agencies to punish the violator by various intermediate sanctions, such as cancellation of government contracts or denial of manpower and material priorities, or could, ultimately, refer the case to the President for final disposition.

During the first year hearings involving forty-nine industries, unions, and defense training programs were conducted in Los Angeles, Washington, Chicago, New York, and Birmingham. These hearings, conducted in the presence of a majority of the Committee and at which the parties charged were permitted to be represented by counsel, served to confirm the allegation that discrimination was rampant in war industry. Seventy-five per cent of these early cases involved Negroes; 10 per cent, Jews; and 15 per cent, other minorities.

ILL-FATED 8802

Of unnatural birth as an involuntary gesture to America's minorities and unloved by its governmental midwives, the first President's Committee was ill-fated from the beginning. In the slightly less than two years that it sought to deal with problems of discrimination in defense industry, it was hamstrung by administrative frictions, financial malnutrition, and inadequate powers and personnel.

The Committee lacked a clear-cut organizational status and was shifted from agency to agency by the President. It was established first in the Labor Division of the Office of Production Management. In January 1942, when OPM was abolished, the Committee was shifted to the War Production Board. In July of the same year it became part of the War Manpower Commission although it theoretically remained an "organizational entity."

These moves did not strengthen the Committee; its place in the administrative structure of the WMC was never well-defined. Once in the WMC the Committee entered into negotiations with Chairman Paul McNutt to coordinate its efforts with the various manpower units of the WMC, as directed by the President in making the transfer. Negotiations dragged on for more than three months until finally in October 1942, an agreement was reached making the President's Committee the sole operating unit in the WMC dealing with discrimination in employment and giving it quasi-autonomous status.

It was not long, however, before the President's Committee's staff accused the WMC of having violated the agreement by continuing to maintain overlapping services and creating new ones. Also, according to the President's Committee, the WMC failed to refer all discrimination cases to the Committee as agreed upon; policies and operational procedures laid down by the Committee were sometimes disregarded by the manpower agency; the field staff of the WMC dealing with problems of discrimination remained separate from the Committee's staff; the Chairman of the WMC called off scheduled public hearings, including the important railroad hearings in January 1943—all in violation of the agreement. This friction and lack of cooperation between the two agencies continued throughout the life of the first President's Committee.[32]

On at least one occasion the State Department interfered with the Committee's work. When a public hearing was scheduled in August 1942 to hear complaints of employment discrimination against persons of Mexican and Spanish-American origin, the Committee was told that the State Department frowned upon such a hearing because the attendant publicity would play into the hands of Axis agents in

---

32. This discussion of the relationship between the President's Committee and the War Manpower Commission is based upon a confidential report issued by the Committee immediately prior to the issuance of Executive Order 9346 which reconstituted the Committee. *Report of the President's Committee on Fair Employment Practice*, Washington (multigraphed), May, 1943, pp. 78-81.

To balance the picture, it should be pointed out that the President's Committee was accused, in turn, of ambitiously attempting to move into all government programs for the furtherance of minority employment in the war effort. The friction within the War Manpower Commission cannot be adequately explained without reference to this internal struggle for power.

Latin America and hamper inter-American cooperation. The Committee was forced to defer to the State Department's wishes on the matter.[33]

In the important field of referring prospective workers to employers, the United States Employment Service did little to aid the antidiscrimination program despite representations from the President's Committee. In July 1942 USES issued Operations Bulletin No. C-45 which instructed field offices to refer workers without discrimination, if possible, but if employers remained adamant, their discriminatory orders should be filled. In southern states the service continued to maintain segregated employment office facilities which permitted the employer to choose his workers by race.[34]

Lack of adequate finances also limited the effectiveness of the first President's Committee. The Committee, financed from the President's emergency fund, was given $43,324 for the fiscal year ending June 30, 1942, during which time the staff was made up of an executive secretary, an assistant executive secretary, and six investigators. For the year ending June 30, 1943, the Committee spent $147,619. In May 1943, just before the Committee gave way to its successor, the staff had reached a peak of twenty-seven professional persons and sixteen clerical employees.[35] The number of cases which could be undertaken was correspondingly small.

It was inevitable that the work of the President's Committee would produce strong tensions in many quarters. The friends of the Committee were impatient for the elimination of discrimination and were, therefore, dissatisfied with its slow progress. On the other hand, industrial corporations and labor unions practicing discrimination resented interference with their hiring and membership policies. On one occasion the railway brotherhoods were accused of joining with the railroad companies in a behind-the-scene campaign to halt hearings involving both parties.[36] Southern newspapers and government offi-

---

33. *Ibid.*, p. 84.
34. *Ibid.*, pp. 85-86.
35. *F. E. P. C. First Report*, Washington: Government Printing Office, July 1943-December 1944, pp. 10 and 102; Frank P. Huddle, "Fair Practice in Employment," *Editorial Research Reports*, I (January 18, 1946), p. 42.
36. James A. Wechsler, "Pigeonhole for Negro Equality," *Nation*, 156 (January 23, 1943), 121-22.

cials also spoke out against the President's Committee in no uncertain terms.

This pressure had its effect upon the Committee. Weaver, a keen and constructive critic, states:

> Faced with the pressure to produce immediate, dramatic results and constantly harrassed by powerful economic and political forces opposed to its existence, the committee concentrated upon those activities which would corral support for it. This resulted in neglect of long-run planning and programming. The most conspicuous example of such neglect was the failure of the committee to pursue fully the possibilities of getting the contracting agencies of the government to enforce the non-discrimination clauses in their contracts.[37]

Protests poured into the White House. The New York Metropolitan Council on FEPC telegraphed:

> The critical nature of the discrimination problem and its relation to war morale require the work of an agency with complete freedom for action. It is a task demanding the exclusive attention of a special agency unhampered by other equally important responsibilities.[38]

Randolph's group threatened another march on Washington. Mass meetings were held in New York, Chicago, and other centers protesting the failure of the government to back up the anti-discrimination program.

Sufficient pressure was generated to force the President to rise to his own defense. He declared, in a public statement, that his intent in making the transfer had been misunderstood and that his wish was to strengthen the Committee and revitalize Executive Order 8802. It was his feeling, he continued, that the Committee would do its work better in close cooperation with the War Manpower Commission where it would have the "friendly supervision of the Chairman of the Commission, Mr. McNutt, whose grasp of the whole problem of manpower utilization will be of great assistance to the Committee on Fair Employment."[39]

The transfer stood but the grumbling did not cease. Mass rallies

37. *Negro Labor*, p. 138.
38. *New York Times*, August 17, 1942.
39. Release No. 6-1198-WP, President's Committee on Fair Employment Practice, August 17, 1942.

became more frequent and grew in size. Statements became more angry. Randolph was quoted in the fall of 1942 as declaring:

Negroes made the blunder of closing ranks and forgetting their grievances in the last war. We are resolved that we will not make that blunder again. Some of our appeasers say that if Negroes persist in fighting for their rights now, they are going to have trouble. Well, Negroes are already having trouble, and a little more trouble won't hurt.[40]

PRESSURE FOR A STRONGER PRESIDENT'S COMMITTEE

Each crisis suffered by the President's Committee provoked an immediate reaction from groups concerned with the elimination of employment discrimination. Negro and sympathetic white organizations watched the work of the Committee with hawk-like eyes. Negro and liberal white newspapers emblazoned every triumph and defeat, major or minor, in screaming headlines. The letters FEPC, standing for the Fair Employment Practice Committee, had become an inspiring symbol of a supposed panacea for all the ills besetting America's minorities. Issues of longer standing, such as anti-poll tax and anti-lynching legislation, were forced to take a back seat.

The first major crisis came with the just aforementioned transfer of FEPC to the WMC following the Birmingham hearings in June 1942, which had aroused considerable ire in the southern congressmen. The move was regarded as a setback for FEPC because it thereby lost its autonomy and became subject to Chairman McNutt's orders. The presidential order came as a surprise; the Committee was preparing to expand its program and staff when the axe fell. Immediately the proponents of FEPC railed against the move and assailed President Roosevelt for yielding to opposition pressures. One writer asserted:

Back of the transfer, as everybody knew, was reactionary Southern pressure. Also involved were top government officials who had been annoyed by FEPC insistence that they put an end to discrimination in their own departments and agencies. Northern industrial interests and "lilywhite" trade unions took a surreptitious hand in the deal.[41]

---

40. Quoted by Charles Williams, "Harlem at War," *Nation*, 156, (January 16, 1943), 86-88.
41. John Beecher, "8802 Blues," *New Republic*, 108 (February 22, 1943), 250.

Despite the President's assurance of better days for FEPC in the War Manpower Commission, the anti-discrimination program made little headway in its new setting. As the Committee attempted to assert itself it was inevitable that new and greater crises would develop. The showdown came on the hearings scheduled by the Committee for December 7-9, 1942, to hear the complaints of Negro railway workers against southern carriers and the railroad brotherhoods for denying experienced Negroes opportunity for employment and promotion in the industry. The administration feared southern repercussions and possible interruption of rail facilities if the Committee held the hearings and issued "cease and desist" orders to the recalcitrant parties. After several temporary postponements WMC Chairman McNutt intervened on January 11, 1943, to postpone the hearings indefinitely which produced a great uproar from the Provisional Committee to Organize Colored Workers, the National Urban League, the National Association for the Advancement of Colored People, and other interested groups.

According to the *New York Times*, Committee members blamed the President for the action:

> Committee members were inclined to ascribe this action to the strengthening of the influence of the Southern Democrats with the Administration since the last election. They felt also that industries and unions which discriminated against Negroes also played a part in the decision of Mr. McNutt, who made no explanation of his action at his press conference today.[42]

The upshot was that several members and key staff members of the President's Committee resigned in January 1943. Federal agencies investigating complaints in the field were withdrawn and interested organizations reported a rise in discriminatory practices as a result of the cancellation of the public hearings.[43]

Will Maslow wrote: ". . . the greatest weakness of the Committee was President Roosevelt's inability to give it full support. As long as the votes of the Southern bloc were deemed indispensable to the winning of the war, it was utopian to expect such support."—"The Law and Race Relations," *Annals of the American Academy of Political and Social Sciences*, 244 (March 1946), 78.

42. January 12, 1943.

43. "Fair Employment Practice Committee Its Development and Trends," undated release issued by the National Council of Jewish Women, p. 2.

Once more the proponents of the President's Committee, increasing rapidly in number and variety, joined to safeguard the anti-discrimination principle and to strengthen the machinery for its application. Among the most vocal were the Federal Council of the Churches of Christ in America, National Urban League, National Association for the Advancement of Colored People, March on Washington Movement, National Catholic Welfare Conference, CIO, National Lawyers Guild, and many Jewish organizations. Proposals were sent to the President for reorganizing and strengthening the President's Committee and personal conferences were arranged with government officials and other key people.[44]

The pressure was effective. On February 19, upon instruction from the President, McNutt called a conference of organizations to discuss reorganization of the President's Committee. Finally the President yielded and issued Executive Order 9346 on May 27, 1943, establishing the second President's Committee on Fair Employment Practice. The reforms incorporated in Executive Order 9346 were based largely upon the recommendations of the organizations consulted by McNutt.

PRESIDENT'S COMMITTEE UNDER 9346

By the new executive order the President's Committee was taken out of the War Manpower Commission and placed in the Executive Office of the President. It was empowered to perform the following duties: to make recommendations to federal agencies, the President, and the War Manpower Commission for full utilization of available manpower; to hold hearings and take appropriate steps for the elimination of discrimination; and to utilize the services and facilities of other private and public organizations. The provision in the old order specifying anti-bias clauses in all government contracts was extended to cover sub-contracts.

To carry out its work a Committee of six part-time members and a full-time chairman was appointed.[45] The work of the Committee

---

44. *Ibid.*, p. 3.
45. Dr. Malcolm S. MacLean, President of Hampton Institute, replaced Ethridge as chairman when Executive Order 9111 was issued May 25, 1942, increasing the number of members to seven. Following Executive Order 9346, Monsignor Francis

was divided into four divisions: administration, field operations, review and analysis, and the legal or hearing division. Under the Division of Field Operations, twelve regional offices and a number of sub-offices were eventually established to handle complaints on the local level. For the fiscal year ending June 30, 1944, the Committee's expenditures jumped to $431,609—small for a government agency but three times as much as the FEPC had had to work with during the previous year.[46] Under these conditions it was possible to do a more effective job.

WARTIME FEPC KILLED

The enemies of the non-discrimination principle did not cease their sniping until the President's Committee was killed. Incident followed incident throughout the Committee's life. In October 1943, for example, Comptroller General Lindsay Warren ruled that Executive Order 9346 did not make it mandatory for contracting agencies to incorporate a nondiscrimination clause in each contract awarded. Such an interpretation, if upheld, would have meant the end of the President's Committee. After a delay of several weeks, however, President Roosevelt notified Attorney General Biddle that the order was mandatory and not discretionary. Unions and companies, too, took advantage of the lack of judicial enforcement powers to ignore the Committee's orders and thus endanger its prestige and effectiveness in future cases.[47]

In Congress the southern opponents of FEPC became increasingly explosive on the subject. In July 1944 Congress, led by Senator Russell of Georgia, attached limiting amendments to Executive Order 9346 in

---

J. Haas, Dean of the School of Social Sciences, Catholic University, was named to head the new committee. When Haas resigned on October 18, 1943, to become Bishop of Grand Rapids, he was replaced by Malcolm Ross, his deputy, who remained with the Committee until its expiration in 1946.

46. *FEPC First Report*, p. 102.

47. Through 1945, compliance orders were issued to employers in 35 cases; 26 of these orders went unheeded. Nine of the 10 unions cited by the Committee also refused to comply.—Huddle, *op. cit.*, p. 43.

The enforcement system broke down when the President and the agencies cooperating with the Committee failed to back up the executive order consistently by cutting off priorities and invoking other sanctions because they feared interference with war production.

the course of approving an appropriation of $500,000 for the agency. Finally, in 1945, the Committee's appropriation was cut to $250,000 after a tremendous parliamentary struggle which almost killed a number of war agencies included in the War Agencies Appropriation Bill with the President's Committee when neither side would yield. This sum did not permit the Committee to see the next fiscal year out.

However, this did not mark the end of FEPC. The struggle over the President's Committee had generated a second movement advocating a permanent FEPC agency with jurisdiction over industries and unions engaged in interstate commerce, as well as agencies of the national government. In contrast with the wartime committees, FEPC proponents advocated adequate enforcement powers and appropriations. War conditions had given birth to a movement which was to write an important chapter of "protest politics" in American history.

CHAPTER **2**   *Organizing for Action*

• RISE OF INTERRACIAL COMMITTEES   • ESTAB-
LISHMENT OF THE NATIONAL COUNCIL   • GEN-
ERAL CHARACTER OF THE NATIONAL COUNCIL
• ORGANIZATIONAL STRUCTURE AND PROBLEMS
• NATIONAL COMMITTEE OF COOPERATING OR-
GANIZATIONS   • CHAIRMAN   • EXECUTIVE
COMMITTEE • EXECUTIVE SECRETARY • STRAT-
EGY AND LEGAL COMMITTEES   • WASHINGTON
OFFICE AND STAFF

THE YEAR 1943 WAS EVENTFUL FOR THE FEPC MOVE-
ment and for race relations generally in the United States. The
failure of the national administration to follow through on its
anti-discrimination policy, coupled with resistance by employers
and unions to the program, contributed to an increasingly explosive
situation. Leaders of minority peoples expressed vigorously their
resentment over their continuing inability to obtain equal treatment
in war industry. Complaints of discrimination in the armed services
added fuel to the fire. On the other side, white workers, especially
migrants from the South to northern industrial centers, showed irritation when Negroes began to penetrate into jobs previously closed
to them. Crowded housing, eating, and recreational facilities in
virtually all industrial communities forced closer social contacts between the races than many people desired with resulting frictions.
Yet responsible authorities did little to alleviate the tensions.

Suddenly, in the summer of 1943, a wave of riots and industrial
strikes swept the country. In Los Angeles, Mexican-American "Zoot-
Suiters" engaged in street battles with sailors until the city was declared out of bounds for the Navy.[1] One person was killed and eleven

---

1. In the fall of 1942 a Los Angeles grand jury "Committee on Mexican Youth"
had found a definite connection between low wages or unemployment and juvenile

injured after a raping in Beaumont, Texas, where it was necessary for the police to escort Negro shipyard workers home to protect them from violence. The worst of the riots took place in Detroit in June when a wild rumor set off an extremely short-fused local situation. By the time the riot had ended twenty-three had been killed and more than six hundred injured. Order was not restored until the President called out federal troops. Industrial strikes over racial issues flared up in St. Louis, Detroit, East Chicago, Columbus, several Maryland plants, and elsewhere.

RISE OF INTERRACIAL COMMITTEES

Between the two world wars a number of Negro, Jewish, Catholic, and interracial organizations had sprung up to propagandize for fairer and more democratic treatment of America's minorities. These committees differed widely in structure, techniques, and areas of operation. Increasingly, however, attention was paid to problems of minority employment; some groups devoted all of their efforts to the solution of specific problems involving employment discrimination.

When the President's Committee was established in 1941, some twenty local committees patterned after it emerged in such cities as New York, Philadelphia, Detroit, Chicago, and Columbus. Usually calling themselves Metropolitan Councils on Fair Employment Practice, they sought to handle the local cases over which the President's Committee had no jurisdiction. The councils were not connected with the Committee and had no official status. In at least one city, Detroit, the council was financed by the Community Fund for several years as a war service. While their structures varied from city to city, the councils were mostly federated bodies of social agencies, civic groups, and labor unions organized for the purpose of coordinating all local efforts to eliminate discrimination in employment.[2] Their chief work was to receive complaints, investigate them, and make recommendations.[3] Lacking legal enforcement powers the councils were forced to

delinquency and had urged equalization of recreational, social, and economic opportunities.—*New York Times*, June 12, 1943.

2. See "Statement of Objectives," New York Metropolitan Council on Fair Employment Practice, November 23, 1945.

3. The Columbus Metropolitan Council heard upwards to 1000 complaints in three years of operation. The Detroit council handled 57 non-war industry cases between August 1943 and August 1945.—*Report*, Detroit Metropolitan Council, 1945, p. 12.

depend upon informal negotiation as their chief remedial technique.

Some metropolitan councils carried on extensive educational programs in addition to the handling of complaints. The Detroit Metropolitan Council, for example, conducted conferences on fair employment practices, participated in forty or more panel discussions, publicized testimony before state legislative committees dealing with
FEPC legislation, and obtained extensive newspaper coverage on the
subject. Furthermore, the Detroit council published pamphlets such
as *Unfinished Business—A Fair Employment Practice Handbook*
which was widely distributed among key leaders of schools, churches,
unions and industry, a *Memorandum* of FEPC information for the
Michigan League of Women Voters, and others.[4]

A National Coordinating Committee on Metropolitan Councils was
set up in 1944; when state and national campaigns for fair employment
practice legislation were launched, the member councils were active in
building local support and exerting pressures upon legislatures.

The shock of the Detroit riot catalyzed interest in interracial cooperation to ward off similar riots in other cities. Many communities
were virtual tinderboxes needing only a spark to set off a conflagration.
For the first time since the riots following World War I, public officials felt it necessary to take official action. New committees, official
and unofficial, were hastily organized; old committees were revitalized.
Twelve months after the so-called "Black Pearl Harbor," the Social
Science Institute of Fisk University was able to learn of the existence
of 224 committees dealing with racial tensions. Among the 166 from
whom the Institute received information, 13 were national organizations, 2 were regional, 16 state, and 135 local. This list included 32
committees appointed by mayors, city councils, boards of supervisors,
governors, and state legislatures.[5] By 1945 it was estimated that approximately 400 official and unofficial committees of all varieties had
been established.[6]

Few of the committees were really effective. Some closed up shop
when the immediate danger of race riots appeared to have passed;

---

4. *Ibid.*, pp. 1-6.
5. *Monthly Summary of Events and Trends in Race Relations*, August-September
1944, p. 23.
6. *News Letter*, American Council on Race Relations, February 1945. In 1945,
the Julius Rosenwald Fund published a *Directory of Agencies in Race Relations*,
describing the organization and work of many of these committees.

others talked of long-range educational programs thus delaying action on immediate problems.[7] Too frequently official committees were established by governors and mayors without proper organization or funds. Many committees became pawns of local and state politics or were so timid in their approach that they accomplished little. For example, New York City's Committee on Unity was pressure-born, but six months after its formation it had no program and had done no committee work to further its objectives. In Detroit the Mayor's Committee was extremely cautious:

With a small budget and staff and with Detroit politics in a hectic state, it treads softly the narrow path between vested political interest and insistent demand from special interest groups. The committee seems torn between two impulses—on the one hand, to publicize racial problems and proposals for their solution, and on the other to avoid "inflammatory treatment" of a still dangerous situation. Local leaders worriedly admit that "Detroit is still dynamite" and that last year's grim experience may be repeated because few fundamental factors have been corrected.[8]

The American Council on Race Relations, interested in setting up local committees, was forced to admit in February 1945 that many of the committees "have not as yet been remarkable for their achievements." It pointed out the value of effective groups and continued, "on the other hand, a committee which merely acts as a front for politicians or as a means of delaying action is probably worse than no committee at all." [9]

---

7. A. A. Liveright, "The Community and Race Relations," *Annals of the American Academy of Political and Social Science*, 244 (March 1946), 106-7. Liveright sums up the criticisms aimed at the committees in this article: "Minority groups are seriously questioning their sincerity and motivation. They ask whether or not such committees really want to face the unpleasant basic factors which must be faced. They wonder, publicly, whether some of these committees may not be doing more to inhibit than to stimulate action. They infer that the official committees have been set up as a buffer for the mayor and city government rather than as a real device to overcome segregation, inadequate housing, employment discrimination, and abuses of civil rights. On the other hand, some officials who have appointed these committees are tempted to let them languish and die rather than face the embarrassing prospect of the inevitable 64-dollar questions which must result from any honest inquiry into race relations questions."

8. Lester B. Granger, "A Hopeful Sign in Race Relations," *Survey Graphic*, XXXIII (November 1944), 476.

9. *News Letter*.

By no means could all of the committees be placed in the failure category. State committees in New York, Massachusetts, Connecticut, and New Jersey set the stage for fair employment practice legislation in their respective states in the following few years. Municipal committees in Chicago and other cities, given adequate financial assistance, were able to hire specialists to aid in planning local programs with commendable results. Even in the communities where strong committees did not come into being, discussion of the principles of fair employment practices and racial justice served to educate and prepare many for the state and national drives for permanent fair employment practice legislation then getting under way.

ESTABLISHMENT OF THE NATIONAL COUNCIL

By 1943 fear of prospective loss of minority wartime employment gains in the postwar period led race leaders and sympathetic groups to seek further safeguards against return to the "last hired—first fired" policy for minorities in industrial employment. Discussion of possible approaches to the problem quickly revealed a notable fact: few leaders were willing to return to the *laissez-faire* approach of advancing the interests of minority groups. Disappointing though the President's Committee had been, it was almost universally agreed by those who concerned themselves with such matters that only through government action could minority groups obtain a guarantee of fair treatment in industry.

Implementation of this common view developed slowly. A. Philip Randolph, the leader of the movement which had coerced the government into establishing the President's Committee, took the first step to set the drive into motion. In February 1943 Randolph called a Conference to Save FEPC in Washington to rally support for the President's Committee, then in the midst of one of its periodic crises. While no action on a permanent FEPC took place here, the idea of a movement for a permanent national FEPC with strong enforcement powers was seriously discussed. At succeeding meetings the thought took root and reached maturity. Finally, at another Conference to Save FEPC attended by representatives of fifteen national organizations on September 13 and 14, 1943, the National Council for a Permanent FEPC came into being.

GENERAL CHARACTER OF THE NATIONAL COUNCIL

The organization was not broad in scope at its inception. The original leadership and support were almost entirely from New York City.[10] In addition to Randolph's March on Washington Movement and Brotherhood of Sleeping Car Porters, the new group drew its early support from the leaders of such liberal, non-Communist New York trade unions as the International Ladies' Garment Workers Union, the Textile Workers of America, the United Retail, Wholesale and Department Store Employees of America, and the United Hatters, Cap & Millinery Workers Union. Also prominent in the formation of the National Council were representatives of the liberal clergy, Catholic, Jewish, and Protestant, and of such Socialist-led organizations as the Workers Defense League and the Post-War World Council.

For months after its establishment the Council continued to exist in name only. Lack of money, staff, and proper direction combined to forestall large-scale operations. A secretary, aided by occasional part-time and volunteer assistance, comprised the entire staff for almost the first half-year of the Council's existence. Adequate funds were not available for even ordinary organizational operations.

The first major undertaking of the Council was the calling of a trade union conference on October 20, 1943, for fund-raising purposes to which representatives of unions with New York headquarters were invited. The invitations came from B. F. McLaurin, acting secretary of Provisional Committee to Organize Locomotive Firemen

---

10. One worker in the field of discrimination reform wrote Randolph early in 1944: "It seems to me from now on that it would be advisable, as your Council members are increased, to have the emphasis on names *outside* of New York City. As you may know (and I know, because I hail from the middlewest) there is a general prejudice in the country against 'radical, Jewish' leadership which is associated with New York City. (The trust in Negro leadership, emanating from New York City is, of course, an exception to the general.)

"It is my belief that you, more than any man, are responsible for all progress along FEPC lines. But at this time I am in doubt about the wisdom and efficacy of having an overloading of first Negro, and second, Jewish representation on the Council's list."—Letter from John Becker, Public Relations Advisor, Council Against Intolerance in America, to A. Philip Randolph, January 26, 1944. The above letter and all others hereafter mentioned are found in the files of the National Council for a Permanent FEPC unless otherwise indicated.

and Randolph's right hand man. The conference followed the failure of the President's Committee to cope with the exclusion of Negroes from "desirable" jobs on southern railroads. Ninety delegates from forty international and local unions of a liberal, non-Communist character with large Jewish and Negro memberships attended and pledged both organizational and financial support.

When the Southwestern Carriers and Railway Brotherhoods defied the President's Committee's directives to cease their discriminatory practices against Negroes, a second conference was called in New York City for December 30, 1943. This time the group composition of the conference was broadened to include civic, church, liberal, and educational, as well as labor, organizations with headquarters in New York City. Approximately fifty representatives of twenty national organizations were present.[11] Before the meeting was concluded, the delegates voted to support the President's Committee by holding a New York mass meeting and by telegraphing President Roosevelt to urge him to take immediate action against the railroad carriers and unions. Furthermore, the delegates endorsed a national conference to be held in Washington to get the drive for permanent legislation under way.

The Washington Conference held on January 20 and 21, 1944, marked the emergence of the movement beyond the confines of New York City and the commitment of a variety of national organizations to support of permanent FEPC legislation.[12] One hundred and twenty-

---

11. The participating organizations included the Relief Association of the Baptist Church, Catholic Interracial Council, Coordinating Committee of Jewish Agencies, Council for Democracy, National Conference of Christians and Jews, National Lawyers Guild, Negro Labor Committee, Post-War World Council, United Hebrew Trades, National Board of the YWCA, New York Metropolitan Council on FEPC, Central Conference of American Rabbis, and several joint boards of New York trade unions.

12. The organizations participating in the Washington Conference included: Union for Democratic Action; CIO, Local 35001; National Catholic Welfare Conference; American Civil Liberties Union; Chicago Unit, MOW; National Association for the Advancement of Colored People; Amalgamated Clothing Workers; Post-War World Council; Ladies Auxiliary, Brotherhood of Sleeping Car Porters, Washington Division; Workers Defense League; March on Washington, Washington Unit; Laundry Workers Joint Board of Greater New York, Amalgamated Clothing Workers; National Council of Jewish Women; Fellowship of Reconciliation; Youth Committee for Democracy; NAACP, Washington Branch; Institute on Race Relations; National Board, YWCA; Labor-Industry Committee, New York NAACP; Alabama Council of the American Jewish Congress; American Jewish Congress;

five delegates from 21 states representing 45 organizations adopted the following resolution:

1) The present FEPC, established under Executive Order, has few and limited sanctions;

2) The present Committee has been publicly challenged as exceeding its constitutional powers. Its authority has been publicly repudiated by sixteen Southern Railroads. If it is left to rely solely on its present limited sanctions, it will be rendered largely ineffective by continued refusals to obey its directives and by time-consuming litigation in the courts;

3) Only an Act of Congress can give to the FEPC a permanency and the resources which it needs to do its important work effectively;

4) Action by the Congress at this time in publicly attacking the problem of discrimination at home would be a symbol to all the oppressed peoples of the world of the sincere and practical determination of the United States to implement the Four Freedoms as quickly and effectively as possible.[13]

While the National Council was building organizational support through the New York and Washington conferences and other efforts, plans for the introduction of a bill in Congress and the establishment of a headquarters in Washington also proceeded apace. After many conferences with congressmen with liberal labor records to secure the most sympathetic and influential sponsors, Representatives Dawson (Dem. Ill.), Scanlon (Dem. Pa.), and LaFollette (Rep. Ind.) were prevailed upon to introduce the National Council's bill in the House of Representatives in January 1944.[14] The task of obtaining a satisfactory senatorial sponsor proved more difficult; it was not until June 23, 1944, that a companion bill (S. 2048) was introduced in the Senate by Dennis Chavez of New Mexico with Senators Downey, Wagner, Murray, Capper, and Langer as co-sponsors.[15]

National Women's Trade Union League; Religion and Labor Foundation; Metropolitan Detroit Council on Fair Employment Practices; Fraternal Council of Negro Churches; Joint Council, Dining Car Employees; Christian Baptist Church, Chicago; Council of Jewish Federations and Welfare Funds; National Association of Colored Graduate Nurses; Tuesday Evening Club of Social Workers; National Alliance of Postal Employees; National Non-Partisan Council on Public Affairs of Alpha Kappa Alpha Sorority; Firemen's Union, Georgia; United Auto Workers, CIO; YMCA; Car Cleaners Union; United Hebrew Trades; United States Student Assembly; Common Council for American Unity; Socialist Party; Women's International League for Peace and Freedom and others.

13. *Report on Activities.*

14. Because only one sponsor is permitted for each bill in the House, the congressmen introduced separate bills which were later dropped in favor of H.R. 3986.

15. It is of interest that early in the search for a senatorial sponsor Robert A. Taft

ORGANIZATIONAL STRUCTURE AND PROBLEMS

At one of the early meetings of the National Council's top leaders, a constitution was adopted setting forth the general objectives of the new organization:

(1) To promote in every possible way the establishment of equal opportunity for employment, to secure hiring with due regard to the already existing skills and experiences of the applicant, equality of wages for the same work, and the full right of upgrading employees within industries regardless of race, creed, color or origin.

(2) To bring about the establishment of a permanent federal FEPC.

(3) To carry on an educational campaign, nationally and locally, to further the Council's objectives.

The manner in which the Council would operate was not well formulated at the outset, but a two-fold job was visualized. In the first place, it was anticipated that the Council would serve as a clearing house for all organizational work in behalf of permanent federal FEPC legislation to assure proper coverage in stimulating public support and to avoid duplication of efforts. Secondly, their plans called for the National Council to spearhead the campaign to enact FEPC legislation through pressure activities on the Washington scene. The question of whether to devote a substantial proportion of the organization's energies to the bolstering of the President's Committee or to concentrate all efforts upon permanent FEPC legislation was not easily resolved. In the early days of its operation the Council divided its energies almost equally between the two areas of operation, but as the issue of permanent legislation assumed national significance, the President's Committee came in for less and less emphasis. This did not meet with the universal approval of the groups concerned and subsequently aroused organizational frictions in the President's Committee's losing battle against congressional antagonism.[16]

---

of Ohio, later to be a vigorous opponent of FEPC legislation with "teeth," signified his willingness to sponsor the National Council's bill but was not invited to do so because he was regarded as a "deadly sponsor."—Letter from Mrs. Stark to Randolph, October 25, 1943.

16. When Leslie Perry of the NAACP requested that the National Council join in opposing the President's Committee hearings on the Capital Transit Company case for fear that such action would injure the chances for FEPC legislation in Congress, the Council's executive committee passed the following resolution in December 1944,

Stated briefly, according to the National Council's constitution, the structure was to be simple: (1) officers, including a chairman and treasurer; (2) a national committee made up of representatives of cooperating organizations interested in permanent FEPC legislation to advise upon the fundamental policy of the National Council; (3) a smaller executive committee of not more than twenty-five representatives from the national committee to act in the latter's behalf on authorized occasions; and (4) an executive secretary and an associate secretary appointed by and responsible to the chairman and the executive committee, whose assignments were to direct the Washington office and to have immediate responsibility for stimulating public support and for lobbying activities.

At one of the early meetings Randolph and the Reverend Dr. Allan Knight Chalmers of the Broadway Tabernacle Church were elected co-chairmen. The arrangement was that Chalmers would lend his name for prestige purposes but that Randolph would be the functioning chairman. Chalmers declined a more active role because he was already on the boards of nearly thirty organizations. William Jay Schieffelin, well-to-do manufacturing druggist active in a number of interracial endeavors, was chosen treasurer. Senators Arthur Capper of Kansas and Robert Wagner of New York agreed to permit their names to be used as honorary co-chairmen. Mrs. Alice Stark was named temporary secretary to be in charge of the New York office until a Washington headquarters could be established.

NATIONAL COMMITTEE OF COOPERATING ORGANIZATIONS

In the actual operations of the National Council, effective authority centered not in the national committee of cooperating organizations but in the chairman and the executive committee. As it later developed, the national committee which grew to contain the names of the repre-

---

which revealed its reluctance to concern itself with the President's Committee's problems: "The sole task of the National Council is the establishment of a permanent FEPC with enforcement powers that would make it unlawful for such violators as the Capital Transit Company to flaunt its directives. The question of timing of hearings is an administrative detail about which the National Council does not feel free to express an opinion."—Letter from Mrs. Anna Arnold Hedgeman to Leslie Perry, Administrative Assistant, NAACP, December 16, 1944.

sentatives of almost seventy national church, labor, civil libertarian, Negro, Jewish, fraternal, and professional organizations had virtually no direct control over the National Council's policies. Once organized the cooperating organizations were rarely called upon, as a group, to share in the making of major decisions.

These cooperating groups were looked upon as conveyor belts to carry to their large memberships the National Council's requests for funds and for local and national political action. Their representatives received frequent action letters from the Washington office making requests for delegations to Washington, letters and telegrams to congressmen, or for testimony before congressional committees. The National Council sought to coordinate all of their FEPC activities so that maximum pressure could be exerted upon Congress at the crucial moments in the legislative campaign.

CHAIRMAN

As has been suggested, the most important single person in the formation and operation of the National Council was Philip Randolph. From the beginning the Council reflected his role as a Negro trade union leader, his personal philosophy, his relations with other leaders and groups, and his general strengths and weaknesses. It can almost be said that Randolph was the National Council.

It is not uncommon in American history to find reform movements built as much around personalities as issues. Single strong leaders or small groups of men with strong convictions often find outlets in initiating movements where they can give full expression to their own personalities. As a result many causes succeed or fail depending upon the strengths and shortcomings of the dominant person or persons in the movement. In the case of the FEPC movement, while the fundamental appeal was based upon a real grievance, it cannot be denied that the leadership of the National Council shaped the character of the struggle for national FEPC legislation.

Randolph, without question, is one of the more influential Negro leaders on the scene today. He is a person of great determination and courage; his idealism and devotion to the advancement of his people have given him considerable stature among both Negroes and whites. In his early career he had achieved considerable prestige as a Socialist organizer and editor of *The Messenger*, a vigorous journal of Socialist opinion. In 1925 he became the general organizer of the Brotherhood of Sleeping Car Porters which has become the most important Negro union in America despite fierce opposition from the Pullman Car Company.[17] He led the BSCP into the American Federation of Labor in 1936 where he has fought the discriminatory policies of many international unions almost single-handedly.

At the same time, his personality and his experience have not prepared him well for leadership of a reform movement containing widely diverse groups. In the first place, his one-man uphill fight in the trade union movement has not conditioned him to share policy-making and leadership with others. The failure of the National Association for the Advancement of Colored People and the Congress of Industrial Organizations to make a greater contribution to the FEPC drive must, in some large measure, be ascribed to Randolph's failure to share responsibility with their top leaders.

Secondly, Randolph is ideologically intransigent. He and the people with whom he surrounds himself are Socialists and New Dealers. His hatred of the Communists is so intense that he will not work with them in social reform movements under any circumstances although their short-range objectives may be identical. When the Communists expressed an interest in FEPC legislation, he went out of his way to exclude them from the movement. While he thereby retained his ideological purity, he also provoked a struggle which did not aid in the passage of the legislation. The National Council suffered when labor unions and Negro and white reform organizations, which leaned to the Communist point of view or abhorred an ideological war over so important an issue, refused to give it full support.

Thirdly, despite his extensive experience in trade union and reform movements, Randolph is somewhat naive about political techniques, a fact which has not engendered full confidence in his leadership. His implicit faith in the March on Washington as an effective technique for pressure campaigns bespeaks an oversimplification of the problem of achieving political objectives. His willingness to align himself with

---

17. See Brailsford R. Brazeal, *The Brotherhood of Sleeping Car Porters*, for a recent appraisal of this union.

would-be third parties, at a time when the National Council's staff in Washington sought to stay out of the party arena and woo both major parties in Congress, also militated against maximum lobbying effectiveness.

Two other facets of Randolph's personality further hampered FEPC progress. One is his tendency to be a "political butterfly," flitting from reform to reform, without sticking to any for very long.[18] He takes on so many causes that he is unable to give much time to any one; for this he is suspect among reform leaders.[19] The National Council's staff in Washington found that one of its major problems was to get Randolph to find time to actually shoulder the responsibilities which he had assumed and which he refused to share with others. His failure to perform properly as a working chairman created many internal frictions over policy and finance.[20] Finally, while he is a stimulating platform speaker and has many admirers, both personal and in the mass, he is accused of "looking down his nose" in his relations with most people. Even Negro newspapermen do not warm easily to his cold, aloof personality despite their similar interests. His "holier-than-thou" demeanor has caused him to be characterized as "Saint Philip."[21] The National Council was indelibly stamped with his personality foibles.

EXECUTIVE COMMITTEE

The executive committee was composed of representatives of approximately twenty-five of the cooperating organizations serving on an indefinite basis. According to the National Council's constitution,

18. See *PM* for April 8, 1946, for a recent third party move involving Randolph.

19. Typical of many communications between the Washington office and Randolph is this excerpt from a letter from Mrs. Hedgeman dated May 22, 1944: "I discover that people generally seem convinced that you are not as interested in this project as you ought to be. . . . They are asking whether you are appearing at the hearings and one important individual came right out and said, 'Is Mr. Randolph really behind this legislation?' "

20. According to the constitution, the duties of the chairmen were "to preside at the national convention, to call special meetings of the Council, as such meetings are required, to advise the executive secretaries, to call together the Executive Committee, to recommend changes in policy to the Executive Council [National Committee], to initiate and supervise the financial policy of the Council, and in all ways to further the work of the Council."

21. *Atlanta World*, April 18, 1944.

the committee's chief function was to "act in place of the Executive Council [National Committee] when quick action is necessary to the extent that the Executive Council gives them authority to so act." In actual practice the executive committee made the organization's policy with only infrequent consultation with members of the national committee of cooperating organizations. This developed as a result of the failure of the chairman to call regular national conventions, as prescribed by the constitution, at which fundamental policy was to be discussed. In addition to the policy-making function which devolved upon it, the executive committee also kept in close touch with the administrative problems of the Washington office through an administrative committee. Other subcommittees concerned themselves with such matters as finance and publicity.

Much of the criticism of the National Council by its supporters, as well as opponents, centered on the allegation that the executive committee did not contain a true cross-section of the groups which supported the FEPC movement.[22] Especially vigorous were the charges that the Negro viewpoint was being represented to the exclusion of nearly all other minority groups and that the committee was dominated by individuals hand-picked by Randolph and loyal to his point of view.[23] Part of this criticism came from the Communists who were

---

22. In addition to the officers, some of the executive committee's most influential members included: Samuel Baron of the Textile Workers Union; Linna E. Bresette of the National Catholic Welfare Conference; George E. Brown of the Dining Car Employees, AFL; Thurman Dodson, lawyer active in the March on Washington Movement; Rabbi Sidney E. Goldstein; Sidney Hollander, President of the Council of Jewish Federations and Welfare Funds; George K. Hunton, Director of the Catholic Interracial Council; Thomasina W. Johnson, Alpha Kappa Alpha; Nathaniel Minkoff, Secretary-Treasurer of the Joint Board, Dressmakers Union, ILGWU; James Myers, Federal Council of Churches; Dorothy S. Norman, *New York Post* columnist and active Liberal Party member; Winifred Raushenbush of the American Civil Liberties Union; Alex Rose, Secretary-Treasurer of the Millinery Workers Joint Board, AFL; Rt. Rev. John A. Ryan, D.D.; Mabel Staupers, Executive Secretary of the National Association of Graduate Colored Nurses; Noah Walter Jr. of the Laundry Workers; Max Zaritsky, President of the United Hatters, Cap & Millinery Workers; Charles Zimmerman, Vice President of the ILGWU; and Willard Townsend, International President of the United Transport Service Employees of America.

23. A newspaper version of this criticism charged: "Support of the National Council for a Permanent FEPC reportedly has dropped off because of its failure to adequately represent minority groups and the indefiniteness of its stand regarding the present struggle of FEPC for a budget. . . .

"Persons interested in a permanent FEPC have questioned the scarcity of minority

bitterly opposed to Randolph's leadership, but much of it came from non-Communist groups and individuals who were concerned lest the the movement fail for lack of appeal to all minority groups.

Succeeding events did little to refute these charges. Although there were some internal conflicts, the executive committee consistently followed Randolph's lead. Key organizations, such as the AFL, CIO, and NAACP, remained without direct representation on the executive committee until the spring of 1946.

Steps were taken to broaden leadership only after the rebuff which the National Council's bill received in the Senate in 1946. After consultation with a variety of political experts in March, the executive committee recommended that its membership be broadened and that a small policy committee be established to give such important leaders as James Carey of the CIO, Walter White of the NAACP, Dr. Allen Knight Chalmers, Dr. Channing Tobias of the YWCA, and several others a share in the responsibility for shaping policy.

The policy committee was formed in April 1946 and served temporarily to quiet the charges of one-man domination. When Randolph suggested that the National Council accept a watered-down FEPC bill sponsored by Senator Robert A. Taft of Ohio to salvage something out of the 1946 legislative drive, White and Carey vigorously rejected the proposal, giving temporary credence to the National Council's claim that the responsibility for leadership had been broadened.[24]

It was not long before charges were flying that Randolph was sidetracking the policy committee and making decisions without consultation with it. For this and other reasons the National Council's control over the FEPC movement steadily dwindled. By the beginning of the Eightieth Congress in January 1947, the organization was forced to reorganize itself by expanding its leadership in order to continue to lead the movement.

---

group representation in an organization reputedly fighting for airing grievances of colored people.

"Tendency of colored executive committee members to dominate meetings attended by Sam Baron of the Textile Workers' Union and George Hunton of the Catholic Interracial Council, both white, has allegedly led to the withdrawal of support by trade unions and other sympathizers."—*Baltimore Afro-American*, April 22, 1944.

24. Telegram from Randolph to Policy Committee, May 20, 1946.

EXECUTIVE SECRETARY

Early in the fight it was recognized that a successful lobbying campaign could not be waged from New York by Randolph and the other god-fathers of the National Council, who were already overburdened with their other organizational activities. Consequently, as soon as the bill was introduced into the House of Representatives in January 1943, steps were taken to establish a Washington headquarters to stimulate public support for FEPC and to guide the proposal through Congress.

To direct the work of the Washington office, an executive secretary and an associate secretary were selected by Chairman Randolph and the executive committee to whom they were responsible. In creating the two positions the executive committee failed to delineate carefully the areas of jurisdiction which paved the way to an early clash between Mrs. Anna Arnold Hedgeman, the executive secretary, and Will Allen, the associate secretary. Finally the dismissal of Allen for failing to carry out the decisions of the executive committee with respect to his work resolved this controversy two months after the Washington office was established.[25] From that time forward Mrs. Hedgeman was able to select her own office staff and to assume sole responsibility for the work of the Washington headquarters.

Mrs. Hedgeman came to the National Council after considerable experience in Negro YWCA work in Springfield, Ohio, Jersey City, Harlem, Brooklyn, and Philadelphia. Immediately prior to her acceptance of the Randolph offer, she had served as special assistant to the Commissioner of Welfare for New York City and as field consultant for the New York Regional Office of Civilian Defense. While she had had no previous pressure group experience, she had established a reputation for being a vigorous and able administrator with wide acquaintance in the organizational world.

In Washington she began as a mere novice in the legislative field, but within the following three years she had gained wide recognition for the aptitude which she had demonstrated for her work. The successes of the National Council were due in large measure to her leadership; the failures, to factors of finance and top leadership difficulties largely

---

25. Executive Committee Minutes, April 10, 1944.

beyond her control. She is an intense person who throws herself completely into her work. She took every FEPC failure as a personal loss. In the period during which she held her post, she frequently clashed with Randolph over his failure to live up to all of his responsibilities as chairman and his general shortcomings already alluded to above.

Mrs. Hedgeman was not without her critics. The foes of Randolph linked her with his policies which, in truth, were the policies of the Washington office. She was accused of giving unwarranted emphasis to the Negro's side in the FEPC movement to the detriment of efforts to involve other minorities in the fight. She did not always cooperate well with other groups which sought to share responsibility for the legislative campaign; the conflict with Malcolm Ross and Will Maslow of the President's Committee on Fair Employment Practice was particularly injurious to the best interests of permanent FEPC legislation.

STRATEGY AND LEGAL COMMITTEES

Upon the suggestion of Roger Baldwin of the American Civil Liberties Union, Mrs. Hedgeman invited a number of legislative representatives of other organizations in Washington to serve on a special strategy committee on FEPC which she could call upon to assist her in reaching decisions on legislative strategy and tactics. Many expressed a willingness to serve and gave the National Council the benefit of their experience on the Washington scene.[26] The meetings of this committee were highly informal, and minutes were kept only occasionally. Some felt that the committee should be formalized with a rotating chairmanship, but the committee remained on a casual volunteer

---

26. The strategy committee contained the following legislative representatives among others: Mrs. Leslie Falk, United Council of Church Women; Mrs. Louis Ottenberg, National Council of Jewish Women; Mrs. James W. Irwin, National Board, YWCA; Mrs. Eunice Hunton Carter, National Council of Negro Women; Mrs. Ted F. Silvey, American Civil Liberties Union; Mrs. Florence Barnes, Women's Trade Union League; Miss Elizabeth Eastman, Common Council for American Unity; Mrs. Claire G. Sifton, Union for Democratic Action; Arthur E. Phillips, National CIO Legislative Committee; Mrs. Helen Loeffler, National League of Women Shoppers; Mrs. Thomasina W. Johnson, Alpha Kappa Alpha Non-Partisan Council; Dr. Francis W. McPeek, Council for Social Action, Congregational Christian Churches; Miss Pauline Myers, Fraternal Council of Negro Churches; Russell Smith, Farmers Union; Ben Marsh, People's Lobby; Marcus Cohen, American Jewish Committee; Leslie Perry, NAACP; and Raymond Wilson, Friends Legislative Committee.

basis.[27] The following excerpts from the minutes of a strategy committee meeting indicate the subject matters with which the participants concerned themselves:

First on agenda was review of legislative background of Dawson-Scanlon-LaFollette Bill. Suggestions were then asked for with regard to names of persons to testify at hearings of House Labor Committee.

Eastman: Analysis of bill should be presented first by somebody like Felix Cohen.

Cohen: I would suggest in this connection that both Mr. Dodson and I be available for advice, etc.

Detzer: Somebody—for instance, a good lawyer—should present the bill at the beginning.

Eastman: Should prepare for objections that we know are going to be raised.

Detzer: After presentation of the bill you want to open with labor, farmers, church leaders, etc.

Johnson: I might suggest that you do not have R—— present the case. He is much too ineffective.

Detzer: Father Haas might do a very good job.

Owens: I prefer Haas to R——. I offer the suggestion that you have labor people there first—before analysis of bill is presented. P——. AFL or CIO.

Detzer: That would make it a communist bill immediately. Couldn't you get Murray rather than P——? . . .

Detzer: We must think of several things. The conventions are coming. Should get good political people to show backing. Get Farley or Sumner Welles—someone with a name in both parties. LaGuardia—just as a type of name to make headlines. Josephus Daniels. A liberal from the South.[28]

To assist with the complicated legal questions involved in framing a bill and in answering the technical objections raised by the opposition, a legal committee was also set up in Washington to be available for occasional consultation with the National Council's staff. Agreeing to serve on the committee were the following outstanding lawyers, four of whom were Negroes and the other a Jew: Professor Andrew Ransome of Howard University; Charles Houston, who had served on the President's Committee on Fair Employment Practice; Thurman L. Dodson, close friend of Randolph and active in the March on Wash-

27. Staff Meeting Minutes, December 26, 1945.
28. Strategy Committee Minutes, May 12, 1944.

ington Movement; Judge William Hastie, who was later to become Governor of the Virgin Islands; and Felix Cohen, brilliant
lawyer in the Office of the Solicitor of the Department of the Interior.
The National Council was well served by this committee.

WASHINGTON OFFICE AND STAFF

Headquarters were established in Washington in February 1944, at
1410 H Street, N.W. where Mrs. Hedgeman and her then small staff
shared a 9 x 15 office with the Workers Defense League. Prejudice
against Negro and white staff members working together made it
difficult to find other quarters. Even at this address, where quarters
were so small that staff members often had to go home to work, the
landlord was prevailed upon to give a dispossess notice to Mrs. Hedgeman when other tenants in the building learned of the mixed staff.
Only when the Workers Defense League got the editor of the *Newark
Afro-American* to discuss the matter with the Mutual Benefit Life
Insurance Company, which owned the building, was the issue dropped.

Finally after about eight months, offices were obtained in the Atlantic Building at 930 F. Street, N.W. which housed the headquarters
of a number of CIO unions with mixed staffs. The offices were located
on the ninth floor of the building in a converted attic or storage
space without elevator service. However, the quarters served the needs
of the staff quite satisfactorily.

The staff itself was of mixed quality. The wartime manpower shortage and the inability of the National Council to pay handsome salaries,
or even to meet payroll commitments regularly, prevented the employment of a staff of fully-qualified, experienced people. Most of the
staff members were women with relatively little experience in the difficult field of reform pressure work. Miss Sidney Wilkinson, Mrs.
Hedgeman's assistant in managing the office, came with a background
of such miscellaneous experiences as assistant to the Municipal Director of Music in Baltimore, secretary to the Vice President of Macy's
Department Store in New York City, secretary to Jascha Heifetz,
concert violinist, and public relations writer for a large lumber association.

The two legislative representatives who were employed by the
Washington office until the spring of 1946 were also women. Miss

Ida Fox had had an active career in Socialist and interracial organizational work. Born and educated in New York City, she came to the
National Council from the Minority Workshop of the Socialist party
in Washington. Mrs. Beatrice B. Schalet was a New Englander with
background in the advertising and social service fields. She had been
the Washington correspondent for the Cooperative League News
Service and an organizer of the Interracial Consumers' Cooperative
Movement. Mrs. Mildred Makover, local council coordinator, and
Miss Margery S. Taylor, general research and legislative worker, were
fairly new to the pressure field. Miss Taylor had served as ferry pilot
during the war and had taught physical education in several colleges
before the war.

Several men were included among the field representatives: William
Leuchtenburg, former general secretary of the U.S. Student Assembly; Milo Manley, former social worker and examiner for the President's Committee; and Charles Toney with a background in journalism. The women representatives included Mrs. Belle Douglas, general
manager of the *New Orleans Informer* before coming to the National
Council; Miss Una A. Squires, social worker; Mrs. Dovey Johnson
Roundtree, former teacher and major in the Women's Army Corps;
Miss Lethia W. Clore, former President's Committee examiner; and
several others.

It might be observed that Negroes and Jews made up most of the
staff; even more significant is the fact that they were very much alike
in their general outlook: believers in democratic socialism, anti-Communist, interracially minded. While there were personality clashes
leading to the resignation of some of the above named people, they
were all agreed on principles and on the objectives of the National
Council.

The duties of the staff members were not rigid; when occasion
demanded, all participated in doing the most pressing job at hand.
Roughly, however, the work of the Washington office was broken
down into three main categories: office, legislative, and field operations. The office operations involved bookkeeping, maintenance of
files, literature inventory, incoming and outgoing mail, and travel
routing and reservations. The legislative work was more varied and
consisted of: constant checks upon the attitudes of senators and repre-

NATIONAL COUNCIL ORGANIZATION UNTIL JUNE 1946

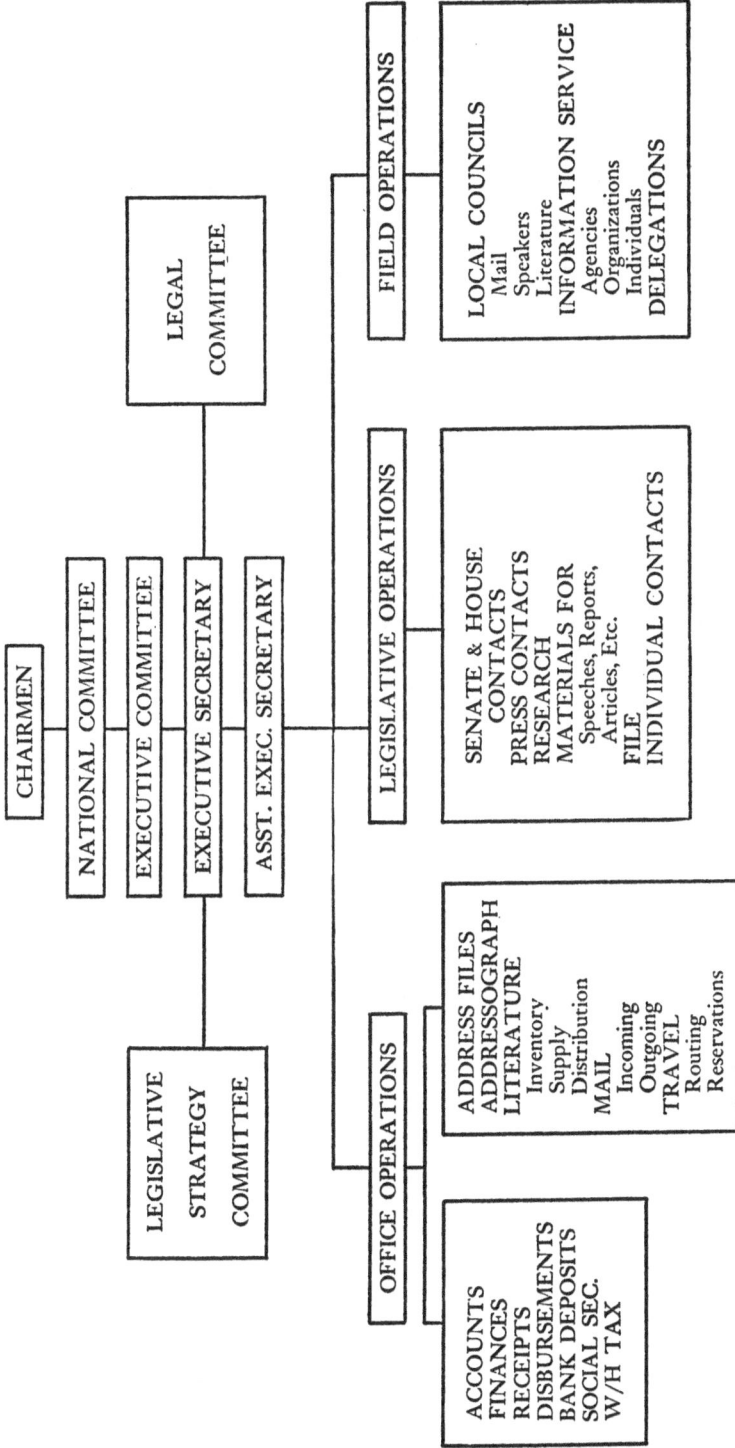

CHAIRMEN

NATIONAL COMMITTEE

EXECUTIVE COMMITTEE

EXECUTIVE SECRETARY

ASST. EXEC. SECRETARY

LEGAL COMMITTEE

LEGISLATIVE STRATEGY COMMITTEE

FIELD OPERATIONS

LOCAL COUNCILS
Mail
Speakers
Literature
INFORMATION SERVICE
Agencies
Organizations
Individuals
DELEGATIONS

LEGISLATIVE OPERATIONS

SENATE & HOUSE CONTACTS
PRESS CONTACTS
RESEARCH
MATERIALS FOR
Speeches, Reports, Articles, Etc.
FILE
INDIVIDUAL CONTACTS

OFFICE OPERATIONS

ADDRESS FILES
ADDRESSOGRAPH
LITERATURE
Inventory
Supply
Distribution
MAIL
Incoming
Outgoing
TRAVEL
Routing
Reservations

ACCOUNTS
FINANCES
RECEIPTS
DISBURSEMENTS
BANK DEPOSITS
SOCIAL SEC.
W/H TAX

sentatives on FEPC legislation with frequent conferences to bring them into line; press contacts; research upon legislative matters; preparation of speeches; reports and other literature to be used by friendly congressmen and to be distributed to the public. Field operations, as far as the Washington office was concerned, involved communication with local councils; arranging for speakers and supplying literature to local councils; cooperation with other organizations and individuals to secure their assistance in the drive by supplying them with information on FEPC; and, finally, arranging for delegations to Washington to coincide with the peak of the legislative drives.

In the field the representatives were called upon to do many jobs. They were to establish local councils wherever possible for the money which they could raise and for the pressure which they could exert upon Congress. They were to engage in educational work by distributing FEPC literature and giving speeches on the objectives of the drive. They were to line up organizational support by securing the adoption of pro-FEPC resolutions at conventions in their territories and, if possible, to involve organizations in active work in behalf of the FEPC movement. They were to make local contacts for the national office to follow up and to size up the local, state, and regional political situations for their bearing upon the possibility of getting the FEPC bill through Congress. Above all, their job was to stimulate as many groups in the local communities as possible to an awareness of FEPC.[29]

---

29. Speaking on the field staff's work at a staff meeting Mrs. Hedgeman said: "It is an over all community job. Pull the whole community together, Japanese, Jews, Negroes, Catholics, Mexicans etc. Watch for the leaders of all communities. Find out composition of community and then work from there. Lean on the Women, United Council of Church Women, YWCA. Watch for Democratic and Republican leaders keeping in mind that this is a political job. Find out who put the guy in office. Write to us and let us know so we can then act intelligently."—Staff Meeting Minutes, October 26, 1945.

CHAPTER 3

Beating the Brush

- SETTING UP LOCAL COUNCILS • COMPOSI-
TION OF LOCAL COUNCILS • LEADERSHIP
- RELATIONS WITH OTHER ORGANIZATIONS •
SOUTHERN COUNCILS AND THE COLOR LINE
- LOCAL-NATIONAL COUNCIL RELATIONS •
EVALUATION OF THE LOCAL COUNCILS

OST PRESSURE GROUPS FIND IT EXPEDIENT TO generate support from back home for successful lobbying. Nothing impresses legislators more than pressure from the people who control their legislative fate.[1] Groups representing established community interests have little difficulty in persuading legislators of the vote-getting possibilities of issues involving powerful segments of the electorate. Reform groups have a special problem in seeking legislative support because legislators are chary of new and controversial issues. Some would not favor a reform unless heavily pressured because of strong personal views against it; others may sympathize with a reform but fear the reaction of opponents in the party organization and at the polls. It is necessary for reform groups to show that a ready market for the new "product" exists and that the "customers" demand its availability.[2]

---

1. "What most members of Congress want more than anything else in the world is to hold on to their $10,000-a-year jobs indefinitely. If they can live long enough, the unwritten laws of precedence in the House will land them eventually in committee chairmanships and they are assured of a footnote in some particularly exhaustive history. They may even be able, with enough breaks, to advance to the Senate, where there is a chance for newspaper publicity and where every member, at least in his own mind, is a potential presidential candidate. Assurance of re-election is therefore the price the average Congressman demands for his services."—Kenneth Crawford, *The Pressure Boys*, pp. 296-97.

2. "The actual influence exerted by pressure groups in nominations and elections is a matter about which there is little precise knowledge. The professional politician, in a sense, makes it his business to estimate the strength of the various interests appealing to him for his support of particular policies. He risks his re-election—and his

Various techniques exist for arousing pressures from back home. Perhaps the easiest and most widely used is the appeal from the central headquarters of a well-established organization to its local branches to buttonhole or write their representatives on issues affecting their group. A second technique, used chiefly when issues cut across economic or social organizational lines, is for a temporary coordinating committee to urge existing branches of all permanent state or national groups interested in the legislation to exert pressure. This technique is favored by many because it helps to avoid organizational jealousies frequently aroused when new groups enter the field even for temporary purposes. The defect in this approach lies in the lack of direct control by the planners of the campaign over the local branches which may or may not bestir themselves as they deem fit.

To ensure more direct control over local phases of a pressure campaign, some temporary coordinating groups have established their own specialized local committees. The potential benefits from such an arrangement are substantial but so are the problems. It focuses greater attention on the issue and facilitates better planning for pressures on a legislative body. The chief drawback is that more time, money, and energy will sometimes go into setting up local committees than the resources of the movement permit.

The National Council was notable for its attempt to build a local organization for purposes of local pressure. The councils became an integral part of the strategy and operations of the National Council despite vigorous criticism by many supporters of FEPC.

SETTING UP LOCAL COUNCILS

The councils came into being through diverse gestation processes. In the early days of the National Council, Randolph went from city to city addressing meetings on FEPC and founding local councils. Later the job of organizing branches was handled chiefly by field representatives operating under instructions from the Washington office. Some of the councils were established by individual enthusiasts who

---

livelihood—on his ability to forecast the strength which can be mustered against him at the polls by the group that the lobbyist represents. Yet the politician acts on intuitive estimates of the situation. The chances are that the bark of most of the organized groups is more terrifying than their bite on election day, but there is little convincing evidence bearing on the question one way or the other."—V. O. Key, *Politics, Parties, and Pressure Groups*, pp. 212-13.

took it upon themselves to push the campaign in their own cities. The National Council encouraged these people by issuing a bulletin on the formation of local councils:

IS YOUR COMMUNITY INTERESTED IN A PERMANENT FEPC?

Is there a local council working for the passage of these bills? (S. 101—H.R. 2232—prohibit discrimination in employment because of race, creed, color, national origin, or ancestry.)

If you have no local council, may we offer the following suggestions for developing one?

I. It is very important that such councils be called: (Name of your city) Congressional Council for a Permanent FEPC. (It is important that you have representatives from every congressional district on your council).

II. Survey your community carefully and call together a group of Catholic, Protestant, Jewish, Negro, and white women and men, representing national groups and civic, labor (CIO, AFL, and Railway Brotherhoods), and foreign language organizations. In other words, the membership in the council should be interracial, interfaith, and truly representative of the community.

III. It would be helpful to have a chairman who is outstanding in the community and who is respected by all of the groups. Of course, such a person must be committed to the need for full employment for all minorities. We are anxious that it be perfectly clear that we want this bill to be for the protection of *all* minorities and not just for the Negro.

IV. This council can plan educational meetings all over the city with a large and effective mass meeting at some designated period.

V. Such an organization can at once arrange for individuals to talk with congressmen about the bill and urge their support of it. This is most important, and it would be helpful for us to know of any contacts you have made with senators and representatives from your state.

VI. It is very important that the National Council for a Permanent FEPC be kept informed of all of your work in order that we may tell other councils about your progress.

VII. Get candidates for Congress to commit themselves (in writing if possible) to work for the passage of this bill.

VIII. We need money in order to carry on an extensive educational program and any financial help that you can give us will be very much appreciated. We promise that the money will be used wisely, and periodic résumés of the work we attempt will be given.

As a result of these activities 100 local councils had been founded in 34 states by June 1946. Texas, Pennsylvania, Illinois, California, New York, and Ohio, in that order, had the largest number of councils although not necessarily the most active. Councils did not emerge in large numbers in the New England, Rocky Mountain, southwestern, and north central states. Some large cities, such as Boston and Milwaukee, were virtually untouched. In spite of oft-stated intentions by the National Council of organizing rural branches, the organization remained chiefly urban in character, following the lines of concentra-

TABLE III

DISTRIBUTION OF LOCAL COUNCILS
JUNE 1946

States With Councils (34)		States Without Councils (14)
States	Number of Councils	
Alabama	3	Arizona
Arkansas	2	Delaware
California	8	Idaho
Colorado	2	Maine
Connecticut	1	Maryland
Florida	4	Montana
Georgia	2	Nebraska
Illinois	9	New Hampshire
Indiana	1	North Dakota
Iowa	1	Rhode Island
Kansas	2	South Dakota
Kentucky	1	Wisconsin
Louisiana	3	Wyoming
Massachusetts	2	Vermont
Michigan	3	
Minnesota	2	
Mississippi	1	
Missouri	1	
New Jersey	3	
New Mexico	1	
New York	7	
Nevada	1	
North Carolina	2	
Ohio	5	
Oklahoma	3	
Oregon	1	
Pennsylvania	9	
South Carolina	2	
Tennessee	2	
Texas	10	
Utah	1	
Virginia	3	
Washington	1	
West Virginia	1	
Total	100	

tion of minority groups, especially Negroes. Councils carried a variety of names including: Birmingham Congressional Committee for a Permanent FEPC; Vallejo (California) Council for Civic Unity; Chicago Citizens' Committee for a Permanent FEPC; Chicago Spanish-Speaking People's Council for a Permanent FEPC; St. Joseph County (Indiana) Committee for a Permanent FEPC; and the Kansas-Missouri Council for a Permanent FEPC.

The councils were, for the most part, very loosely organized. Some drafted constitutions and set up highly formal machinery including offices for headquarters, but the majority operated upon the theory that this was a short-run effort which did not call for an extensive organizational superstructure. The number of active members varied widely with perhaps an average of fewer than forty attending meetings.[3] As might be expected there was a great turnover in membership. In response to a questionnaire from the Washington office, the Mobile (Alabama) Council wrote:

You will note that total membership and frequency of meetings are not stated in exact numbers. That variation is due to the fact that all members who have maintained an interest in the organization are very busy people; while they sympathize with the movement, they do not find time to attend meetings frequently. The number who can meet varies so until it is difficult to fix a number as members. If we are permitted to use such a term as "floating members," we could claim fifty whose names are on the roll.

For a while we met every week; later twice a week, or as the need presented itself. Sometimes it is once every two weeks, etc. However we have fulfilled every suggestion from your office with respect to sending telegrams and letters to the senators, representatives, and President Truman. Also we have passed the request on to other organizations that did likewise.[4]

---

3. "Numerically, the membership varies from ten to 1500. The smaller number constitutes the officers and the committee chairmen, usually, some ten to twenty persons who have assumed responsibility for the activity of the Council. The larger number represents mailing list names, a large percentage of which can be counted upon as 'regulars' to attend public meetings. Many are 'on call' for special assignments as occasions arise.

"Thus, a member of a Local Council means an individual familiar with the program and responsible to calls for committee work, drives, public meeting attendance and directives for communications to the Congress."—From a *Survey of Local Councils*, Mrs. Mildred Mackover, National Council staff member, June 18, 1946.

4. Letter from Miss V. L. Blount, Secretary of the Mobile Council, March 23, 1946.

The Mobile Council was typical. Membership and activity rose and fell with the congressional tide. When the life of the temporary wartime FEPC was threatened, or when the bills proposing a permanent agency reached a crucial stage, the councils reached a peak in activity. Between crises some councils continued in name only while others carried on educational and fund-raising campaigns and built for the future.

It fell in with the National Council's plans to have organizational fluidity with peak strength when FEPC was "on the Hill." In this way local leadership and activities could be altered more easily to meet changing pressure requirements than if there were organizational rigidity. In Dallas, when the council's co-chairmen failed to develop a program, the National Council's field representative was able to step in to divert control from them:

> We did not wish to offend them, so we set up a campaign committee that would really in time become the actual Council, and it would facilitate matters if you [Washington office] would clear through the officers of the campaign committee. We really want the other officers to atrophy.[5]

On the other hand, the Washington office permitted a wide degree of local autonomy where the National Council did not feel a vital interest. When the chairman of the Cleveland Council asked Randolph to assist in selecting new officers, Randolph replied by telegram: "Don't feel qualified to suggest changes of committee chairmanships for Cleveland local. Policy of council is to have locals democratically develop their own committee composition and procedure."[6]

COMPOSITION OF LOCAL COUNCILS

While there was no standardization of council membership, a pattern tended to emerge. The backbone of nearly every council, not surprisingly, was composed of Negroes. In the South many councils were almost wholly confined to the Negro communities.[7] The limited

---

5. Field Report, Mrs. Anna Belle Douglas, October 20, 1945.

6. Telegram to C. L. Sharpe, March 2, 1946.

7. Exceptions included: Fort Worth Council which claimed to be "truly representative of all Fort Worth in that all labor, religious, civic, professional and political groups are represented."—Letter to National Council, May 14, 1945.

The New Orleans Council had representatives from the following organizations

interracial cooperation in the southern councils followed the general social pattern of the region. Where intergroup cooperation did develop it came chiefly from CIO unions, the Catholic hierarchy, and Jewish groups.

In northern communities, too, many councils were not representative of the entire community. The original impetus came from Negro groups almost everywhere, but in many cases the Negro leadership lacked the social opportunity or experience necessary to draw in all segments of the community. Utica, New York, was a case in point. Surveying the local situation, a National Council field representative complained:

> Any work that you can say was done in the name of the Utica Council for a Permanent FEPC has been confined to the Negro community. The groups need broadening. . . . Utica is hopelessly lacking in the type of Negro leadership that can move in a mixed group. . . .[8]

Contributing factors to the unrepresentative character of many councils were the haste and lack of planning attendant upon their establishment. Randolph, himself, was perhaps the most derelict in this respect.[9] He spent little time in any single city and usually drew upon his MOWM contacts for his local nucleus, thus antagonizing would-be supporters in many cities. Some of these councils underwent one or more reorganizations before becoming working organizations; others were moribund from the date of birth. In analyzing the future needs for council growth in June 1946, the local council coordinator finally came to the conclusion that:

---

present at a meeting in April, 1946: International Union of Marine Shipyard Workers; New Orleans Classroom Teachers; International Ladies' Garment Workers Union; B'nai B'rith (Ladies' Auxiliary); Urban League; Methodist Church; Baptist Church; YWCA; and the New Orleans Youth Conference.

8. Field Report, Una Squires, December 28, 1945.

9. National Council Staff Meeting Minutes, December 29, 1945.

Representatives of the Texas councils, in a special caucus, blamed the lethargic campaign in Dallas, Houston, and San Antonio partially on: "1. Insufficient advance preparation for Mr. Randolph's first organization meetings, which resulted in very small, non-representative attendance; 2. The impetus (encouraged by Mr. Randolph) toward formal organization at the earliest possible moment. The Dallas group, for instance, elected an inept panel of officers from among the non-representative audience at the first meeting. These officers, and they were a poor bunch, held control for several weeks, necessitating a complete reorganization before the more responsible community leaders could be attracted to the program."—Letter to National Council from a local supporter, September 22, 1945.

A full community blueprint should be built before a local Council organization is attempted. Few community individuals have the scope or skill to assess the working potentials of a community. Often, an individual has no concept of all of the forces which exist where he lives. The national office must do this evaluating from its perspective. The names and record of accomplishments of local chapter people must be obtained from the offices of our national cooperating organizations. The nature of the community, from the standpoint of industries and types of citizens, must be explored. The relationship of the area to a political set-up must be examined. The leaders of church, civic, trade union, and other such organizations must be determined. The temper of the federal and state legislators must be studied. Commitments of aid from national organizations must be obtained before work is begun.

When the field person enters a town or an area with such vital information blocked out beforehand, the task is already begun; and the individuals who will make up the membership have only to add their zeal and not their ingenuity.[10]

Aware as the National Council was of these important factors, it lacked the time and resources to bring them to fruition.

All of the local councils did not fall into this unrepresentative category. In metropolitan centers and states, where experience along interracial and interfaith lines was well-developed, councils were often highly representative. The character and timing of the FEPC movement made it perhaps the best balanced interracial movement in many years. The demand for economic equality did not tread on as many toes as did drives for greater social equality and the urgency of the war brought some white groups into the fold which ordinarily would not have extended themselves.[11]

LEADERSHIP

The leadership of the local councils came chiefly from already existing organizations. The National Urban League, the March on Washington Movement, the Negro Baptist Church, the labor movement and community service bodies, such as the YMCA and YWCA, supplied a large number of officers. Council leaders included Negro attorneys, school teachers, insurance men, newspaper publishers, and

---

10. *Survey of Local Councils.*

11. Various straw polls have revealed that whites are far less antagonistic to economic equality for Negroes than other forms of racial equality.

welfare workers; Catholic clergymen; Jewish businessmen, attorneys and welfare workers; and white Protestant ministers, university professors, and representatives of many other groups. Often the officers and executive committees of local councils were not truly representative of the council membership because an effort was made to put FEPC's best foot forward by studding the roster with the names of leaders of all community groups whether they were active or not. For this reason white and Negro co-chairmen were frequently elected.[12] Where the choices were made without reference to the fitness of the candidates for pressure work, the local units were severely handicapped. In addition there was always the problem of getting busy key community people to take on new responsibilities on top of their other obligations. The result was that leadership was not always of the highest calibre.

Despite the altruistic reform aspects of the movement, FEPC was used as a grinding stone for the axes of local as well as national groups and individuals. The struggle for power and prestige goes on within reform movements as well as in all other human institutions and movements. For example the Minnesota council, notwithstanding its general effectiveness, suffered from municipal as well as personal rivalries. St. Paul and Minneapolis, the "Twin Cities," became rivals in FEPC as in other things.[13] In Portland (Oregon), Indianapolis, Richmond, Philadelphia, Chicago, and Galveston the local FEPC efforts were injured by similar conflicts. Sometimes the rivalry involved personalities; sometimes organizations such as the NAACP and Randolph's Brotherhood of Sleeping Car Porters and MOWM attempted to run the show which did not please the other groups. Ideological conflicts created frictions in Philadelphia and elsewhere.[14]

---

12. A typical slate of officers of a better than average council, the East St. Louis Congressional Council, included: Chairman—Haney, Negro, Pastor of Mt. Zion Baptist Church, Negro Baptist Ministerial Alliance, and President of the Interracial Baptist Ministerial Alliance; Vice-Chairman—Hall, Negro, Catholic, member of Aluminum Workers Union; Honorary Vice-Chairmen—Hudson, white, Methodist, President of the YWCA Board of Directors; Harris, white, Pastor of First Methodist Church; Zuroweste, white, Pastor of St. Joseph's Catholic Church, Editor of the *Messenger*, Belleville diocesan weekly; Secretary—Langford, Negro, Methodist, YWCA staff worker; Treasurer—Staley, white, President of the CIO Council.

13. Field Report, Charles Toney, December 7, 1945.

14. In Philadelphia the first group in the picture was the small Citizens' Committee for Equal Job Opportunity during the defense period which made little headway in

RELATIONS WITH OTHER ORGANIZATIONS

The degree of skill in interorganizational relationships on the part of local council leadership did much to determine success or failure in mobilizing community support for FEPC. Considerable efforts were made to draw local Negro groups, labor unions, and churches into the FEPC fray.[15] Others were by no means neglected. Local branches of national organizations which had evinced some interest in FEPC were often included in councils as affiliated organizations, thus permitting them to retain the highly prized autonomy for final action.[16] The Southwestern Connecticut Council, typical of many, included representatives of the Stamford Jewish Center, the Stamford

the community. A metropolitan council was set up when a regional office of the President's Committee was established in Philadelphia and became, for a time, the important local FEPC committee. Then, however, the United Citizens' Action Committee, a leftist group, which had been interested in housing and eliminating police brutality seized upon FEPC as a good issue to promote its own growth. Friction developed between these two committees, both of whom were interested in local, state and national FEPC. In order to emphasize local FEPC, another group came into being, chiefly under Jewish auspices. Finally, a faction broke off from the UCAC and set up the Bi-Partisan Committee for FEPC, further complicating the local picture.

When the National Council sought to get local action, it found that factionalism had nullified all efforts. After considerable work an armed truce was established which prevailed through June 1946 and enabled the National Council to stage some mass meetings and financial drives in Philadelphia.—Interview with Milo Manley, National Council field representative in that area.

15. See Part II, *infra*, for a fuller discussion of the activities of these groups.

16. "We do not have a membership plan for, as you know, such a plan is very difficult to work out mechanically, since we have a very small office force. For that reason we are not attempting to solicit memberships. We are anxious rather to secure contributions for the whole national educational program. We are essentially working through already organized groups in order that the expense of our educational program may be cut somewhat. In your local community you perhaps find that your major task will be one of stimulating organizations already established to plan and carry out educational programs. It is easier to get cooperation if people do not find themselves thinking in terms of another organization. In other words, the task of your council is the continued stimulation of the entire already organized community toward action and education for this Bill."—Letter from Anna Arnold Hedgeman to Miss R. E. Arnold, Chairman of the Kansas-Missouri Council for a Permanent FEPC, May 1, 1944.

On the other hand, the National Council's chief handbook stated: "Since the Councils will exist only for the period of time it requires to obtain passage of the Bills S. 101 and H.R. 2232, we recommend that a Local Council be established, rather than have an already existing community organization merely add the FEPC issue to its agenda. In this way, the issue will receive full attention and will have the combined influence of a fully bi-partisan, interfaith and interracial core of American citizenry."—*Manual of Strategy*, p. 4.

Negro Center, the Norwalk NAACP, and the Stamford-Greenwich YWCA. In some communities the bulk of the work was carried by almost completely independent organizations. In Dayton, Ohio, especially in 1944, the Frontiers Club, a Negro businessmen's organization, was active in behalf of FEPC through its contributions to the National Council and its pressure on Ohio senators. The student bodies of several universities, such as Antioch and Wilberforce in Ohio and the University of Michigan at Ann Arbor, formed the nucleus for local activity in their communities.

While interorganizational cooperation on FEPC was encouraged, it was not always successful. Local groups often tend to divide their energies among a number of projects, to the great disgust of coordinating committees charged with a single program. When the chairman of the Dayton Frontiers Club FEPC Committee wrote to Mrs. Hedgeman asking her to postpone her speaking and money-raising trip to Dayton because of the local campaign being waged to abolish discrimination in the school system, Mrs. Hedgeman replied somewhat sharply:

> I can understand the importance of your school discrimination program, and merely wrote you because you suggested that you would like to know when I would be in the vicinity. Toledo is so close to Dayton that I thought perhaps some of your leaders might be interested in the latest dope on our FEPC legislation, which might be most helpful in making it possible for our kiddies to stay in school—if we can mobilize enough sentiment to pass it.[17]

Relations between committees for state legislation and the National Council left much to be desired. In the face of their common interest in FEPC, each regarded its area of operation as the more important. A National Council field representative visiting Boston wrote the Washington office:

> No one in Boston, even our most ardent supporters, will consider the federal FEPC fight as anything but an adjunct of the fight for a state

---

17. Letter to W. D. McLoud, January 25, 1945. Another example of conflicting organizational interests is found in a letter from the chairman of the Roanoke Council: "The basic reason why I did not ask an offering for FEPC Sunday was because the YW is in a drive to finish a mortgage and there were those in the audience who would not reconcile sending money away when, as they think, we need it here. And one of the big donors of the YW was in that audience. She is not in sympathy with our efforts for FEPC".—Letter from a local supporter, January 28, 1946.

FEPC. Boston liberals have made a poorer showing than any other group in the country and they know it. . . . This State FEPC idea is a complete obsession with about half the liberals in Boston. . . .[18]

National Council experience in Pennsylvania, California, and other states was similar. Nor did the National Council secure full cooperation from the metropolitan councils. Organizational jealousy often hampered effective local collaboration. The Cleveland local council was forced to split the proceeds of a financial campaign with the metropolitan council in that city to salve the latter's hurt feelings over being ignored by the National Council. Co-Chairman C. L. Sharpe wrote the Washington office:

We shall pay the reasonable expenses of the campaign out of the money collected, and turn over a portion of the funds to the group here who are sponsoring the Ohio FEPC at Columbus.

This last step was agreed upon to prevent friction between our group, which Mr. Randolph organized, and the Metropolitan Council for FEPC. They (the Metropolitan) feel that twice they were by-passed by Mr. Randolph when he came here. They also feel that no other organization in Cleveland should use the term FEPC in their name.[19]

Personality conflicts resulted in a serious split in Detroit. Relations were not entirely satisfactory in Chicago and elsewhere.

SOUTHERN COUNCILS AND THE COLOR LINE

The southern councils are of especial interest because of the additional handicaps under which they had to operate.[20] It was not long before they came to the realization that serious and effective political work could not be undertaken in the South. After several attempts to deal with southern congressmen through the delegation technique, the Jacksonville Council observed:

18. Field Report, William Leuchtenburg, October 20, 1945.
19. Letter to Mrs. Hedgeman, April 10, 1945.
20. Even in the formation of southern local councils special problems were encountered. In the minutes of the executive committee of the National Council the following notation is found: "Mr. Randolph reported on his Memphis meeting, which had been held in the church of Rev. Long, the only one who would lend his facilities. The meeting had been very successful, but Rev. Long had suffered immediate repercussions in the press and in the form of investigation of his church by the Fire Department. It was generally agreed that every possible assistance would be given in the event of a need arising for funds for immediate repairs, etc., which would help preserve the Church."—Executive Committee Minutes, April 10, 1944.

It was the thinking of our Council, based upon my experience in Washington at the last conference and my attempts to contact Senators and representatives from the State of Florida, that we could best serve the Council and the fight by financial aid. We are keenly interested and will continue to write and wire our representatives for their assistance.[21]

Following paralleling experiences, the active Fort Worth Council decided to go directly to the House Rules Committee instead of working upon the Texas congressional delegation:

We received your wire and are following part of the suggestions made therein. We are wiring Senators Connally and O'Daniels requesting that they vote for an appropriation for the present committee. It is the general feeling that it will be a waste of money and time to wire our Congressmen again in regard to the petition. It is for this reason that we requested via telegraph this afternoon that you send us the names of the committee members who opposed bringing the bill to the floor of the House. We feel that we will be able to get better results if we concentrate our attention on these six persons. We have already begun preparation of letters, wires and air mail special delivery letters to send to these persons with the hope that one of them will reconsider and vote for the action.[22]

The border state of Missouri, where the Kansas City and St. Louis Councils were able to obtain commitments from their senators, was an exception to this general pattern.

As a result, the chief emphasis in the South was placed upon fundraising and the stimulation of public opinion to an awareness of FEPC and a willingness to back the movement in any way that the National Council deemed desirable. The southern regional representative summed up the work in the South:

We ask the groups to do three things: to work for the organization and mobilization of public opinion; to see that people make known to Congress their desire for a bill; and to raise funds. Their first reaction is that it is a futile effort, but it is most important that Congress know they are aware of what is going on and that no Congressman be able to say that no one in his district is interested in this. Congress must not be able to say, "This is not something which the Negro wants. No one from the South has ever stated that he wanted this. This is something that Northern agitators brought down here."

21. Letter from J. Leonard Lewis, Chairman of the Jacksonville Council, February 6, 1946.
22. Letter from Fort Worth Council, June 13, 1945.

The councils also work for interracial cooperation on a little different basis than in the past. A third task is to work for financial contributions for the support of the national organization here. Every one of our twenty-eight councils has agreed to raise a financial contribution varying from $1,000 in the smaller communities to $10,000 in the larger communities.[23]

The low educational level of southern Negroes, especially in the small towns, handicapped the National Council's mobilization campaign. The concept of FEPC was new and fairly complicated.[24] Without the expenditure of considerable energy to acquaint the people in backward areas with FEPC, these people could not be fully activated.[25] Chiefly for this reason the National Council confined the bulk of its organizing efforts to the larger southern cities.[26]

Notwithstanding these barriers, the councils were able to go quite far in promoting interracial cooperation for FEPC. In fact on occasion councils were surprised at the degree of freedom which they found available in some southern communities. The Fort Worth Council, which enjoyed unusual success in interracial and interfaith cooperation, marvelled:

Frankly, we are going farther than we thought possible in a southern town. To the contrary of what we expected, our biggest obstacle here is Negroes who are nursing petty individual jealousies against each other

23. Report of Mrs. Anna Belle Douglas before national FEPC conference, *Digest of Working Conference*, September 12 and 13, 1945, p. 2.

24. One of the most difficult tasks was to clarify the distinction between the President's temporary wartime committee and the drive for a permanent FEPC with enforcement powers.—National Council Staff Meeting, October 22, 1945.

25. At least one confidence man attempted to take advantage of the vague general interest of southern Negroes in FEPC to line his own pockets. The chairman of the Little Rock Council wrote: "At the last meeting of the Little Rock Council for a Permanent FEPC, we were visited by a white man who is sponsoring an organization (incorporated under the laws of Nevada) embracing the same principles and objectives as our organization and said organization is to work among and organize Negroes.

"From questioning the man we could arrive at no conclusions other than the main objective is to exploit gullible Negroes. Of course he got no encouragement or comfort from our organization, yet it will be an easy matter for him to sell his scheme in small and rural communities."—Letter from J. C. Gray, Chairman of the Little Rock Council, October 22, 1945. Thereafter the National Council provided its field staff with letters of credentials.

26. "In the smaller towns the pattern of the work shifts a little from what it has been in the larger towns. The people are so far removed from national problems and interest in them that you have to do a tremendous amount of educational work. In fact, I am beginning to wonder if we haven't just about reached the point of diminishing returns in the South."—Field Report, Douglas, November 28, 1945.

and attempting to retard the program by not giving and influencing their friends not to give.[27]

In this connection it should be emphasized again that there are as many economic and social divisions among Negroes as among whites. More than one local council failed to succeed because of divisions among Negroes in the labor movement and those in business and professional groups. All in all, considerable experience was thus stored up for future pressure group action in the South, but the old lines were still too tightly drawn during the battle for FEPC to permit any immediate political successes.

LOCAL-NATIONAL COUNCIL RELATIONS

Theoretically, the spark of the FEPC movement was to come from the local councils; the national office was to act only as a clearing house and a pressure spearhead. In actual practice most of the councils, being composed of political amateurs, were only as active as the national office was able to stimulate them to be. This was not for want of enthusiasm, for there was considerable interest in FEPC in most communities, but rather because of lack of knowledge of what to do with their steam once generated. Meetings were built around National Council staff members who visited the various local councils. Letter-writing and fund-raising campaigns ensued only after "Action Letters" or telegrams were received from the national office.[28]

Virtually no originality in the preparation of literature and pressure techniques developed in the local councils.[29] The "willingness-to-be-led" attitude simplified the national office's control problems but also increased its work load. Eventually more and more staff was placed in

---

27. Letter from Almita S. Robinson, Secretary of the Fort Worth Council, June 22, 1945.

28. "As soon as I received your wire Thursday last I called Mr. Anderson and organized a telephone campaign for contact with the proper Civic, Church and Labor groups in the City and asked them to send the required five telegrams to Washington. I personally contacted ten groups and he had an equal number to call."—Letter from Laura Davidovich, Secretary of the Detroit Committee for a Permanent FEPC, November 19, 1945.

29. Exceptions included the well-done illustrated multigraphed "FEPC Bulletin" printed by the Birmingham Congressional Committee for a Permanent FEPC, describing the President's Committee and its work in addition to the status of the permanent bill in Congress, and finally listed the things which supporters could do. Also, the delegation sent by the Minnesota Council to Washington served as the prototype for all succeeding delegations.

the field and the Washington office became as much a supply depot for the hinterlands as it was a headquarters for pressuring Congress.

The chief medium of communication between Washington and the local councils was the mails. Because sufficient funds for an adequate field staff were not available, many problems had to be handled by correspondence. The National Council issued frequent releases to councils and individuals on its mailing list, attempting to keep them abreast of the progress of FEPC legislation and to stimulate local action. A typical release read, in part:

NEWS FROM WASHINGTON

April 25, 1946

WHERE DO THE FEPC BILLS STAND NOW?

The Bills can come to the floor of BOTH HOUSES OF CONGRESS in *this* session,—because, in the HOUSE OF REPRESENTATIVES, only 40-odd signatures still remain to complete Discharge Petition #4;
—because, in the SENATE, S. 101 is still on the Senate Calendar and can be re-called to the floor.

WHERE DO WE GO FROM HERE?

Political-Action-at-Home . . . . (now that election campaigns are under way) . . . . is just about everybody's answer to that question.

WHY IS "POLITICAL-ACTION-AT-HOME" OUR MAIN JOB?

Because every member of the House of Representatives and one-third of the Senate are up for re-election this year. They will spend every available moment, beginning with the Easter holiday, AT HOME WHERE THE VOTES ARE. . . .

HOW DO YOU PROCEED WITH "POLITICAL-ACTION-AT-HOME"?

1: While Senators and Representatives are *at their homes* ORGANIZE DELEGATIONS TO SEE THEM.

Where the *Senate* is concerned, the enclosed report of your Senator's roles during the filibuster will help your approach.

Where the *House* is concerned, remember that the remaining signatures, about 45, will have to come from the Republican Side. You are bound to meet opposition on the ground that FEPC is of no direct concern to these Representatives since there are not many minorities in the areas of those who have not signed. Your assignment is to tell them, as well as Republicans who have already signed, that FEPC is A NATIONWIDE PARTY ISSUE and should be supported by the Party as a unit. Anything less is a DENIAL OF THE 1944 REPUBLICAN PLATFORM.

2: Check the primaries and *make FEPC an issue* on which candidates for nomination for House and Senate MUST TAKE A STAND.

Publicize that information, so that the people know whether these men are for or against FEPC.

Every member of the House of Representatives and one-third of the Senate is up for re-election this year.

Are they willing to face the voters without a strong record on FEPC?

Now is the time to throw the spotlight of publicity on every individual who wants to *represent* YOUR DISTRICT OR YOUR STATE in the Congress of the United States.

3: Get on record with the ward, county and State leadership of BOTH political parties that FEPC MUST BE IN THE FOREFRONT OF ANY POLITICAL PROGRAM.

Get word through individual contacts and through delegations and follow up by mailing a *written declaration.*

4: Call a full meeting and PLAN YOUR PROGRAM OF ACTION. Make specific individuals responsible for specific assignments. Set dates ahead for progress reports. Do not fail to let the National Council here in Washington have a continuous report of your plans and your progress. . . .

The "Action Letters" and "News From Washington" releases were fairly successful in stimulating the sending of telegrams and letters to Congress. On occasion the councils were asked to send delegations to Washington with rather good results. Nevertheless, the efforts of the National Council to resolve local problems through the mails left much to be desired. Frequently issues involving local rivalries were too delicate to be handled by correspondence. Lack of an adequate staff in the field permitted some of these situations to drift until the councils involved became inactive. The Washington staff was so small and had taken on so many functions that local councils failed to receive answers to their letters for periods of time up to a month.[30] This tardiness, though explainable, contributed neither to the morale of the local councils nor to the solution of local problems.[31]

One of the important communications from the Washington office

---

30. Letter from Jerry O'Gillian, Secretary of the Norfolk Council for a Permanent FEPC, November 5, 1945.

31. Considerable use was made of the long distance telephone and the telegraph which aided in establishing better contact with local councils than the mails alone would permit.

to the branches was the *Manual of Strategy* issued in October 1945 to give the councils a handy reference pamphlet to guide them in their work. The *Manual* sought to make up for the lack of an adequate field staff by providing the answers to common questions. It contained a section on local council organization describing the desired composition of a local group, its officers, committees, and its contacts with authorized field agents. It called upon councils to help in fund-raising by setting a quota for their communities and suggested ways and means of meeting the quota. Educational programs, publicity, and political action were also dealt with in the *Manual*. The guide book also contained digests of the bills before Congress and other handy materials. For the most part it was a well-done and informative pamphlet, but in itself it was not sufficient.

While the field workers must be given credit for doing a fairly good job of establishing and energizing local councils, they were limited by their lack of numbers and experience. At no time were there more than seven representatives in the field. These seven were assigned to thirty-six states, the others being virtually untouched. Their territories were so large and their itineraries so crowded that little time was spent in any one place.[32] Few of the field workers brought with them previous experience in comparable lines of endeavor and consequently did not always perform this extremely difficult job satisfactorily.

Another technique used for coordinating local councils was the national strategy planning convention held in Washington. The first, in September 1945, was attended by 125 delegates from 27 states and the second, in February 1946, by 28 delegates from 20 states. The conventions served several worthwhile ends: they helped to create a feeling of belonging, they enabled the National Council to learn what the local councils were thinking, and finally brought forth important suggestions for future activities.

Many alert local councils were not satisfied with the services being rendered them by the National Council and did not hesitate to make

---

32. One field agent feeling the need for a more coordinated effort, reported: "It is very important that these local groups be made to feel a close connection with the National office in Washington. They need to feel tied to something more stable than a roving crusader with an office in a brief case."—Field Report, Thelma Nickens, December 21, 1945.

their feelings known. A correspondent reporting for a group of Texas councils listed the following criticisms:

Insufficient liaison between the various local councils and between the local councils and the National Council. Belle Douglas [field representative] was invaluable but it was impossible for her to spread herself thin enough to spend enough time with any one group. . . .

I believe it would be tremendously helpful in the Texas campaign if there were some agency to tie together the efforts of the various local councils. The state is so large that each local group feels isolated and half-forgotten ("alone and crying in the wilderness," as one delegate expressed it) unless it can remain in more or less close touch with its sister councils. If, as seems likely, the local councils are going to be semi-permanent bodies, at least until the national fight is settled, it is probably advisable for us to arrange state planning conferences from time to time.

There is great need for a coordination of all the liberal forces in Texas behind the fight for a permanent bill. At the present time we do not have even the semblance of united liberal front pressure. The time is near at hand when we will need exactly that. This again should be a further responsibility of the above-mentioned liaison agency.[33]

Field representatives reported breaks in the communication line and urged closer contacts. The southern representative wrote, "I enclose a list of the officers of the Oklahoma City Council. They say they have never heard from the office and were feeling quite rejected. I suspect that Mr. Randolph forgot to tell the national office of their existence." [34]

The lack of coordination proved most serious in the field of finance. From Oklahoma City came the report:

Some time ago the Oklahoma City Council had $1,500 in its treasury. I have heard since then that the money is being badly handled by the local council. Did they ever send the office any money? I'd like to know so as to get in touch with the right people out there and salvage whatever is left for the national office.[35]

Another southern council was even more disorganized and removed from National Council supervision:

The ———— Council is the worst we have. They have not had a meeting in months. The chairman has no following, and I believe is really afraid

33. Letter from Jackson Valtair, September 22, 1945.
34. Field Report, Douglas, July 16, 1945.
35. *Ibid.*, November 13, 1945.

to call a meeting and is just sitting around using the name of the Council to get money for which he is making no accounting. The porters were justified, I think, in questioning the handling of the funds.

The chairman had refused to open a bank account or to have the treasurer bonded. When the porters got ready to hand over the money they had raised the chairman wanted them to make a personal check to the secretary. I didn't attempt to interest any new people in the ——— Council as it seemed to me that we'd just be making it easier for ——— to get his hands on more money.[36]

Still, situations of the latter type were rare and notwithstanding them, the morale of the local councils was fairly high. The thought that they were part of a national movement aiming at a fundamental adjustment of minority grievances served to buoy the spirits of National Council supporters.

EVALUATION OF THE LOCAL COUNCILS

Despite the large number of problems and the additional work created by the local councils they were not without value. They served as a means of directing local enthusiasm into constructive channels in behalf of FEPC. This guided enthusiasm resulted in pressures upon congressmen which in many cases paid off with signatures on House petitions and other congressional support of both the President's Committee and permanent FEPC legislation. The councils helped to educate their members and local communities on the implications of FEPC. Of great importance is the fact that approximately 40 per cent of the total receipts of the National Council came from local council solicitations.[37] Without the councils the Washington office would have had to depend upon the tenuous support of cooperating organizations which perhaps would have required as great an expenditure of time and money on the part of the National Council.

Nevertheless, the existence of the local councils was a source of irritation to many well-established organizations. It is conceivable that if the councils had not been established these organizations would have been more willing to permit their groups to be used in the FEPC campaign. Had there been such a division of labor, the National Council

36. *Ibid.*, October 18, 1945.
37. See Chapter IV, *infra.*

could have confined its activities to the Washington scene with more effective results.

The National Council was aware of these criticisms and the short-comings of the local branches. But once it had embarked on the local action program it refused to retreat. Always there was the hope that sufficient funds would be forthcoming from supporters to make a really potent local system possible. Yet the existence of councils in itself served to limit contributions from some important national organizations. The local council coordinator, as late as June 1946, following the disastrous filibuster, still looked ahead to a strong system of local councils:

> . . . the very fact that local councils have been formed and kept alive with so little professional help, makes us realize how potentially enormous this kind of operation can be. If, in only two years, we have been able to move this group of nebulous organizations to an expression of the will of the people, it does not require too much imagination to fathom what compelling results we could have with a nation-wide operation. We hold in our hands the nucleus for a great educational program, affording to the average citizen a means of expressing his concern for fair employment practice legislation where it will be meaningful and productive. It is a challenge that requires only an intelligent plan of operation and the resources to do it.[38]

It is quite possible that had the National Council had the staff and resources the local council organization could have been molded into an extremely effective pressure adjunct; as it turned out, it remained a promise rather than a realization.

---

38. *Survey of Local Councils.*

CHAPTER 4

Greasing the Wheels

• EARLY PROBLEMS   • TECHNIQUES FOR RAISING
MONEY   • WHY THE WELL WAS DRY   • WHO
CONTRIBUTED   • EXPENDITURES AND CONSE-
QUENCES

THE RELATIVE STRENGTH AND INFLUENCE OF A
pressure group are not necessarily proportionate to its expenditures.[1] More important are its ability to deliver votes and its weight with the party organizations. It cannot be denied, however, that the monetary contributions which the group makes directly or indirectly to party campaigns and its expenditures for programs to generate popular support have a bearing upon the success or failure of its lobbying activities.[2]

Unquestionably, some money is required to put over even the most powerful of ideas in a democratic system where political power is widely diffused. Without an extensive organization it is difficult to activate amorphous public opinion, even when sympathetic, for an assault upon legislative bodies. Therefore, it has become standard procedure for pressure groups to establish central offices to serve as clearing houses for campaigns and to guide proposals to fruition through the use of planning and research staffs, field organizers, public relations workers, and legislative lobbyists. In addition, issues are promoted by the utilization of all available media for persuading key groups to give their active support to the desired proposal.

The machinery for persuasion comes dear. Economic interest groups regard pressure activities as good investments and do not stint in estab-

---

1. Religious, patriotic, veteran, and charitable organizations have an influence far out of proportion to their pressure expenditures because they reflect the *mores* of the majority of the community. In addition, among groups having large sums to spend, there is considerable waste in high salaries and unnecessary expenditures.

2. It is difficult to say whether pressure groups are successful because they have money or have money because they are successful.

lishing elaborate machinery. Reform groups may make up for lack of money, in part, through their enthusiasm for their cause and their willingness to undergo personal sacrifices to advance it; but, as one student of reform pressure groups has observed: "Reform organizations, even those devoted to the Lord's work, cannot, like the Children of Israel in the desert of Paran, rely upon manna from heaven. They must have money." [3]

EARLY PROBLEMS

From the beginning the National Council was plagued with problems of finance. Only on rare occasions did it have a bank balance sufficient for two or three months' operations; most of the time it operated on a week to week basis.[4] Under these conditions it was not possible for the Washington office to do the job which it laid out for itself.

As stated in Chapter II, in the early days Randolph sought to draw upon his New York City trade union friends for financial assistance. The first conference called by the National Council on October 20, 1943, was a money-raising meeting to which international and local unions with headquarters in New York City were invited. Some ninety delegates attended, representing forty unions claiming a membership of more than a million.[5] The conference, led by trade unionists who had been active in the FEPC movement from the beginning, resolved unanimously to support the National Council "organizationally and financially." [6] A trade union committee was appointed to help raise a budget of $25,000 for the Council. Immediate pledges totalling $5,050 were made by the International Ladies' Garment Workers Union; United Retail, Wholesale, and Department Store Employees; Brotherhood of Sleeping Car Porters; Textile Workers of America; and the Joint Board of the United Hatters, Cap and Millinery

---

3. Peter Odegard, *Pressure Politics*, p. 181. Odegard quotes an Anti-Saloon League leader as saying that at the height of the campaign for national prohibition the League was spending about $2,500,000 a year—quoted from W. B. Wheeler, "The Inside Story of Prohibition," *New York Times*, March 29, 1926.

4. *Digest of Findings from a Working Conference of Local Councils*, September 12 and 13, 1945.

5. *Report on Activities*, National Council for a Permanent FEPC, September, 1943-February, 1944.

6. *New York Times*, October 21, 1943.

Workers—all of whom are staunch advocates of racial equality. A trade union committee, made up of Samuel Wolchok (URWDSE), David Dubinsky (ILGWU), and Randolph (BSCP), was formed to serve as a liaison committee between the National Council and the trade unions. A budget committee was established composed of the members of the liaison committee together with Nathaniel Spector (Mgr. Jt. Bd. Mill. Wkrs., AFL), Frank Crosswaith (Negro Labor Committee), William Wolpert (United Hebrew Trades), and Abe Miller (N.Y. Jt. Bd. Amal. Cl. Wkrs., CIO).

Even this small budget was not raised. By February 1944 only $4,-976.28 had been received from the New York trade unions.[7] Mrs. Stark, the first National Council secretary, observed later to her successor:

> They did promise to raise the budget of $25,000—and the screws should be put on them as much as possible. A great many assignments made by them—and stated in the minutes of the TUC—were never properly carried out and Randolph was never around long enough to call other meetings or follow through, which they wanted him to do on the main. And it would serve a good morale purpose too—they should not be permitted to feel that once they had made some contribution, their responsibility or involvement was over. . . .[8]

As a consequence, the National Council had only a token existence until well into 1944. No large-scale operations were possible; the New York staff was composed of merely a full-time secretary and a part-time office worker.[9]

A complicating factor in the trade union drive was the decision by the trade union conference to raise a total of $30,000, of which $5,000 was to be allotted to special committees formed for the defense of two soldiers alleged to be victims of persecution in the armed forces.[10] This resulted in competition for fund priorities and considerable bookkeeping complications as the money came in. In November 1943 the National Council's secretary wrote Randolph:

---

7. *Report on Activities.*
8. Letter from Mrs. Alice Stark to Mrs. Hedgeman, July 21, 1944.
9. Letter from Mrs. Stark to Thurman L. Dodson, November 5, 1943.
10. The Workers Defense League took over the case of Alton Levy while the Lynn Committee to Abolish Segregation in the Armed Forces was formed to aid Winfred Lynn's fight to test the legality of the alleged Negro quota by which Negroes were inducted into segregated units in the Army.

.... The allocation of the money is merely academic so far as we're concerned, except for $5000. However, now that there is the emergency situation of the Levy case and far more than the percentage of returns due the WDL has already been given, I think clarification of general policy and future procedure is necessary, if for no other reason than to clear up my own position in the matter and those of other individuals. Morris [Milgram] sort of feels it's personal persecution on my part if I object to turning over 100 or even 50% of returns until the full quota is paid the WDL. His own concern with the urgency and immediacy of the Levy case seems to blind him to the fact that I cannot act without authority, nor can I act at all, having no recourse to withdrawal of funds, and that we have no money either. Also, if this committee should not succeed in collecting the full total of $20,000 we would sort of be left holding the bag, while having expended time, energy and money in helping get this money collected.[11]

The skeleton organization fumbled along even after Mrs. Hedgeman was hired to serve as executive secretary and a Washington office was established. The promise of an immediate budget of $25,000 given to Mrs. Hedgeman when she accepted the job was not fulfilled.[12] Funds for large-scale operations did not become available until the appeal was broadened in 1945.

TECHNIQUES FOR RAISING MONEY

The National Council and its supporters showed no great originality in their money-raising schemes. All of the traditional techniques were employed. Because of the group's inability to break into the charmed circle of large contributors, emphasis was placed largely upon appeals to the "little people" of the country.

On the national level a finance committee headed by Dorothy Norman, *New York Post* columnist, supplanted the New York trade union committee when the latter proved unsuccessful in its efforts to raise the desired funds. Appeals were made through Mrs. Norman's column, occasional advertisements in national liberal magazines such as the *New Republic* and through individual solicitation by mail or personal contact with organizations and individuals.

Locally the devices employed were more diversified. Special finance

---

11. Letter from Mrs. Stark to Randolph, November 12, 1943.
12. Interview with Mrs. Hedgeman.

committees were appointed by some councils to raise money. The Cleveland Council in launching a drive for $10,000 set up forty teams of ten persons each and offered $450 in war bonds to team captains and workers as prizes.[13] In the New York metropolitan area a finance committee headed by Noah Walter, Negro trade union leader, was organized in January 1945.[14] In order to reach all segments of the population, but especially Negroes, this committee set up the following divisions: Bar and Grill; Beauticians; Brooklyn Businessmen; AFL; CIO; Corona; Dentists; Drug Stores; Jamaica; Legislative; Liquor Stores; Manicurists; Morticians; Government Workers; Negro Press; Nurses, Physicians; Real Estate Brokers; Employment Agencies; Postal Employees; Recreation Leader Group; Teachers; and Women. To raise its share of the fund, the Corona and Jamaica divisions held a "Cocktail Party and Parade of Stars" in March 1945, charging FEPC supporters $1.20 admission to be entertained by Avon Long of Uptown Cafe Society, Bill Kenny of the Ink Spots, and "others of stage, screen, and radio fame."

Other benefit performances of plays and variety entertainment were staged. The Buffalo Council took over the opening performance of the play "On Whitman Avenue," starring Canada Lee on April 10, 1946.[15] The Columbus (Ohio) Council produced a "Mammoth Variety Show and Recognition" with "16 professional and amateur acts—song, dance, instrumental, choral and novelty numbers. Clever staging, fast moving, unique lighting, professional direction."[16] Some were good money-raisers, others involved so large an investment that the local councils staging them were fortunate to break even.[17]

Elsewhere solicitations at mass meetings, Negro movie houses, and social organizations, as well as church, sporting events, and door to door collections were employed extensively. The traditional chicken dinners, Christmas parties, and church socials also played their role.

---

13. Letter from Co-chairman C. L. Sharpe, April 10, 1945.

14. Co-chairmen were Judge Jonah S. Goldstein, Judge Stephen S. Jackson, and Father Shelton Hale Bishop; Lillian Sharpe Hunter served as campaign director.

15. Letter, March 27, 1946.

16. Letter, November 5, 1945.

17. The Buffalo Council raised only $300 on its play sponsorship when the theater manager drove a hard bargain.—Letters from Buffalo Council dated April 5 and June 7, 1946.

When the Dayton Frontiers Club inquired about fund-raising suggestions, the Washington office replied:

> You ask for suggestions as to ways and means of securing additional funds. I thought I would tell you of some of the things which other communities are doing and you can decide which ones might be effective in Dayton. One city is approaching all of the ministerial associations, white, Negro, Spanish-speaking, Catholic, Protestant and Jewish to get them to call an FEPC Day in their churches. They have tried to get it for the same day in as many city churches as possible. They have also asked that these churches take up offerings for the Permanent FEPC on that day. In the afternoon of FEPC Day, they have held a large community interracial, interfaith Rally with prominent speakers and have called that Rally meeting "Fifth Freedom Rally"—"Freedom to have a Job." In addition to this they approached the local radio stations for announcements. This same community has formed a committee of 100 representatives of all of the kinds of groups in the community to work on securing the interest in the Mass Meeting. They issued a booklet with 10 contribution receipts in it. On the top of these receipts was the statement "I believe in the American-Way. I am for a Permanent FEPC, which would make it possible for people to secure work without regard to race, creed, color or national origin. I make my contribution to the 'Fifth Freedom' of all Americans, 'Freedom to have a Job.'" Then there is a space for name, address and amount. The committee of 100 each took one of these books and promised to get a minimum of 10 people to give at least $1.00. . . .[18]

At the suggestion of the Finance Committee of the September 1945 Planning Conference, the National Council had a large number of "FEPC buttons" manufactured and distributed to the local councils to be sold for 25¢ or more. A "flash bulletin" regarding these buttons was sent to the councils listing possible ways to sell them:

PROCLAIM AN FEPC DAY: Plan an FEPC Day, with the Mayor proclaiming such a Day. Have the papers carry the story and a picture of the Mayor buying the first button. Enlist the support of churches, schools, stores, trade unions, civic organizations. Use streamers, banners, posters, placards, bulletin board notices, car stickers and every outdoor and indoor publicity spot possible.

ASK THE PULPIT TO HELP: Ask ministers, priests and rabbis to make the texts of their sermons a plea for fair chance at jobs and the blessing of interracial unity. Exchange sermons of the clergy at each others' churches

---

18. Letter from Mrs. Hedgeman, October 7, 1944.

can be a forceful demonstration of interfaith unity . . . . and good copy for the local press.

PASS THE AMMUNITION: Instead of the usual collections, the collection plate filled with buttons could be passed—each person to take a button and leave a quarter.

MOVE IN ON THE MOVIES: Booths selling FEPC buttons in lobbies of local movie houses attract an ever moving stream of people. Try to get a flash announcement on the screen before each feature showing.

GO WINDOW-SHOPPING: Ask shopkeepers—both downtown merchants and neighborhood grocers—to fill a box with FEPC buttons in a prominent part of the store window and give a prize for the guess closest to the amount of buttons. Point out the excellent publicity advantage of such a display for the store.

ASK BOOKSTORES TO COOPERATE: Have bookstores promote button sales along with displays of such social problem best-sellers as "Deep River," "One Nation" and others.

LINE UP YOUR VOLUNTEERS: In addition to members of your own groups, try to get coordinating organizations to appoint button committees. Try to promote the services of union men each giving one hour of button selling time each week.

MAKE YOUR TURNOVER RAPID: Get behind your button re-consignments and collect the quarters quickly. Don't wait until all buttons are sold to collect the total amounts. Avoid entanglements in finances and send in returns in small units as you receive them—five dollars, ten, twenty and so on. . . .[19]

From time to time other money-raising schemes were considered by the National Council. One interesting proposal was to buy a list of names from a New Yorker specializing in lists of potential contributors to causes and organizations. At a National Council staff meeting this possibility was discussed:

Zatkind said Behrend wanted to do his usual business, he gets $1000 before he starts. He has an excellent list. He has one 5000 name-list from which we could get a good 500 list. He wants $400 in advance for the use of this mailing list. We would have to operate on speculation on his part and get from him a full statement before we go ahead. Zatkind told Behrend that we can not speculate with the nickels and dimes given for our use by individuals all over this country. Since, while he feels sure he can do a substantial job for us, he can not give us a guarantee in advance that we will realize money on our investment. Behrend then said he would take the job without our putting up any money, but would then take a larger

---

19. "Flash Bulletin," National Council for a Permanent FEPC, November 2, 1945.

percentage of the fund raised, say about 7½%. In this way we will get less money but whatever we get will be pure gravy because we have put up nothing.[20]

Schemes to raise upwards to $500,000 for the FEPC fight proved impossible. The most raised in any single year was $68,110.33 in 1945; the total amount raised by the National Council was less than $133,000, which proved insufficient to carry on an extensive national campaign for a period of almost three years.

WHY THE WELL WAS DRY

The same reasons which prevented full cooperation by labor and reform organizations in the pressure drive served to limit contributions to the National Council. The National Council suffered most from the frictions and suspicions engendered by organizational, ideological, and personal rivalries in its fund-raising efforts.

The priority given to state FEPC movements in many states also diminished prospective collections. For example, the California group set a budget of $125,000 for the state campaign and refused to aid the National Council financially until its budget was attained.[21] The CIO, NAACP, and American Jewish Congress were far more active in many state drives than in the struggle for national legislation. This can be explained, at least partially, in terms of the friction between these groups and top leadership of the National Council.

Another important reason for the inability of the National Council to raise money was the fact that tax exempt organizations feared the loss of their exemptions if they contributed to the National Council since the latter's efforts were primarily legislative rather than educational in form. When national educational groups were asked to subscribe, most of them begged off giving this as their reason. The Council for Democracy replied to such a request:

Among other organizations, we have received your appeal of April 29 for support of the proposed permanent FEPC. We wish to assure you that we are very strongly in favor of this and regard it as an important step, but since the provision for this can be made only by enabling act of Congress, the Council for Democracy cannot, under its charter, its tax

20. National Council Staff Meeting Minutes, November 7, 1945.
21. Field Report, Roundtree, November 20, 1945.

exempt status and long settled policy support or oppose specific legislation, especially of a highly controversial nature as this is. To do so would be dangerous and unwise with respect to our status in this regard. We keenly regret that this is so, but we know no escape from it.[22]

Recognizing this as a serious barrier to fund collections, the National Council sought and found an interpretation which alleviated the problem somewhat. In soliciting the American Jewish Committee, a staff member wrote:

As I told you on the telephone, I have made considerable investigation at the Bureau of Internal Revenue regarding the status of tax-exempt organizations like yours which might make contributions to us. I was particularly eager to have an interpretation of the word "substantial" under the wording of the tax laws. The only case on record, it was discovered, was that of the Twentieth Century Fund, which had its tax exemption taken away for two years because it had devoted 50% of its funds one year, and one third of its funds the next year to a campaign on changes in the laws governing credit. I was unofficially advised that if a tax-exempt organization devoted no more than 10% of its outlay to legislative activities it would not strain its tax exemption in any way.[23]

The following month the American Jewish Committee contributed $1500 and other like organizations were prevailed upon to make contributions.

WHO CONTRIBUTED

Unlike many other reform movements which have enjoyed the indulgences of wealthy "angels," the National Council raised a bare 5 per cent of its total revenues from individual contributions of $500 or more.[24] There were only two contributions of $1,000, one of $621.60 and eight of $500 each. A total of $7,465.00 was raised from contributions from $100 to $500; $12,038.34 came from donations of less than $100. Much of the latter came in trickles of quarters and

---

22. Letter from Ernest Angell, President of the Council for Democracy, May 2, 1944.

23. Letter from Mrs. Beatrice Schalet to John Slawson, Executive Vice President, American Jewish Committee, May 7, 1945.

24. The Anti-Saloon League, for example, was able to stay afloat in its early years through the contributions of E. W. Metcalf and A. I. Root of Elyria, Ohio. Up to 1913 the Root Bee Company had contributed approximately $30,000 to the League. By 1919 the Rockefeller family admitted to contributions of $350,323.67 to the League. —Odegard, *op. cit.*, Chapter VII.

dollars to the Washington office. The lack of tax exemption for such contributions may have had something to do with the small amount from large donors but other reasons were probably more important. Especially pertinent is the fact that the FEPC movement was not the type of cause which would appeal to most people of means. Furthermore, the failure of the National Council to completely satisfy potential contributors as to the soundness of the leadership and planning of the movement had its adverse effect. So many demands are made of them that donors of large sums, as a rule, make careful investigations before going all-out in support of a cause.

Organizational contributions came to $54,430.23, or 41 per cent of the total raised through June 1946. Yet this sum is not very significant when the total resources of the contributing groups are considered.[25] Labor unions, usually heavy contributors to reform movements, contributed $30,475.40, or less than 23 per cent of the $132,700.35 solicited from all sources. Of the labor contributions, $25,321.40, or all but 4 per cent, came from the two AFL unions closest to Randolph, the BSCP and the ILGWU. Outside of the New York City metropolitan area, financial support from the AFL was practically non-existent. Contributions from affiliates of the powerful Congress of Industrial Organizations came to a mere $2,724. In the case of the AFL, the established pattern of discrimination in at least twenty-one of the international unions precluded strong financial support. The refusal of the National Council to work with Communists probably prevented collections from CIO unions where this group has strength. More important, however, was the CIO's general lack of confidence in Randolph's leadership of the National Council.

The pattern of non-cooperation by national Negro organizations is even more significant. The only contribution of any consequence was a total of $2,146.59 from the National Association for the Advancement of Colored People. To be sure, there were other contributions from various Negro groups, but the generalization that national Negro organizations did not see fit to give full support to the leadership of the National Council in the fight for FEPC must stand.

25. The only person who resembled an "angel" in the case of the National Council was the treasurer, William Jay Schieffelin, who made a personal loan of $5000 to the organization which, incidentally, had not been paid off at the time of Mrs. Hedgeman's resignation in July 1946.

TABLE IV

NATIONAL COUNCIL FOR A PERMANENT FEPC
CHRONOLOGY OF CONTRIBUTIONS

NOVEMBER 1943—JUNE 22, 1946 INCLUSIVE

Date	Total Contributions	Local Council Contributions
1943		
November	$ 2,540.00	—
December	571.65	56.65
1944		
January	1,332.55	230.55
February	2,216.53	—
March	1,319.00	5.00
April	492.00	—
May	2,415.27	—
June	292.00	20.00
July	2,381.00	—
August	2,607.50	—
September	1,616.01	137.01
October	1,859.00	157.00
November	3,826.90	500.00
December	2,509.50	—
Total 1943 and 1944	$25,978.91	$ 1,106.21
1945		
January	1,437.50	—
February	4,031.27	1,302.15
March	4,369.50	1,000.00
April	15,499.07	10,276.00
May	8,300.74	6,058.00
June	11,455.85	4,855.00
July	6,702.12	2,330.00
August	2,387.00	2,035.00
September	1,921.00	1,800.00
October	5,103.00	4,979.00
November	3,882.28	2,561.00
December	3,021.00	2,400.00
Total 1945	$68,110.33	$39,596.15
1946		
January	$ 5,192.28	$ 2,110.81
February	9,515.69	3,321.28
March	14,139.00	1,410.00
April	1,886.09	1,275.00
May	5,077.05	955.73
To June 22	2,821.00	2,370.00
Total 1946 to June 22	$38,611.11	$11,442.82
Grand Total	$132,700.35	$52,145.18

Jewish organizations contributed a total of $7,111. The American Jewish Committee and the Anti-Defamation League each donated $2,750; the Jewish Labor Committee of New York, $1,000; the B'nai B'rith and miscellaneous Jewish organizations, a total of $611. The important American Jewish Congress was conspicuous for its absence from the list of National Council supporters. It made its contributions directly to the FEPC fight and chiefly to state campaigns.

A breakdown of contributions to local councils is more difficult because in most cases the local councils forwarded the proceeds of fund-raising drives without specifying the sources. From available evidence it is probable that small contributions, chiefly from individuals, comprised the bulk of the $52,145.18 raised by the local councils. The *New Orleans Weekly* reported on January 27, 1945, the following contributions in a drive in New Orleans:

Miss Mary B. Allen, $30; Ephesus Seventh Day Adventist Church, $50; NAACP, $50; Dr. Taylor Segue, $10; Frank Pania, $20; Dr. E. P. Jimson, $10; Benevolent Daughters of Louisiana, No. 1, $54; Mrs. Ruby Bell, $6; Dr. K. L. Douglas, $10; Rev. H. T. Primm, $15; St. John Divine, B.C., Rev. A. J. Bebelle, pastor, $44.40; C. L. Belfield, $10; solicited by James Howard, $40.17; solicited by Miss Arnetta Ellis, $40; Douglas Insurance Co., $50; T. L. Miller, $5; E. L. Marsalis, $2; Dr. N. R. Davidson, $5; Ira Cantrell, $5; George Lone, principal McCarty School, $5; Mr. M. Prevost, $1 . . . ILA, 1419, $500; Mt. Zion Methodist Church, $100; Knights of Peter Claver Council 59, $10; Brotherhood of Sleeping Car Porters, $10; E. A. Fabacher, $50; Robert McClean, $5; Brotherhood of Car Cleaners, $37.25; Rev. Bazile Jolicour, $10; and E. A. Marigney, $5.

Some local councils were far more active in fund-raising than others. A few branches conceived of their work as being chiefly to bring political pressure and therefore made only modest financial contributions. Among the largest money-raisers were the New Orleans and Chicago councils, each raising more than $5,000; Fort Worth contributed almost $5,000; and Norfolk, Houston, St. Louis, and the Kansas-Missouri councils, $2,000 or more. In general the southern councils, composed chiefly of Negroes, outshone the more representative northern councils in this field. One difficulty which sometimes developed was the failure of councils to send in money to Washington once collected. A few desired to send in their whole quota at once to make a grand flourish while others sought to retain at least part of the money for local activities. With the National Council living from month to month and on occasion from week to week, this holding back resulted in frequent appeals from Washington for immediate transmission of funds.

EXPENDITURES AND CONSEQUENCES

The National Council, consequently, was unable to operate in the free-handed manner typical of many pressure groups. Prospective expenditures had to be scanned carefully and often rejected in favor of some more pressing obligation. There was little margin for experimentation or indulgence in novel approaches. The expenditures, for the most part, were for minimum essentials.

TABLE V

NATIONAL COUNCIL FOR A PERMANENT FEPC
CONTRIBUTIONS RECEIVED FROM NOVEMBER 1943 TO JUNE 22, 1946

LOCAL COUNCILS		$ 52,145.18
AMERICAN FEDERATION OF LABOR		
ILGWU	$17,730.00	
BSCP	7,591.40	
United Hatters, Cap & Millinery Workers	1,155.00	
Hotel & Restaurant Employees	670.00	
Miscellaneous AFL unions	605.00	
		27,751.40
MISCELLANEOUS ORGANIZATIONS		14,697.24
CONTRIBUTIONS UNDER $100		12,038.34
CONTRIBUTIONS OF $100 TO $500		7,465.00
JEWISH ORGANIZATIONS		
American Jewish Committee	2,750.00	
Anti-Defamation League of B'nai B'rith	2,750.00	
Jewish Labor Committee	1,000.00	
B'nai B'rith	445.00	
Miscellaneous Jewish Orgs.	166.00	
		7,111.00
CONTRIBUTIONS OF $500 AND UP		6,621.60
CONGRESS OF INDUSTRIAL ORGANIZATIONS		
United Auto Workers	805.00	
Amalgamated Clothing Workers	700.00	
United Retail, Wholesale & Dept. Store Employees	610.00	
Textile Workers of America	425.00	
Miscellaneous CIO unions	184.00	
		2,724.00
NAACP		2,146.59
TOTAL CONTRIBUTIONS		$132,700.35

TABLE VI

NATIONAL COUNCIL FOR A PERMANENT FEPC
EXPENDITURES: APRIL 1, 1944—APRIL 30, 1946

Salaries	$ 57,014.54
Out of Town Travel and Maintenance	19,371.31
Local Taxi and Miscellaneous	1,110.02
Telephone and Telegraph	14,343.51
Printing, Mimeograph and Promotion	18,256.39
Newspaper and Clipping Service	1,003.88
Postage and Express	5,280.76
Office Supplies and Equipment	2,253.73
Rent and Electricity	1,641.80
Professional Fees	940.62
Tax Expense	904.43
Buttons	3,816.74
General	1,222.84
Total	$127,160.57

Salaries comprised almost half of the expenditures and yet were not inordinately high. After April 1945 Mrs. Hedgeman as executive secretary was paid $5,000 a year, the two legislative representatives and the office manager received $3,000 for their services, and the office secretary, $2,000 for the year. Salaries of the field representatives and other staff members were also modest.

The flatness of the organization's purse evidenced itself in many ways. One of the most crying needs was for a well-planned public relations program, yet the most that the National Council could do was to hire a public relations counsel for three months beginning September 26, 1945, for the sum of $3,500. Three months proved insufficient for the planning of a "public relations program suited to arouse and guide public opinion in the direction of the enactment of legislation for a permanent FEPC" as specified in the counsel's contract.

The National Council also ran into a situation often confronting pressure groups. Congressmen and senators who push a group's legislation frequently expect support in campaigns for re-election. However, when Senator Chavez, leading FEPC standard-bearer in the Senate, asked for $5,000 from the Council to help finance his re-election bid, the National Council was able to give him only $500.

An alleged case of unusual application of "senatorial courtesy" further serves to reveal the tight margin on which the campaign was conducted. Following a speech by Senator ——— in Chicago, the executive secretary of the Chicago Council Against Racial and Religious Discrimination wrote the Washington office:

> Your letter of December thirteenth to Mr. Weiss relative to Senator ——— expenses while in Chicago has remained unanswered simply because it has taken us these two weeks to calm down after reading the Senator's expense account!
>
> You indicate that Sen. ——— advised you that his hotel bill which he paid for was $53.30. That sounded rather high for one night's lodging and in checking with the La Salle Hotel we found that his bill was $9.20! You also indicate that you paid out $148.06 in railroad tickets for the Senator and his wife.
>
> This total bill of more than $200 is excessive. We are not blaming the National Council, although you might have warned us in advance and you might have indicated to the Senator that whatever senatorial courtesy might be, the FEPC campaign can only be won on sacrifice and not on the spending habits of a maharajah.[26]

Expenditures more than kept pace with income throughout the life of the National Council. In many periods of fiercest activity, the Washington office was unable to meet its payroll and was forced to carry its staff along without pay until a contribution trickled in. At times the morale of the staff became strained by its hand-to-mouth existence but held up fairly well under the circumstances. When the executive committee decided in January 1946 to let the field staff go, the latter volunteered as a group to "serve gratuitously during the present financial crisis of the National Council . . . in spite of the fact that we as ordinary people have the responsibilities of ordinary people."[27]

The Washington office staff blamed Randolph for the failure to raise sufficient funds to stay afloat. When a last-effort meeting with potential contributors in July 1946 proved unsuccessful, Mrs. Hedgeman offered as one of her reasons for tendering her resignation:

> . . . Our contacts with potential big givers last week were fruitless because of this apparent lack of responsibility in planning ahead for a national program of the character and scope of this fight. I wrote you

---

26. Letter from Dr. Homer A. Jack to National Council, December 31, 1945.
27. Memorandum from the field staff to Mrs. Hedgeman, January 24, 1946.

in January that I could not assume responsibility for the legislative, educational and administrative ends and also raise funds. While you did not answer that letter, your verbal acceptance of the responsibility for the fund raising has made this situation an acutely embarrassing one for us as we attempt to interpret our present need to the public. It is imperative that funds be available immediately to pay already incurred obligations, including salaries, vacation pay, rent, the Schieffelin loan, printing, postage, etc., which roughly amounts to $18,000. It seems regrettable that after the amount of personal interest and sacrifice which has been put into this fight and just at a time when this achievement has been recognized to the extent that we were able to secure commitments from Luce, Donovan, Poletti, Rosenberg, Quigley, and others, we must now abandon it simply for lack of funds and permit some other organization to carry it to fruition. . . .[28]

This marked the end of the first, and unsuccessful, phase of the National Council's life. However, the Randolph group did not withdraw from the fray; rather it prepared for the 1947-48 legislative campaign, hoping by broadening its leadership to obtain the funds and support necessary for a full-scale drive.

---

28. Telegram to Randolph *et al.*, July 15, 1946.

PART II

The Factor of Social Cohesion

CHAPTER **5** *Negroes and the Crusade*

* NEGROES IN GENERAL * NAACP * NATIONAL
URBAN LEAGUE * MARCH ON WASHINGTON
MOVEMENT * BROTHERHOOD OF SLEEPING
CAR PORTERS * NEGRO SOCIAL ORGANIZATIONS

REFORM MOVEMENTS USUALLY CUT ACROSS MANY
social, political, and economic lines, making necessary the manipulation of paralleling groups for the achievement of victory
in a pressure campaign. To establish an entirely new organization to
mobilize mass support would require sizeable resources and considerable time. Moreover, people are more easily moved when appealed
to in terms of familiar and trusted affiliations than if a new organization attempts to establish rapport.

The resources of the National Council being decidedly limited,
speed was considered imperative to take advantage of the current
interest in FEPC to secure congressional approval of permanent legislation. Therefore, the Randolph group sought to draw existing organizations into association with itself in the FEPC fight. To ensure
broad coverage a great variety of groups was approached: racial,
social, nationality, economic, and religious.

Because of the jealousy and apprehension which established groups
manifest towards newcomers in the organizational field, the leaders
of the National Council sought to assure potential supporters that
the Council was not to be a permanent membership group but rather
a temporary coordinating committee for all FEPC action. Once the
goal had been attained, the Council would be dissolved.

The National Council centered its sights upon top leadership of
organizations in preference to the rank and file, on the theory that,
in what they hoped would be a short campaign, endorsement by prominent organizational leadership would be sufficient to impress Congress
with the strength of the movement so that the necessity for a time-

consuming and expensive educational campaign would be obviated. While this is not an unfamiliar approach in pressure campaigns, it is extremely risky when a new issue is being pushed because even though officers usually set the pace for an organization, the group's effectiveness will frequently depend upon the average member's understanding of his organization's program and the degree of intensity with which he supports his leaders.

The National Council asked a number of things of cooperating organizations, depending upon their structure and means. Money was an item which all organizations were asked to contribute; the prestige of official endorsement was another. Then, depending upon the organization, active lobbying, local pressures on congressmen and party leaders, testimony before committees, preparation and distribution of literature, letter writing, and delegations to Washington were solicited. In general the National Council sought to leave the activation of members to the national headquarters of cooperating organizations, fearing the charge of interference with internal affairs.

The National Council was not highly successful in its efforts to coordinate the would-be supporters of FEPC. Many groups whose interests logically lay with the movement gave mere lip service or even opposed the National Council's strategy on FEPC. Herein lies an important key to the failure of national FEPC legislation through 1947. Part I of this study dealt, in part, with the organizational shortcomings of the National Council, while it is the general purpose of this section to describe and analyze its interaction with some of the important social groups and their organizational manifestations, as well as to examine the critics and opponents of the movement. Because the reaction of groups, like individuals, to outside stimuli will depend in large measure upon internal factors, a thorough analysis must touch upon organizational motivations, structures, and *modi operandi*. It is readily admitted that the analysis is not all-inclusive. Even so, such an analysis is necessary in accounting for the failure of the movement at the time of writing.

NEGROES IN GENERAL

Reform movements are commonly associated with altruistic endeavors to correct injustices. While altruism did play a part in the motivation of many groups in the FEPC campaign, for Negroes it was a "bread and butter" movement. The promise of a change in economic status through permanent FEPC legislation elicited a response from low income Negroes which the anti-poll tax, anti-lynching, and other movements have not been able to evoke.

Even among non-laboring Negroes, the intensity of feeling on FEPC was infinitely greater than among whites in comparable economic and social classes. Racial awareness, forced on the Negro, overcame most class barriers. Negro businessmen, for example, generally favored FEPC and supported the movement through financial contributions and organizational activities, while their white counterparts were almost uniformly opposed. Negro businessmen, as businessmen, are no more friendly towards the general theory of government control of employment policies than white entrepreneurs, but racial segregation has bred a desire for racial advancement which frequently has run counter to prevailing business *mores*. The same is true for other upper-class Negroes.

How was this intensity of feeling manifested in the FEPC movement? In spite of their interest, low income Negroes failed to capitalize fully upon their bitterness towards the existing system and their desire for change because they, in common with low income whites, were generally politically illiterate and inarticulate. At the same time it marked a high-water point in political activity for them. For the first time in their lives many low income Negroes were attending mass meetings and making small contributions to a pressure movement. However, as was to be expected, the bulk of the Negroes' FEPC work was carried on by middle and upper class Negroes: trade unionists, businessmen, insurance agents, teachers, physicians, lawyers, welfare workers, and government employees through the temporary local branches set up by the National Council and through the older permanent Negro organizations.[1]

NATIONAL ASSOCIATION FOR THE ADVANCEMENT OF COLORED PEOPLE

Perhaps the leading Negro interest group in the United States is the National Association for the Advancement of Colored People, founded in 1909 as a repudiation of the Booker T. Washington phi-

---

1. See Horace Cayton and St. Clair Drake, *Black Metropolis, passim,* for an excellent discussion of social and economic classes among the Negroes of Chicago.

losophy that the white community would voluntarily give equal rights to the Negro if he would but demonstrate his capacity to assume equal social responsibilities. The NAACP believes in pressure activity to promote recognition of legal rights, especially the suffrage, the theory being that once these rights are attained the Negro can begin to move forward. In the past, while this organization has engaged in some educational work to create race pride and has frequently ventured into the legislative field, it has laid its chief emphasis upon defensive legal battles largely concerned with specific cases involving disfranchisement, segregation, discriminatory legislation, court injustices, lynchings, and peonage.[2] At all times it attempts to work within the framework of the American Constitution, even though many white southerners look upon the NAACP as a radical "carpetbagging" organization.[3]

The NAACP has been interracial in composition from the beginning; whites serve on its board of directors and as members and officers of its 1,195 local branches, 254 youth councils, and 48 college chapters throughout the nation.[4] The executive secretary, Walter White, is regarded by many Negroes as the leading spokesman for their people. He has close relations with national leaders and is the White House's most frequent consultant on Negro problems.

The NAACP was one of the first national Negro organizations to recognize the need for government action to safeguard equality of opportunity in employment. During the defense period it not only in-

2. See James E. Pierce, *The National Association for the Advancement of Colored People—A Study in Social Pressure, passim,* unpublished master's thesis, Ohio State University, 1933.

3. This, in turn, has led to severe criticism by some students of Negro movements. The sociologist, Guy B. Johnson, in a brilliant article, has said: "Sociologically the weakness of the movement is inevitable and incurable: it attempts to undo the folkways and mores of the southern caste system by attacking the results and symptoms of the system. Paradoxically, if it leaves the attitudes and folkways of the white man out of the picture, it is doomed to fail; and if it takes those attitudes into account, it is either forced back to the gradualistic and conciliatory position of Booker Washington or forced forward into revolutionary tactics. One wonders then, whether its chief function, aside from its value in actually obtaining racial rights, has not been to serve as a catharsis for those discontented, impatient souls who, while they see no hope of normal participation in American life, feel that they must never give in and admit that they are beaten down spiritually."—"Negro Racial Movements and Leadership," *American Journal of Sociology,* XLIII, (July, 1937), 67.

4. Quoted by Arnold Rose in *The Negro in America,* from a letter from Julia E. Baxter, Division of Research and Information, NAACP, July 21, 1947.

stituted legal action in individual cases of employment discrimination, but also cooperated with other groups to mobilize pressure climaxing in the issuance of Executive Order No. 8802.[5]

When the campaign for permanent FEPC legislation got under way, the NAACP took a lively interest in its progress. Walter White threw the weight of his prestige behind it. Leslie Perry of the NAACP's Washington bureau served on the National Council's strategy committee. Roy Wilkins and other NAACP leaders testified for the legislation before congressional committees. Some money came from NAACP affiliates. In the state campaigns the national office backed its own model state FEPC bill and local branches played prominent roles in many state drives, both financially and politically.

These activities notwithstanding, the NAACP was never fully integrated into the National Council-guided campaign for federal FEPC legislation. The all-out cooperation of which the NAACP was capable was not forthcoming. Some critics of the National Council charged that the chief reason was Randolph's refusal to share the limelight with Walter White. *Manuscript*, a weekly newsletter purporting to give inside information on Washington politics as it affects the Negro, alleged that the National Council's work was being hampered by Randolph's desire "to prove he was big enough to do the job without Walter White." [6] Others charged an ideological conflict between some members of the NAACP's national board and Randolph, an outspoken anti-Communist.[7]

Most of the time the NAACP followed the lead of the National Council even though it lacked full confidence in the latter's leadership. However, after the 1946 defeat, the NAACP's national board adopted

5. In 1944, for example, the NAACP was able to get a Providence, Rhode Island, judge to hold that "Jim Crow" auxiliary unions, established especially for Negroes by the Boilermakers' Union, were illegal in Rhode Island, and that Negroes must be considered members of regular locals.—Roy Wilkins, "The Negro Wants Full Equality," *What the Negro Wants*, p. 125.
6. No. 50, February 26, 1946.
7. Asking for figures on the Senate cloture vote in 1946, a National Council supporter wrote: "The reason why I wanted it is that John ——— and Judge ——— as left wingers on the Board of the NAACP are bringing some heavy criticism against the National Council for a Permanent FEPC, and I wanted to show that it has been more successful than was the organization set up to back Marcantonio's bill to outlaw poll taxes a year ago."—Letter from ——— to Morris Milgram, Workers Defense League, March 5, 1946.

a resolution advocating a new FEPC committee to carry on the fight on the ground that Randolph's group had been given its chance without interference and had failed.[8]

Throughout the interorganizational conflict White, personally, gave statesmanlike leadership and refused to permit these rivalries to interfere with FEPC's prospects for victory. At crucial times he pledged the support of the NAACP to the National Council's program. At the Washington strategy conference in September 1945, he told the assembled delegates, "I want to join with the others in pledging the support of the organization which I represent—the National Association for the Advancement of Colored People—with 900 branches and 500,000 members." [9] He reaffirmed his support at the conference held in February 1946 following the disastrous filibuster. White did not approve of the resolution to set up a new committee passed by his national board in his absence on the West coast; at all times he sided with Randolph's group in its legislative strategy when criticized by the opposition.[10]

NATIONAL URBAN LEAGUE

The National Urban League is generally looked upon as the leading exponent of the indirect technique of promoting Negro advancement.[11] Instead of dealing directly with racial issues through political or other pressures, the Urban League has usually been content to prevail upon existing social agencies to make more services available to Negroes and to engage in research to prepare data which can be used by those who are interested in advancing the Negro cause. For many years it

---

8. *Manuscript*, No. 52, March 12, 1946.

9. *Digest of Working Conference.*

10. For example, as in his speech before the Southern Conference for Human Welfare, September 24, 1945.

11. It was formed in 1910 for the following purposes, according to the *Directory of Agencies in Race Relations*, p. 51: "(1) to coordinate efforts in behalf of the Negro to avoid duplication; (2) to investigate social conditions among Negroes in cities in order to determine what services were needed; (3) to persuade existing social agencies to include Negroes in their programs of work, but failing in this, to conduct demonstrations of needed social work activities with the idea eventually of getting agencies committed to such work to include Negroes in their program; (4) by fellowships and publicity, to encourage further training and experiences of Negroes in social work for fuller participation in attaining the objects sought by the League."

has maintained an Industrial Relations Department to promote Negro employment opportunities. Much of its energy has been directed towards changing the attitudes of white employers and workers through counseling with unions, executives, and supervisory personnel. It has also made studies of Negro industrial performance in the League's Industrial Laboratory and has conducted "Vocational Opportunity Campaigns" since 1930 to guide young Negro workers and to make more jobs available to them.[12]

The League is national and interracial in scope with over 25,000 people giving support or service to it. A national office is maintained in New York and local branches in fifty-six industrial centers throughout the country. The annual budgets of the national and local Urban Leagues total well over $500,000; the national budget alone in 1947 was $184,000, including the cost of *Opportunity*, its general publication. More than thirty-two branches receive assistance from local community funds.[13]

The conservative approach taken by the League has given it considerable respectability and support from leading whites and Negroes. Even in the South, the League is not regarded as a radical organization. Yet, at the same time, the indirect, conservative approach has prevented the Urban League from making an important contribution to Negro political pressure movements. In the case of the FEPC drive, the League's contribution was not commensurate with its size and prestige. It did endorse the National Council's bill before congressional committees but privately urged alteration of its terminology. Local League members gave a measure of cooperation to the National Council, nevertheless the character and philosophy of the organization prevented its full integration into the FEPC movement.

MARCH ON WASHINGTON MOVEMENT

The March on Washington Movement was the most spectacular Negro action group since Marcus Garvey's ill-fated United Negro Improvement Association of the World War I period.[14] Born out

12. Alphonse Henningburg, "Adult Education and the National Urban League," *Journal of Negro Education*, XIV (Summer Number, 1945), 396-402.
13. Statistics are drawn from the *Directory of Agencies in Race Relations*, and the *National Urban League, Thirty-Sixth Annual Report*, 1946.
14. The leaders of the MOWM denied any resemblance to Garvey's movement yet the parallel is not far-fetched.

of the desire for government action to promote employment opportunities for Negroes, the MOWM swept Negro communities off their feet. It was audacious and positive in its demands. Negro groups, impatient for progress, were dazzled and intoxicated by the uncompromising stand taken by the MOWM on FEPC. Local "March" units sprang up in many cities, mobilizing many previously unaffiliated lower class Negroes and also bringing middle and upper class Negro groups into the fold, at least temporarily.

The MOWM was a one-man organization; Randolph was its alpha and omega. The MOWM embodied Randolph's philosophy of mass political action with its strong as well as naive elements. The backbone of the MOWM was Randolph's own Brotherhood of Sleeping Car Porters which helped to organize and direct local chapters of the movement. The MOWM attracted Randolph's Negro admirers and was opposed by his critics.

The MOWM followed Randolph's theory of direct action to achieve results. Randolph termed it "non-violent goodwill direct action," which apparently meant mass marches and picket lines around political capitols to force capitulation to Negro demands. Randolph saw in the "March" a means to achieve racial gains which conciliation and education had not been able to accomplish for the Negro:

> The immediate, positive and direct value of mass action pressure consists of two things: One, it places human beings in physical motion which can be felt, seen and heard. Nothing stirs and shapes public sentiment like physical action. Organized labor and organized capital have long since recognized this. . . . Mass demonstrations against Jim Crow are worth a million editorials and orations in anybody's paper and on any platform. Editorials and orations are only worthwhile and effective when they are built around some actual human struggles for specific social and racial rights and against definite wrongs.[15]

While a broad program was worked out in time, the essence of the MOWM program of action was cited by Randolph before the 1942 Detroit convention:

> 1. A national conference for the integration and expression of the collective mind and will of the Negro masses.

---

15. "MOWM Presents Program for the Negro," *What the Negro Wants,* pp. 153-54.

2. The mobilization and proclamation of a nation-wide series of mass marches on the City Halls and City Councils to awaken the Negro masses and center public attention upon the grievances and goals of the Negro people and serve as training and discipline of the Negro masses for the more strenuous struggle of a March on Washington, if, as, and when an affirmative decision is made thereon by the Negro masses of the country through our national conference.

3. A march on Washington as an evidence to white America that black America is on the march for its rights and means business.

4. The picketing of the White House following the March on Washington and maintain the said picket line until the country and the world recognize the Negro has become of age and will sacrifice his all to be counted as men, free men.[16]

Although the MOWM did not advocate Negro nationalism of the Garvey type, it provided a unique example of racial exclusivism in a period when joint action across racial lines was emphasized by most groups. In explaining the exclusion of whites from MOWM, Randolph told his supporters in 1942:

And while the March on Washington Movement may find it advisable to form a citizens committee of friendly white citizens to give moral support to a fight against the Poll tax or white primaries, it does not imply that those white citizens or citizens of any racial group should be taken into the March on Washington Movement as members. The essential value of an all-Negro movement such as the March on Washington is that it helps to create faith by Negroes in Negroes. It develops a sense of self-reliance with Negroes depending on Negroes in vital matters. It helps to break down the slave psychology and inferiority-complex in Negroes which comes and is nourished with Negroes relying on white people for direction and support. This inevitably happens in mixed organizations that are supposed to be in the interest of the Negro.[17]

The "March" viewed the FEPC movement as the fruit of its early efforts and, therefore, its private preserve. National Council workers, not surprisingly, resented and resisted this paternalism. After some local brushes with the "March," the Council's southern field repre-

---

16. *Proceedings of Conference Held in Detroit,* March on Washington Movement, September 26-27, 1942, p. 9.

17. *Ibid.,* p. 6. Another reason for limiting membership to Negroes cited by Randolph on a number of occasions was to prevent the movement from being dominated by Communists, although paradoxically, Negro Communists were not expressly excluded.

sentative reported, "I did learn to steer clear of the MOW, and from then on [Richmond] I've inquired if there's an MOW in town and carefully avoided it." [18] In Richmond a coalition of the MOWM and the Brotherhood of Sleeping Car Porters had stolen the show from the field representative and had set up a slate of officers of their own choosing. The National Council's Washington staff finally resolved this particular problem by tactfully asking the coalition's choice for chairman to retire from her MOWM office to give full time to the local council, thus lessening the antagonisms of anti-MOWM groups in the community.

Friction resulted when a prominent MOWM leader, embarked upon a tour of the southwest where he sought to organize local councils on his own initiative. The Washington office was especially incensed when he established a local council at El Paso, Texas, and accepted $25.00 of the $37.31 collected at the first meeting for his expenses. It was some time before the office even knew of the existence of the local council.[19] Mrs. Hedgeman addressed a letter to him, the point of which could not be mistaken:

The National Council is very grateful for the work you have done around the country. Because I know you are likely to be on the road soon, I would like to make one very special request of you. *Please do not organize any local councils.* I understand exactly why you did it, but have not had the opportunity to explain to you that we are setting up a regional representative system. Mrs. Belle Douglas is organizing local councils throughout the South and is completely responsible for that area. She has spent considerable time in the Washington office and is in constant contact with us on the political situation here and its relation to the local community. We have already secured people for similar work in the Midwest, Northwest, Southwest, and East. We hope to correlate their efforts in the same way we have been able to accomplish the work in the South. We are most grateful for all of the interest you have been able to arouse and we hear a great deal about your excellent speeches, and therefore hope that you will not stop talking about FEPC wherever you go and in your usual dynamic fashion.[20]

This MOWM leader was also an irritant in Chicago where the local

18. Field Report, Douglas, April 16, 1945.
19. Letter from Mrs. Marguerite F. Walker, El Paso Council Secretary, July 2, 1945.
20. Letter, August 27, 1945.

council said that it could raise $25,000 "if they could get————out of the picture." [21]

The story of how the threat of a March on Washington in 1941 helped to force the issuance of Executive Order No. 8802 was related in Chapter I. MOWM leaders never tired of retelling the tale of their victory. It seemed to them to demonstrate completely the efficacy of their technique for political action. From that time forward, whenever a crisis confronted the President's Committee or the legislation for a permanent FEPC, "March" leaders could be expected to call upon other organizations to join them in a mass descent upon the nation's capital. But, as time passed, these organizations became more and more reluctant to join hands in such a venture, feeling that the victory in 1941 had been due to a bluff which could not work twice and that tried and tested pressure techniques should be employed instead of staking all upon the not too definite prospect of mobilizing thousands of people for such a trip.

Furthermore, the MOWM's aggressive approach rubbed many older organizations the wrong way. They resented the fact that MOWM had become a competitor for local and national leadership and took exception to the "March's" racial exclusivism. It was not long before the blush of initial triumph wore off. The prestige of the MOWM declined when the failure of the President's Committee on Fair Employment Practice to cope adequately with problems of discrimination in employment rendered the 1941 achievement somewhat less lustrous. Beyond this, local MOWM leadership failed to hold the confidence of the general Negro communities. By 1943 the old organizations had recovered from their temporary back seat position and many MOWM units had dropped from the picture.

BROTHERHOOD OF SLEEPING CAR PORTERS

Randolph's trade union, the Brotherhood of Sleeping Car Porters, also took a proprietary attitude towards the FEPC movement. In Dallas, Richmond, and other cities the BSCP was responsible for the establishment of local councils. Wherever present, BSCP

---

21. Field Report, Thelma E. Nickens, November 8, 1945.

representatives took the lead in planning local programs and raising money for FEPC. While their assistance was generally appreciated by the National Council, it sometimes interfered with the latter's plans. Trained in trade union tactics, BSCP leaders often sought to run the pressure campaign as they would a union drive, thereby irritating the National Council staff which had other thoughts on the matter.

Friction sometimes developed over credit for money which was raised locally. Because each had a quota, some Councils resented the fact that the BSCP collected money in its own name in their territories. The Secretary of the Denver Council complained:

On Wednesday of last week, the President of the Denver Division of the Brotherhood of Sleeping Car porters, handed me a receipt to Mr. J. R. Benoit, Secretary of the Division from the National Headquarters for the $267.00 sent in from the Denver Division, which was money raised in an FEPC Mass Meeting. I was instructed by the members of the Denver Council for a Permanent FEPC to ask you if this money is being given credit towards the Denver Council's quota.

There was much discussion in the community, as well as dissatisfaction in the Council because of the way in which the money was collected and sent in, instead of their cooperating with the Council, since the Council was in the midst of a financial drive and was expected to raise a certain amount of money for the National.[22]

NEGRO SOCIAL ORGANIZATIONS

The great multitude of national and local Negro fraternal orders, sororities, and clubs are primarily social in function, but most also like to think of themselves as organizations for advancement of the race. Consequently they stress service to the Negro community in their programs. For example, the twelve national Negro college fraternities and sororities representing a small segment of the colored populations, have their "service" emphases—"the Kappa Alpha Psis concentrating on vocational guidance in accordance with their slogan, 'Guide Right'; the Alpha Phi Alphas stressing an annual 'Go to College Week'; the Phi Beta Sigmas standing for 'Bigger and Better Negro Business.' "[23]

22. Letter from Mrs. Thelma Freeman, Denver Council Secretary, to the National Council, April 15, 1946.
23. Drake and Cayton, *Black Metropolis*, pp. 536-37.

In actual practice, few of these select groups or their more plebian brothers actually give much time to community work, since the bulk of the members are far more interested in the social opportunities which membership can afford. In this respect Negro social organizations are not different from their white counterparts. Where Negro societies have played outstanding roles in public affairs, their activities have usually stemmed from the personal concern of individual leaders, rather than from active interest of the rank and file. Public service remains, in most cases, "window dressing" to give prestige to the club and to help justify its existence.

In the drive for permanent FEPC legislation these groups played a relatively minor role. A number of Negro social organizations, including Sigma Gamma Rho and the Negro Elks, went on record as favoring FEPC.[24] Their pressure and financial contributions, however, were minute. The Negro Elks are a powerful group claiming 600,000 members; J. Finley, its grand exalted ruler, is a prominent Republican who served as chairman of the National Voters Independent Committee for the Election of Dewey and Bricker in 1944. Yet attempts to obtain the cooperation of the lodge in lining up Republican support in Congress were virtually fruitless.[25]

On the other hand, several groups in this general category made useful contributions to the FEPC movement. Robert Kearse, Negro Postmaster of Vauxhall, New Jersey, and Grand Master of the King Hiram Grand Lodge, Ancient, Free and Accepted Masons, Incorporated, staged a one-man campaign for FEPC in New Jersey, using his lodge's name to raise money and pressure congressmen. In 1944 he raised $500 by sponsoring a "Victory Benefit Show" for the National Council for a Permanent FEPC, importing Negro performers from the New York entertainment world. During the 1944 campaign he polled all of the candidates for Congress in New Jersey and parts of New York by mail and telegraph to ascertain their positions on FEPC. During the legislative campaign Kearse bombarded New Jersey's congressmen with telegrams demanding posi-

24. *Chicago Sunday Bee,* September 2 and December 17, 1944.
25. A Negro Elk leader reported having contacted Senator Robert Taft of Ohio at the request of Randolph but begged that his cooperation not be publicized.—Letter, January 4, 1945.

tive action. However, it remained a personal campaign by Kearse rather than a rank and file membership project.

The Alpha Kappa Alpha Sorority, far more than most social organizations, has taken an active hand in national politics. The sorority maintains a National Non-Partisan Council on Public Affairs in Washington with able Mrs. Thomasina W. Johnson as legislative representative until 1946. The Non-Partisan Council is partisan to the extent that its major objective is to obtain equal treatment for the Negro in all areas of American life. It is unusual for a social organizational adjunct in that it is far more interested in the political rather than the educational approach to Negro equality. According to the *Directory of Agencies in Race Relations* it employs the same sophisticated techniques used by the major pressure groups:

> The Council helps to coordinate the work of existing agencies concerned with public affairs; assembles, distributes, and interprets information; prepares testimony for public hearings and participates in public hearings; interviews public officials; builds programs and gives advice on programs and projects of social action; keeps its members informed through regular news letters and calendars of public affairs; maintains a clipping service; and releases materials to the press.[26]

The wide experience of the sorority's leadership was put to work in behalf of FEPC. Mrs. Johnson served on the National Council for a Permanent FEPC's strategy committee and aided in the lobbying work. The Non-Partisan Council also watched the voting record of congressmen on FEPC and other controversial issues and published the record vote for the sorority's membership. Alpha Kappa Alpha, in general, was useful in the FEPC pressure drive.

---

26. *Op. cit.*, pp. 49-50.

CHAPTER **6**   *Other Minorities*

• JEWISH ORGANIZATIONS AND THE FEPC MOVEMENT • AMERICAN JEWISH COMMITTEE • ANTI-DEFAMATION LEAGUE OF THE B'NAI B'RITH • NATIONAL COUNCIL OF JEWISH WOMEN • AMERICAN JEWISH CONGRESS • SPANISH-SPEAKING AMERICANS AND FEPC

CONOMIC DISCRIMINATION IS BY NO MEANS SOLELY a Negro incubus. Jews in the United States have continued to suffer the discrimination which has been their historical lot. According to a study of 1,000 sample complaints involving employment barriers in the New York metropolitan area, economic discrimination is practiced against this group in a wide variety of industries and occupations: financial institutions; professions, including accounting, advertising, engineering, and law; machinery and metal occupations; chemical and allied trades; printing and publishing plants; employment agencies; food industry; and many others.[1]

Early operations of the President's Committee on Fair Employment Practices revealed considerable discrimination against Jews in the aircraft, instruments, shipbuilding and repair, iron and steel, ordnance, machinery, and construction industries. During the fiscal year from July 1, 1943, to June 30, 1944, Jewish complaints comprised 6.3 per cent of all those docketed by the Committee. The complaints, in order of numerical importance involved: refusal to hire, discrimi-

---

1. J. X. Cohen, *Who Discriminates and How?* American Jewish Congress, undated, p. 17. Cohen also quotes reasons given by employers for refusing to hire Jews: the president of a large banking institution in New York: "Jews, through mind and heart, are congenitally disqualified to be bankers"; the vice-president of a large restaurant chain: "We jealously guard the atmosphere of our places; Jewish cashiers, hostesses and waitresses can't fit into this atmosphere because they're short, dumpy creatures"; the vice-president in charge of personnel of a great New York public utility: "We cannot hire Jewish girls to handle our large office equipment because their arms are too short," p. 6.

• 101 •

natory dismissal, discriminatory working conditions, discriminatory application forms and refusal to upgrade.[2]

Because of the low ceiling on employment opportunities, the majority of the approximately 5,000,000 American Jews have been concentrated in trade and small business; light manufacturing, especially the garment industry; and in certain services and professions where greater opportunities for entrance are available.

JEWISH ORGANIZATIONS AND THE FEPC MOVEMENT

Jews have been slow in organizing to combat the economic manifestations of racial and religious prejudice against them. The reason for this, it is sometimes alleged, is the general unwillingness of Jewish leaders to meet problems involving prejudice against their group head-on; they prefer to pretend that the problem does not exist and thereby hope to prevent further discrimination. In addressing the American Jewish Congress in 1937, Rabbi J.X. Cohen took these Jews to task:

> There are some Jews who would—and do—counsel a do-nothing policy in dealing with discrimination. They advise silence: "sha-sha" [quiet, quiet] is their pass-word. *No Irish Need Apply* was a slogan in the nineteenth century. The Irish did not rest until that slogan lost its currency, even though in some few areas today the policy may still prevail. And here, too, the opposition was not to the Catholic religion. The antagonism was racial—as in the present case of the Jews. Shall American Jewish leadership sacrifice the future for a quasi-peaceful present? What kind of leaders would they be if they traded self-respect for inaction? The American people as a whole would not wish a cowardly, supine group as a component of the great American commonwealth. On the contrary, we can earn increased respect by evoking the American sense of fair play in a free field.[3]

The first sustained effort to deal with the problem came with the establishment by the American Jewish Congress in 1930 of a Commission on Economic Discrimination headed by Rabbi Cohen. The Commission has engaged in research on discrimination, received and

---

2. *First Report*, p. 101.
3. J. X. Cohen, *Helping to End Economic Discrimination*, the second report on Jewish non-employment, presented to the adjourned session of the American Jewish Congress, Washington, D. C., November 28, 1937, p. 13.

investigated complaints often with satisfactory results, and supervised the establishment of local committees in many cities to deal with the same problems.[4] From this beginning, Jewish organizations advanced and had developed machinery and a good working knowledge of the field by the time World War II loomed on the horizon.

In 1941 the Coordinating Committee of Jewish Organizations Dealing with Employment Discrimination in War Industries was established by the Jewish Occupational Council to coordinate the work of local and national Jewish organizations and to publicize Jewish employment problems in defense industries.[5] Implementing the Coordinating Committee's work, Jewish vocational service agencies "tried to facilitate occupational readjustment by establishing information bureaus on job and training opportunities, setting up consultation centers for small business men seeking employment, devising programs for the adjustment of those entering war industries, and expanding guidance programs for youth of school age." [6]

Many Jewish organizations interested themselves in FEPC from the beginning. The Coordinating Committee served to unify and direct their interest along constructive channels. When the President's Committee was threatened by recurring crises, the Coordinating Committee was in the forefront in its defense. Jewish groups generally agreed that promotion of fair employment practices should become a permanent function of government. In the drive for federal legislation Jewish organizations were important for their financial and pressure contributions. On the other hand, not all of them were fervent supporters of the National Council for a Permanent FEPC, nor did all make constructive contributions to this coordinated effort in behalf of FEPC. It is necessary to examine some illustrative organizations to properly evaluate the group's mixed contributions to the advancement of FEPC legislation.

---

4. *Ibid.*, pp. 4-5.
5. Harry Schneiderman, "Judaism and Jewish Communal Affairs," *American Year Book*, 1943, p. 660. By 1945 the Coordinating Committee had been absorbed by a broader organization, the National Community Relations Advisory Council, established for the coordination of national and local Jewish agencies engaged in community relations activities.
6. Harry Schneiderman, and Julius B. Maller, "Judaism and Jewish Communal Affairs," *American Year Book*, 1945, p. 731.

AMERICAN JEWISH COMMITTEE

The American Jewish Committee was organized in 1906 "to safeguard the civil and religious rights of Jews, to combat discrimination and allay prejudice, to aid victims of persecution and discrimination."[7] It is of special interest in that it is the leading non-Zionist Jewish organization. While it is pro-Palestine in temper and contributes towards the establishment of a center for Judaism in Palestine, it is anti-nationalist and refuses to advocate the setting up of a Jewish state.[8]

The Committee is an affluent and conservative organization. According to Horace Kallen it belongs to the groups "whose tradition is to think of the community as a somewhat hierarchical body governed by its elders—elders by virtue of birth, wealth, power, station and superior education—who would act *for* their fellow Jews on their own authority, according to their own judgment."[9] It is charged that the Committee is not broadly representative of American Jewry. In recent years the American Jewish Committee has discussed the advisability of broadening the membership base to strengthen the organization.[10] But following its withdrawal from the American Jewish Conference, a consultative body for effecting

7. Maurice J. Karpf, *Jewish Community Organization in the United States,* pp. 62-63.

8. John Slawson, Executive Vice President, expressed the organization's viewpoint on Zionism when he said: ". . . the philosophy that appears to be the expression of the American Jewish Committee point of view at the present time is that of cultural assimilation which opposes both a Jewish nationalistic doctrine and the assimilationist approach of the escapist variety. . . . We do not accept escapism of any form, either into Jewish nationalism or into an aggressive melting pot assimilation process. We assert that the democratic process calls for cultural integration of the Jew into the American scene with every possibility for the exercise of devoted and loyal citizenship, but at the same time retaining the religio-cultural adherence to, and preservation of Judaism."—Address before the thirty-seventh annual meeting of the General Committee of the American Jewish Committee, held in New York, January 30, 1944, published in the *American Jewish Year Book,* 5705, September 18, 1944 to September 7, 1945, pp. 580-81.

9. H. M. Kallen, "National Solidarity and the Jewish Minority," an article in *The Annals of the American Academy of Political and Social Science,* 223 (September 1942), 25.

See Harry S. Linfield, *The Communal Organization of the Jews in the United States, 1927,* pp. 120-21, for a description of the structure of the American Jewish Committee.

10. *Ibid.,* p. 546.

unity of action with respect to Jewish problems, as a result of disagreements on Zionism and other matters, it lost the support of important Jewish leaders and 42 out of its 420 affiliated organizations in 1944.[11]

The Committee was interested in the FEPC movement from the standpoint of benefits obtainable for Jews. Its pressure contributions were not outstanding, although it sent representatives to testify in behalf of permanent FEPC legislation before several congressional committees and was represented on the National Council's strategy committee. It was more important for its financial contributions which, while not huge, were of considerable assistance to the National Council. In a sense it is representative of a number of organizations which seek to substitute money for strenuous political pressure work.

ANTI-DEFAMATION LEAGUE OF THE B'NAI B'RITH

The Anti-Defamation League sponsored by B'nai B'rith, a major Jewish men's organization, aided the FEPC movement in several ways. While it claims to be educational in character and "does not engage in political activity, but believes that anti-Semitism must be eliminated through an educational process and not through militancy," it assisted the National Council's pressure program through financial contributions and educational literature. The League's contribution of $2,750 was one of the larger ones received by the National Council. Especially important was the League's contribution to the National Council's extremely inadequate supply of FEPC literature. The reprint from *Look* magazine which was widely circulated by the National Council was obtained from the Anti-Defamation League.[12] In addition, the League gave the Randolph group full rights to use posters and pamphlets prepared by its own research, educational, and literature departments. Finally, the League cooper-

---

11. Some of the influential organizations which withdrew included: B'rith Sholom, Free Sons of Israel, Hadassah, Independent Order B'rith Abraham, Progressive Order of the West, Rabbinical Assembly of America, Union of Orthodox Jewish Congregations, United Synagogue of America, Women's Branch of the Union of Orthodox Jewish Congregations, Women's League of the United Synagogue of America— *American Jewish Year Book*, p. 557.

12. "Prejudice: Our Postwar Battle," *Look*, May 1, 1945.

ated by underwriting the cost of an FEPC pamphlet and was responsible for the publication of a widely circulated *FEPC Reference Manual*.

Nevertheless, the Anti-Defamation League's chief interest is in Jewish rights and it disagreed with the alleged tendency of the National Council to emphasize Negro rights almost to the exclusion of all other minorities. On one occasion the League refused to underwrite a proposed National Council pamphlet because it placed stress almost solely upon Negro problems.

NATIONAL COUNCIL OF JEWISH WOMEN

The National Council of Jewish Women, representing 65,000 members organized in more than 300 branches in all parts of the country, is the leading Jewish women's organization participating in public affairs. Its five departments promote interest among the members in welfare work, social legislation, international relations and peace, contemporary Jewish affairs, and service to the foreign born. Its work in the field of race relations proceeds from the belief that it is necesary to eliminate all forms of discrimination if Jewish rights are to be maintained.

The National Council of Jewish Women took an active interest in the FEPC movement and cooperated closely with the National Council for a Permanent FEPC. Helen Raebeck, the organization's Washington representative, assisted the Randolph group in planning and executing strategy. Beyond this, the NCJW claimed:

> Our support of FEPC has not been confined to the adoption of a resolution. Our National Committee on Social Legislation has implemented our endorsement with testimony, letters and telegrams. But we also realize that our greatest strength lies in the active participation of our 300 Sections through direct contact with their Senators and Representatives.
>
> We have therefore kept our Sections informed of all major developments through our regular bulletins and special calls to action. We told them of the activities of the President's Committee on FEPC, and asked them to help support and strengthen it. As soon as the bill for a permanent FEPC was introduced, we endorsed it and called for action from our members. They have responded to our every call, and sent a barrage of letters and telegrams to their Congressmen and to the President.

AMERICAN JEWISH CONGRESS

The American Jewish Congress is an exceptionally alert and active confederation of a great variety of Jewish organizations which takes a leading role in representing Jews in American public affairs. Its Commissions on Community Interrelations, Economic Discrimination, and Law and Social Action have pioneered in the development and application of action programs based upon opinion measurement, diagnostic surveys, social psychology, legal research, and other advanced techniques for social action.

However, because of its own well-defined ideas about how social reform is accomplished and because of personality conflicts, the American Jewish Congress remained almost completely outside of the pressure structure erected by the National Council for a Permanent FEPC. In fact considerable bitterness accompanied relations between the two organizations.

The clash between Will Maslow, Director of the Commission on Law and Social Action of the American Jewish Congress, and National Council leadership was an insurmountable barrier to cooperation between the two organizations. Before Maslow had joined the Congress in 1945, he had served as Director of Field Operations for the President's Committee on Fair Employment Practice and had acquired a low opinion of the ability of the members of the National Council's Washington staff in his contacts with them. When he moved to the Congress he carried with him this lack of confidence in the National Council and proceeded to translate it into Congress policy.[13]

Maslow, in a letter to the author, categorized his complaints against the National Council as follows:

(1) The National Council never attempted any real publicity or educational campaign and never had a publicity or educational director.

(2) It never worked well with the CIO and thus cut itself off from its most important support.

(3) It never enlisted the wholehearted support of Negro groups such as NAACP, Negro Elks, etc.

(4) Because of the personality of Hedgeman, it antagonized most of the members of the FEPC staff from Ross down.

---

13. There is evidence of differences of opinion between the AJC and the National Council before Maslow's arrival on the scene.

(5) In the field the Council insisted upon organizing its own local groups even though there were other organizations already in existence which could have been utilized to support FEPC. This created friction, duplication, etc.

(6) Finally, the Council from director down were third-rate, unable to do an intelligent job on anything they attempted.[14]

One squabble between Maslow and the National Council involved American Jewish Congress representation on the Council's executive and strategy committees. When Maslow asked for an invitation to serve on the committees, a National Council staff member replied vaguely:

> As you know, the Strategy Committee has no regular schedule. It meets on call as frequently as the situation warrants—sometimes on only 24 hours' notice. There will be no further meetings until Congress reconvenes. We shall try to give you sufficient notice to insure your representation on all future meetings.
>
> As for the Executive Committee appointment, your request must be put before the Executive Committee itself. This we shall do at its first fall meeting.[15]

Although Maslow was appointed to the strategy committee shortly thereafter, the National Council showed its feelings towards him by failing to send him notices of meetings. In connection with a disagreement over legislative strategy, Maslow wrote angrily:

> The whole business has a jealous organizational aspect which is disturbing for those more interested in getting an FEPC than in the pretensions of any individual organization.
>
> What disturbs me personally, however, is that although I was appointed a member of the Strategy Committee of the National Council on August 28, 1945, I have not been asked my views on this question of strategy, have not been invited to any meetings of the Strategy Committee, and am informed of important strategy decisions after they are made. Certainly that is no way to enlist the cooperation of the members of the Strategy Committee or the organizations they represent.[16]

Another major area of conflict involved legislative strategy. Maslow agreed with those who favored the "House First" and "Calendar

---

14. Letter, September 6, 1946.
15. Letter from Ida Fox to Maslow, August 17, 1945.
16. Letter to Mrs. Hedgeman, December 4, 1945.

Wednesday" approaches, rather than the National Council's "Senate First" plan. This difference of opinion proved injurious to the FEPC cause and diminished the chances for victory. Local affiliates and representatives of the American Jewish Congress took their cue from Maslow and propagandized for his strategy while National Council representatives in the same communities were advocating the opposite approach—the inevitable result was division of energies and confusion.

The National Council resented the fact that the Congress vigorously pushed state FEPC legislation and gave considerable assistance to state movements. The National Council preferred that all energies be centered on federal legislation first; in 1945 it sought successfully to persuade the American Jewish Congress to postpone the Missouri drive.

It is difficult to assess final responsibility for the friction between the two organizations, but it appears that the National Council was not always frank and forthright in dealing with the Congress and failed to subordinate personality clashes and differences of opinion as a good coordinating committee must do. On the other hand, Maslow was intransigent in his views on strategy and was not an easy person to "coordinate." Their failure to cooperate fully on FEPC resulted in duplication of efforts in some areas, confusion among rank and file members over strategy and tactics, and general injury to the entire cause; whereas, proper clearance and collaboration could have aided the movement immeasurably.

SPANISH-SPEAKING AMERICANS AND FEPC

The approximately 3,000,000 Spanish-speaking people in the United States have been second only to the Negro minority as sufferers from social and economic discrimination. In large sections of western Texas, New Mexico, Arizona, Colorado, and southern California the Spanish-speaking minority, chiefly of Mexican origin and at least half of whom are American citizens, are subjected to a severe form of segregation and discrimination. They are refused service in "white" restaurants, are denied access to "white" recreational facilities, both public and private, and are relegated to common labor and other menial occupations.

Recognizing the plight of the Spanish-speaking peoples, the National Council sought to mobilize them behind the drive for permanent FEPC legislation. In 1944, at the suggestion of Senator Chavez of New Mexico, the National Council approached Ernest Maes, Director of Inter-American Cooperation in the Department of Interior, to explore the possibilities for a field trip by him to awaken Spanish-American interest in the legislation and to "(1) mitigate the popular impression that the Permanent FEPC is solely a Negro issue and (2) block the attempt of the Southern coalition to join hands with Western members of Congress in opposing the bill, as has hitherto been the practice in legislation of this type."[17] Maes, who was deeply interested in the problem, secured a furlough from the government and embarked upon a field trip of several months duration to sell FEPC to the leaders of Spanish-speaking organizations and to establish local councils for Spanish-speaking peoples. Later, to supplement this initial venture, the National Council prepared a few items of literature in Spanish and sought to reach the Spanish-Americans through its field representatives and other media.

It was not long, however, before the National Council realized that it had undertaken a gargantuan task, one beyond its resources or capacity to complete. In September 1945 Carlos E. Castaneda of the President's Committee's San Antonio office, wrote the National Council:

Frankly, not 1% of the population of the Southwest knows or understands what FEPC is or means to them. This is the reason why the response of the Latin-Americans as concerns support to the National Council has been negligible. The Spanish press has had very few notices of FEPC. Consequently, the rank and file of the Spanish-speaking population of the Southwest is almost unacquainted with the existence of FEPC. . . . The

17. Letter from Mrs. Beatrice Schalet, National Council legislative representative, July 26, 1944, to Horace M. Marston of the Anti-Defamation League of B'nai B'rith in reply to the latter's objections to the field trip. Marston had written on July 25, 1944, in part: "With regard to the educational program of a general pro-democratic nature, we fail to recognize how it is possible to achieve any beneficial results with a fairly substantial foreign language minority in this country on the basis of a fourteen week trip through the respective areas. In addition, it is our opinion, based on many years of experience in the field of education, that the program you have set up for activities amongst the Spanish-speaking minority is all too vague to permit any proper evaluation of the ultimate purposes that are to be achieved as well as of the methods you want to employ."

Spanish-American who reads English depends for his source of information on the white press which in the South and Southwest has seldom reported anything concerning the merits of FEPC and has taken notice of it only to present the views of its opponents.[18]

Maes' field trip apparently had only scratched the surface. Castaneda continued:

I was in California in August of 1944 when Mr. Maes was there and since that time I have had an opportunity to contact many of the local Latin-American Councils which he organized from California to Texas. Mr. Maes did a splendid job of organization, but he was not in the field long enough, nor did he succeed in transmitting his enthusiasm to the local councils. I know from personal experience and observation that in Texas, Colorado, and Arizona the local councils organized by Mr. Maes have been practically inactive for the last six months and that only recently was there a sign of activity in Denver. Outside of California the only active Latin-American Council of those organized by Mr. Maes is the Chicago Council, thanks to the deep interest of Frank X. Paz, who unfortunately is now in the Armed Forces of the United States.

The Mexican-American local councils established by Mr. Maes need to be recontacted and reactivated, as well as the various state and inter-state Mexican-American organizations throughout the Southwest.[19]

Other evidence also exists which indicates that efforts made in Chicago, Kansas City, Denver, and other northern cities to reach the Spanish-Americans generally met with little success. For example, the Denver Council secretary asserted:

A sub-council of Spanish speaking people was organized in Denver last August. At that time, it was the understanding of the group already organized, or the city-wide council that this group would work with the city-wide council, or in fact, that all the minority groups and those interested in minority problems would work together, combining forces for strong team work in interest of a permanent FEPC. However, I do not think that this point is clear to the sub-council group. Notwithstanding the fact that we made the chairman of the sub-council the co-chairman of the city-wide council, we are not getting the cooperation of this group, and just what work they are doing, we do not know.[20]

---

18. Letter, September 22, 1942.
19. *Ibid.*
20. Letter from Mrs. Thelma S. Freeman, Denver Council secretary, to Dorothy S. Norman, National Finance Secretary, October 21, 1944.

In the southwest, where the bulk of Spanish-Americans of recent origin reside, there was almost no cooperation between this group and Negroes. Effective collaboration could have given these groups political power in some areas, but time-weathered social barriers have prevented a joining of forces. Spanish-Americans were invariably organized in their own local councils in the southwest. In San Antonio, where both Negro and Mexican councils carried on operations, considerable rivalry existed between the two over financial drives and other matters.[21]

One major difficulty in dealing with the Spanish-speaking peoples lay in their lack of political awareness and maturity. Senator Chavez complained that he got no letters favoring FEPC from his Spanish-American constituents despite economic discrimination against them.[22] A National Council staff member, in stressing the need for a program to energize and educate them, pointed out:

> Because they are so inarticulate as a group, their representatives in Congress have not been made aware of the relationship between the FEPC and the situation of their Spanish-speaking constituents. That is why, for instance, that Senator Edward Johnson, of Colorado, voted against the FEPC appropriation even though he is very active in his own state on behalf of the Spanish-speaking citizenry. That is why, also, the leadership of the opposition to the permanent FEPC bill in the House has been taken by Congressman O. C. Fisher, even though he has a mainly Spanish-speaking constituency in Texas.[23]

In many areas of the South, too, the Spanish-American vote is machine-controlled. The National Council's southern field representative reported:

> In so far as Texas Congressmen are concerned, influencing them in '46 is a dream. It is true that the Latin-American vote combined with the Negro vote could defeat Kilday in San Antonio *if it were solid*, but the Negro vote and about 60% of the Latin-American vote is sold out to the machine. Castaneda and Perales do not have the majority of the L-A vote. . . . In Corpus Christi where your L-A vote is powerful it is controlled by the Lu-Lacs whose leadership is reactionary.[24]

---

21. Field Report, Douglas, September 23, 1945.
22. *Ibid.*, Leuchtenburg. May 16, 1945.
23. Letter. Schalet to Marston, *op. cit.*
24. Field Report, Douglas, October 5, 1945.

The last is a reference to the leadership of their social organizations which is, for the most part, in the hands of rich conservatives whose economic status does not lead them to encourage their less fortunate brethren to engage in political reform movements.

A few of the Spanish-American groups did respond to the National Council's appeals. The Committee of One Hundred, describing itself as a "strictly political organization," with headquarters in San Antonio, sent telegrams to President Truman and the senators from Texas and asked leaders of other organizations throughout Texas and the southwest to do likewise.[25] *La Prensa*, a leading Spanish-language newspaper, published two articles in its November 18 and 25, 1945, editions by Alonzo S. Perales, Chairman of the Committee of One Hundred, asking Latin-Americans to telegraph their representatives in Congress on FEPC. The League of Loyal Americans at Pottet, Texas, did so and received an unfavorable reply from Senator Lee O'Daniels, which was not unexpected.

Nevertheless, these activities were exceptional. The great majority of Spanish-Americans were untouched and unmoved by the appeals. The National Council's efforts were doomed from the start. Its critics were probably correct when they asserted that this tremendous job would best be left untouched unless the National Council had the resources to do it properly. The National Council was never able to throw sufficient money and workers into the field to make real headway with this group. The time and energies spent could probably have been utilized with more telling effect in other channels.

---

25. Letter from Alonzo S. Perales, Chairman, November 30, 1945.

CHAPTER 7   *Civic Action Groups*

• AMERICAN CIVIL LIBERTIES UNION • NATIONAL
FEDERATION FOR CONSTITUTIONAL LIBERTIES
• AMERICAN COUNCIL ON RACE RELATIONS
• SOUTHERN CONFERENCE FOR HUMAN WEL-
FARE • COUNCIL AGAINST INTOLERANCE IN
AMERICA • COMMON COUNCIL FOR AMERICAN
UNITY •WORKERS DEFENSE LEAGUE AND POST-
WAR WORLD LEAGUE •WOMEN'S GOOD GOVERN-
MENT AND REFORM ASSOCIATIONS • NATIONAL
LEAGUE OF WOMEN VOTERS • OTHER WOMEN'S
ORGANIZATIONS

IN RECENT YEARS A VARIETY OF NATIONAL ORGAN-
izations have come into being whose announced aims are to preserve
civil liberties and improve race relations in an age filled with tensions produced by wars, depressions, and industrial strife. In most cases
they have no economic or special group axe to grind; sponsored by
intellectuals and having small followings, they nevertheless have been
able to undertake important projects of many types because of the
beneficence of large donors. Most of these organizations are educational in character, but some have also participated in legal and legislative battles. Their contributions to the FEPC movement were chiefly
educational and advisory, but their backing was eagerly sought by the
National Council for what prestige, money, and active support they
could muster.

AMERICAN CIVIL LIBERTIES UNION

The American Civil Liberties Union was formed in 1920 for the
defense of civil liberties as an outgrowth of the World War I
American Civil Liberties Bureau. Over the years it has established a

• 114 •

reputation for being the leading private organization dedicated to the preservation of basic rights in the interest of the democratic way of life.[1]

The ACLU's techniques for action include legal proceedings, conferences with public authorities, education through publication of literature and staging of public meetings, cooperation with other organizations with similar interests and, on some occasions, indirect aid to legislative campaigns. On February 1, 1946, the Union had 6,749 members scattered throughout the country.[2] Most of the supporters came from professional and intellectual groups with a heavy weighting of educators. In 1945 the ACLU's income reached the high-water mark of $66,000 for both the operating and special purposes funds, the average contribution being about $8.00.[3] Ten organizations represent the Union in local cases and five other local groups cooperate closely with it. The ACLU also has correspondents in all states who secure information and give advice on local matters. On the national level the ACLU maintains eleven committees, each of which is responsible for an important area of civil liberty.

Identifying the demands of racial minorities for greater recognition in war industry employment and the armed forces with the struggle for civil rights, in 1942 the Union formed a Committee on Race Discrimination, whose work was to "help coordinate the many organizations in the field and to formulate a program to tackle phases of other than Negro discrimination as part of the democratic struggle."[4] Pearl S. Buck served as chairman and Winifred Raushenbush as secretary of the committee. Beginning with 1942 the Committee held annual conferences on discrimination attended by representatives of almost thirty national organizations. After the Detroit riots the Committee distributed 13,000 copies of a pamphlet entitled *How to*

---

1. In 1945 the Union was active in the following fields: racial minorities; international civil liberties; censorship; conscientious objectors; labor's rights; war prosecutions for speech and publication; military power and civil rights; freedom of speech and assembly; radio; un-American activities; freedom in schools and colleges; freedom in the colonies; rights of aliens; Jehovah's Witnesses; political rights; restraints on communications; and rights of women.—*From War to Peace, American Liberties, 1945-46*, annual report of the American Civil Liberties Union, July 1946.

2. *Ibid.*, p. 64.

3. *Liberty on the Home Front*, ACLU report, July 1945, pp. 62-63.

4. *Directory of Agencies in Race Relations*, p. 6.

Prevent Race Riots in Your Home Town. In general the Committee sought to cooperate with the programs of other organizations and to supplement them where it was deemed desirable.

The ACLU joined with other groups in support of continuance of the President's Committee on Fair Employment Practice early in the war period. When the drive for permanent FEPC legislation was initiated, the Union cooperated with the National Council for a Permanent FEPC. In fact Roger Baldwin, Director of the Union, was one of Mrs. Hedgeman's earliest and most influential advisors. It was Baldwin who suggested the formation of a strategy committee of Washington lobbyists stressing that "the main point is to get persons with experience in lobbying who represent voting strength."[5] Baldwin also made use of his local representatives, committees, and state correspondents to urge letters to Congress for action on FEPC. In addition, he was instrumental in getting a $1,000 contribution from the Robert Marshall Civil Liberties Trust for the educational work of the National Council.[6] Finally, a Washington representative of the ACLU, Mrs. Ted Silvey, aided the National Council's staff by interviewing congressmen to ascertain their views on FEPC and to secure their commitments, if possible.

On occasion Baldwin was also a critic of the manner in which the FEPC campaign was being handled. He took the National Council to task in December 1944 for not clearing lobbying plans with Malcolm Ross, Chairman of the President's Committee, and for not "putting Jews, Catholics and Mexicans to the front" in making an appeal to the country.[7] He further questioned the desirability of a mail campaign to revive the drive for permanent FEPC legislation after the 1946 Senate defeat.[8]

The total contribution of the ACLU to the FEPC drive was limited. Being a tax exempt organization it could not contribute heavily to the National Council's war chest, nor could it participate

---

5. Letter to Mrs. Hedgeman, March 14, 1944.
6. *Ibid.*, July 11, 1944.
7. *Ibid.*, December 29, 1944.
8. Roger Baldwin wrote Mrs. Hedgeman on May 7, 1946: "We have considered your telegram of May 3rd and do not feel that the FEPC bill can be revived by a shower of letters and telegrams. A much more careful campaign needs to be worked up to gain serious attention or to have political effect. We have consulted Mrs. Silvey who agrees with this view and you better talk with her if you wish our further cooperation."

openly in the lobbying campaign. Taking these factors into consideration, the ACLU cooperated as closely with the National Council as its structure and objectives permitted.

NATIONAL FEDERATION FOR CONSTITUTIONAL LIBERTIES

The National Federation for Constitutional Liberties formed in 1940 was one of the more aggressive civil libertarian organizations produced by the crisis of war. According to the Federation it engaged in many activities during the war which were "essential to victory over the Axis, and to an enduring peace." It claimed to fight "discrimination and denial of constitutional rights wherever and whenever found" and to expose and isolate "defeatists, seditionists, anti-Semites and all purveyors of Nazi-inspired race hatred who would divide the American people."[9]

A federation of national, regional, and local groups having similar objectives, it carried on its work through conferences, publications, meetings, radio programs, and field trips. It sought to work through existing organizations—educational, church, trade union, farm, professional, minority, and community groups—informing and stimulating them to action.[10] It provided "action letters" and bulletin services for its members. In addition to the national office in New York, a Washington bureau was maintained to secure information on developments in Congress and to lobby for bills favored by the NFCL. The voting record of every member of Congress was kept by the Washington bureau. An Academic Division composed of educators was also formed to concern itself with problems of academic freedom and discrimination in the educational field.

The NFCL made FEPC one of its chief planks and cooperated with the National Council on most occasions. Through its "action letters" it kept Federation members informed on FEPC progress and sought to assist the drive by organizing letter-writing and fund-raising campaigns.[11] It also participated in congressional lobbying efforts.[12]

---

9. From cover of a reprint of an article entitled "Race Discrimination and the Law" by Carey McWilliams.

10. *Directory of Agencies in Race Relations*, pp. 46-47.

11. From column by Bascom N. Timmons in the *Pasadena Independent*, November 1944.

12. Letter, July 23, 1945, from Frances M. Williams indicates that Mrs. Seller,

On at least one occasion, however, the NFCL did not clear its signals with the National Council and was subsequently hotly attacked by Representative Charles M. LaFollette of Indiana, FEPC supporter who helped make National Council strategy. This episode took place in December 1945, when the big offensive against Congress was being planned. While the National Council was assiduously wooing Republican support, the NFCL caused concern by charging that the failure of Republican congressmen to sign the petition:

... lends strong credence to the charge that the majority of Republican Congressmen are withholding their signatures . . . until a few months before election so that they may claim the Negro vote while nevertheless preventing passage of the bill, since it will leave too little time for the bill to pass both Houses of Congress before the end of the session.[13]

When LaFollette was written to in a similar vein, he replied to George Marshall, NFCL chairman, charging that the Federation was pursuing the Communist party's line on FEPC strategy and had no sincere interest in securing passage of the bill:

The activities of your organization, together with those of Max Yergan and his National Negro Congress and the local activities of Hoyt Haddock, legislative representative of NMU (National Maritime Union), are driving me to the conclusion that you people do not want this legislation, but would rather have an issue with which to agitate Negroes.[14]

Whether or not LaFollette was correct in his Communist charges, the incident does present a good example of the difficulties involved in coordinating a large number of diverse organizations in a campaign requiring careful execution of strategy.

AMERICAN COUNCIL ON RACE RELATIONS

The American Council on Race Relations was organized in the summer of 1944 by a group of prominent leaders in the field of race relations, including Clarence E. Pickett, Will W. Alexander, A. A. Liveright, and others, to serve as a coordinating and advisory agency for organizations dealing with race relations problems on the com-

---

NFCL Washington secretary, "has been working in close teamwork with the members of your organization [National Council] and others from day to day in the terrific fight which has just been waged with some degree of success."

13. *PM*, December 9, 1945.
14. Letter, December 19, 1945.

munity level. Establishment of the Council was made possible by grants from the Julius Rosenwald Fund and the Marshall Field Foundation. By August 1946 the Council had a broad, chiefly educational program underway which included: police training in race relations; minority veterans' problems; Japanese-American affairs; establishment and servicing of both official and unofficial local race relations councils; studies of the feasibility and effectiveness of municipal fair employment practice ordinances; integration of minorities into non-production employment; techniques for fighting restrictive covenants; and many others.[15] Both popular and technical pamphlets on race relations have been published by the ACRR. Field representatives have been sent to many parts of the country to aid in the solution of local problems. The Council asserts that all this activity is for the purpose of "arousing a large number of individuals to passionate concern and aggressive action for establishing a working democracy that will include all elements of the population on an equal basis."[16]

Employment discrimination has been one of the chief interests of the Council. Local race relations organizations are urged to tackle local discrimination problems. The national staff aids these organizations by field service consultation and by giving assistance on employment integration. Materials such as *Negro Platform Workers*, an objective pamphlet analysis of the Philadelphia transit strike, are issued to present the facts on racial discrimination in employment.

At the same time, the ACRR refused to become involved in the pressure campaign for a permanent FEPC in any direct manner. As with many other groups, the tax-exempt nature of the Council stood in the way. When A. A. Liveright, Executive Director, was asked to publish a pamphlet advocating FEPC over the American Council's name, he declined because it would "very definitely be a contravention of the limitation placed on tax exempt corporations which prohibits them from actively attempting to influence legislation."[17] For this reason the Council was only indirectly helpful to the movement. It did publish several pamphlets dealing with the battle for FEPC

---

15. *American Council on Race Relations Programs Under Way*, (mimeographed), August 22, 1946, p. 4.
16. *Directory of Agencies in Race Relations*, p. 9.
17. Letter to Mrs. Hedgeman, November 20, 1944.

legislation which could be interpreted as favoring FEPC although the materials assumed an objective pose.[18] Individual members of the Council's staff aided the National Council by giving advice, sending in field reports on FEPC activities observed by them, and by other unpublicized assistance.

SOUTHERN CONFERENCE FOR HUMAN WELFARE

Some groups found in the FEPC movement an opportunity to expand their membership by playing up their efforts in its behalf. An example was the Southern Conference for Human Welfare, an interracial organization working for a "more prosperous and more democratic South" through biennial conferences on southern problems and its publication, *The Southern Patriot.* It was no doubt sincere when it attempted to stir up pressure for FEPC by calling for letters and telegrams from state and local affiliates:

When the filibusterers seized control of the Senate floor, holding up the vital war agencies appropriations, they claimed to speak for the "solid" South in their opposition to the FEPC. Chapters of the Southern Conference, in Georgia and Tennessee, however, were skeptical. They arranged for the "silent" South to be heard.

In two days, the Davidson, Tennessee chapter secured more than 1700 names from every Southern state to a petition urging the creation of a permanent FEPC. Since it was a rush job, signers had to invest in a telegram to our Washington representative, authorizing their signatures. Mr. Bilbo was unhappy about that list of names, which included outstanding Southern citizens of every profession.

The Committee for Georgia, affiliated with the Southern Conference for Human Welfare, cooperated in securing names of more than 1000 Georgians to a similarly impressive petition.[19]

Nevertheless, it was accused of using the FEPC issue to advance its southern organizational drive. Mrs. Douglas, the National Council's southern field representative reported:

---

18. *Manual For Official Committees,* 1945, suggested that local groups push for municipal and state legislation if existing employment discrimination bans are inadequate, p. 17; *State FEPC—What the People Say,* 1945, presented the arguments for and against the New York Ives-Quinn bill introduced during the legislative hearings; *Confidential Report on Ives-Quinn Hearings, New York,* drew conclusions applicable to FEPC drives in other states.

19. *The Southern Patriot,* vol. 3, no. 7, July 1945, p. 7.

Dombrowski of the Southern Conference for Human Welfare is trying to move into Texas on the strength of what they have done for FEPC. They are using the petition that came out of Atlanta as a selling point for themselves. Just what, specifically, has the Southern Conference done for FEPC, and didn't that petition originate with the Atlanta Council?[20]

The Southern Conference for Human Welfare was trying to get the same people on whom we depend for support to finance the Conference's coming into Texas on the strength of what they might be able to do for FEPC. They wrote Dombrowski that they would welcome his coming but could assume no financial obligation. So that's that.[21]

COUNCIL AGAINST INTOLERANCE IN AMERICA

The Council Against Intolerance in America is an organization which proclaims itself to be purely educational in character yet finds it possible to participate in an occasional pressure campaign. For the most part the Council seeks to promote national unity by placing educational materials in the hands of teachers and by holding rallies, celebrations, and other public events.[22] In the case of the FEPC movement, however, the group went afield. Before the National Council for a Permanent FEPC began large-scale operations, the Council Against Intolerance had already held a mass meeting to "Save the FEPC" on November 10, 1943, at Hunter College. In June 1945 the organization staged another "Save the FEPC Rally" at Town Hall in New York City which received favorable messages from President Truman and labor leaders Philip Murray and William Green. Throughout the campaign the Council Against Intolerance cooperated splendidly with Randolph's organization by sending telegrams and exerting other pressures at the National Council's request. Apparently, warm personal relations between Director James Waterman Wise and the National Council's leaders made close collaboration possible.

COMMON COUNCIL FOR AMERICAN UNITY

The Common Council for American Unity exemplified the type of civil libertarian educational organization which refused to participate in the pressure campaign despite its lively interest in the FEPC cause. The Common Council has a broad program for the protection

20. Field Report, Douglas, July 30, 1945.
21. *Ibid.*, August 1, 1945.
22. The Council sponsored two nation-wide celebrations, The Bill of Rights Sesqui-Centennial in 1941 and the Thomas Jefferson Bi-Centennial in 1942.

and advancement of refugees, foreign-born, and minority groups.[23]
But, beyond taking a strongly favorable public position on FEPC
and distributing information on the movement for nationality and
minority group leaders through its *Interpreter Releases*, the Common
Council remained on the sidelines. Its reaction to pressure demands
by the National Council was more typical of the average civil libertarian educational organization than was that of the Council Against
Intolerance in America discussed above.

WORKERS DEFENSE LEAGUE AND POSTWAR
WORLD COUNCIL

Reform movements are frequently as guilty of "interlocking direc-
torates" as giant corporative holding companies. Prominent persons
of liberal inclinations often serve as officers or board members of at
least several reform organizations. When this is done to excess, it may
result in such a diffusion of energies that no one organization receives
proper leadership. On the positive side, this overlapping of personnel
may tie a number of organizations together and promote harmony
among them.

The Workers Defense League was closely linked with the National
Council from the beginning through such a duplication of leadership.
Many WDL leaders, including Nathaniel M. Minkoff, Max Delson,
Alfred Baker Lewis, A. Philip Randolph, Willard S. Townsend, Norman Thomas, Morris Milgram, and Winifred Raushenbush, were
either directly or indirectly prominent in the National Council. Much
of the early planning for the formation of the National Council took
place at WDL executive board meetings. The National Council's first
headquarters in Washington were shared with the WDL. The

23. Publisher of *Common Ground*, the leading American magazine dealing with
interracial and intercultural problems, the Common Council also: (1) services the
900 foreign-language newspapers and 146 radio stations in this country with a weekly
educational news service attempting to promote a better understanding of the democratic system; (2) takes stands on specific issues involving discrimination; (3) supplies
interested organizations and individuals with a legislative bulletin on pending legislation affecting nationality and racial groups; (4) works with government agencies
interested in foreign origin groups, giving various types of information; (5) assists
more than five hundred new arrivals each month in making adjustments to the American scene; and renders many other services. In a sense, it is quasi-governmental in
that it carries on work started by the federal government in 1918 to promote national
unity—From "America's Explosive Idea," membership leaflet, undated.

League's leadership continued to serve as the planning core of the National Council throughout the latter's operations.

A complicating factor was the ideological persuasion of this "interlocking directorate." The WDL, which calls itself the National Non-Partisan Defense Agency of the Labor Movement and devotes its major energies to the defense of labor and minority rights, is a Socialist organization. Because of the leadership link, the National Council was associated by many with the Socialists, giving rise to controversy with the Communists, their bitter antagonists. In other words, while ideology served as an interorganizational link betwen the National Council and such organizations as the WDL and the Post-War World Council, another Socialist affiliate, it also militated against the emergence of a truly non-partisan movement in behalf of FEPC.

WOMEN'S GOOD GOVERNMENT AND REFORM ASSOCIATIONS

In addition to the organizations which represent women in their racial, national, or religious aspects, there are those which take a general interest in public affairs and work to promote good government, to safeguard consumer rights, and to advance international cooperation, as well as for various domestic reforms. These groups have considerable prestige because of their non-partisan efforts for community improvement. They also have considerable weight in politics because of their fancied or real influence with women voters. For these reasons the National Council sought to bring women's organizations into the fold.

NATIONAL LEAGUE OF WOMEN VOTERS

The National League of Women Voters is probably the most prominent women's organization in the public affairs field and its support is eagerly sought by other groups. It is a national organization with members in more than 1500 communities and subsidiary Leagues in 34 states and the District of Columbia. The membership is chiefly urban upper middle class. It is a non-partisan group which does not seek to speak for women alone but for good government for all. Activities include: promotion of study groups, interviews with candidates, pressure for approved legislation, preparation and distribution of materials on important issues, and other work to inform women voters and to secure their active participation in politics. The programs of both the national and state Leagues are adopted by delegates at annual conventions. These conventions select issues for emphasis on the state and national levels by placing them on an "active list" which is binding upon all League affiliates.

The National Convention held in Chicago in April 1944 placed nine items on the "active list," one of which was "preservation of civil liberties and protection of minority groups against discrimination." Specific legislative proposals were not mentioned in connection with this broad item. As a result, some local Leagues interpreted it to imply endorsement of FEPC legislation and proceeded to plan support of the pressure campaign for the bills in Congress and the state legislatures. However, the National Board, meeting in November 1944, issued a statement in which it withheld League support for the FEPC bills then before Congress. The statement read:

The National Board of the League of Women Voters endorses the principle of equal economic opportunity for minority groups and recognizes that it has widespread significance both nationally and in our relations abroad.

Though it approves the objectives of a permanent FEPC, it believes it would be unwise to support the proposed legislation which would establish an independent agency with mandatory powers and enforcement penalties. It believes that such legislation would be unenforceable on a country-wide basis at this time and might cause repercussions which would damage the cause of racial understanding.

The Board recommends that there be a continuation of the type of work done by the present FEPC, preferably through empowering an established governmental department rather than through the creation of a new, independent commission.

The Board believes that there is need at this time for a widespread educational program by the League and other organizations interested in equalizing work opportunities. It recognizes further that an insufficient number of Leagues are prepared to support mandatory legislation with enforcement provisions and therefore that suitable materials for discussion should and will be prepared.

Meanwhile, it should be constantly pointed out that our Federal Government contract provisions against employment discrimination are establishing the principle of equality of work opportunity.[24]

---

24. Release, November 17, 1944.

Immediately protests from several local Leagues were heard. The Minorities Committee of the District of Columbia League addressed a communication to be given to the National Board in which it took exception to the latter's position. A field representative of the American Council on Race Relations wrote the National Council:

You will be interested in knowing that the Milwaukee group was very much disturbed over the "on the fence" attitude and position which the national Washington office took in regards to a permanent FEPC, namely, that the National League of Women Voters felt that this was not the opportune time to foster such legislation but that it would be better to devote a longer period to educating a larger segment of the people in regards to its advisability. The women with whom I spoke felt that the national office had not sufficiently canvassed the local League of Women Voters throughout the country and, further, believe that there were many local groups who were desirous of the national organization taking a positive stand on the passage of the bill.[25]

The argument raged until the National Board felt obliged to defend its action by addressing a letter to all League presidents in March 1945.[26] The letter admitted that the minority groups provision had been adopted by the 1944 convention but declared that "it is the duty of the National Board to follow the emphasis given by the Convention to certain items above others" and that the Board has the obligation to emphasize action in those fields "(1) in which the League has had a continuous interest and wherein the League is best prepared to carry on the broader type of action program (2) of greatest importance at the present time (3) in which it is most likely to be effective." Therefore, the letter continued, it would be unwise for the League to divide its energies and budget by carrying on all-out action on a measure which has not been studied carefully and which is opposed by large segments of our population. The Board did admit that the "active list" authorization made it possible for state Leagues to support state proposals for FEPC "if they adopt it as part of their state program of work so that adequate time and energy may be allocated for its support." In terms of political activity this meant that until the national convention would endorse the permanent

25. Letter from L. Howard Bennett to Mrs. Hedgeman, December 7, 1944.
26. Letter from Anna Lord Strauss, March 28, 1945.

FEPC legislation no active assistance from the League would be forthcoming for the national drive.

OTHER WOMEN'S ORGANIZATIONS

Other women's organizations were less cautious than the National League of Women Voters and gave their support to the National Council and the FEPC movement. The League of Women Shoppers, a vigorous consumers and public affairs group, contributed some money and sent letters to national leaders urging the enactment of FEPC legislation. The Women's International League for Peace and Freedom, United States Section, was active through Dorothy Detzer, its national secretary, who served on the National Council's executive committee and testified in favor of a permanent FEPC at Senate hearings on the proposal. The well-known Women's Trade Union League of New York aided by applying pressures upon New York congressmen to secure House petition signatures to force the release of the FEPC bill from the Rules Committee. The Young Women's Christian Association was helpful on both the national and local levels. The National Board supported the FEPC bill in 1944 by writing in its behalf to Chairman Mary T. Norton of the House Labor Committee.[27] Local YWCA's promoted discussions and action on FEPC. In 1946 the YWCA's Public Affairs Committee pointed out to members the necessity for contributions to the National Council if the movement were to continue.[28] Finally, the American Association of University Women demonstrated its interest by endorsing FEPC legislation before Congress although it did not follow up its endorsement with more active support.

---

27. Letter from Mrs. Henry A. Ingraham, June 15, 1944.
28. "Public Affairs Post-Convention News Letter," March 29, 1946.

CHAPTER 8   *The Christian Church*

• NEGRO CHURCH   • PROTESTANT CHURCHES
AND AUXILIARY ORGANIZATIONS   • ROMAN
CATHOLIC   CHURCH   AND   AUXILIARY   ORGANI-
ZATIONS

CHURCHES ARE NOT ISOLATED FROM AMERICAN
political life. With the state increasingly regulating morals, aspects
of family life, and other phases of community living, it is natural
that churches should seek to influence public policy. Progressive
churches have long recognized that religion cannot be rigidly sepa-
rated from politics. Peter Odegard quotes a minister who recognized
the affinity as declaring: "We ought to mix religion and politics. What
is religion worth if it is not mixed with life? Our political life is of tremendous importance, and if religion and politics are not mixed, politics
becomes rotten and religion a superstition."[1] Today every major
church is represented in political centers through auxiliary organizations which have been established for the purpose. Many of these organizations are well-financed and are skilled in lobbying techniques.
Because of the large number of voters which these groups represent,
the legislator is rare who chooses to ignore their wishes when considering the desirability of specific items of legislation.

Yet interdenominational cooperation in politics is not highly developed. With some exceptions doctrinal and institutional barriers
have prevented joint operations on matters which should be of common concern to all churches.[2] There is conflict between Protestants, in
general, and Catholics; within the Protestant Church, between funda-
mentalists and progressives. Jewish church groups tend to move in

1. Sermon by Dr. Charles E. Jefferson preached at the Broadway Tabernacle,
October 27, 1929, quoted in *The American Public Mind*, p. 76.
2. Exceptions include the National Conference of Christians and Jews, primarily
an educational organization, and the Federal Council of the Churches of Christ in
America, a group with a wide range of interests.

• 127 •

their own channels, seeking outside cooperation only when their own interests are at stake. This lack of cooperation has reduced the effectiveness of the church in politics.

One of the proudest boasts of the National Council for a Permanent FEPC was that it had succeeded in involving churches and their auxiliary organizations in the FEPC drive to a degree seldom before attained by a reform movement.[3] Unlike the prohibition movement which was almost a single church monopoly, the FEPC drive is remarkable for its support by a broad cross-section of American churches representing many denominations. In accounting for this unprecedented success, due credit should be given the National Council's efforts. At the same time it should be mentioned that many churches had been interested in the field of race relations and minority group problems for a number of years and that they did not find it difficult to move from the discussion to the action stage under the stimulus of appeals based upon religious ethics and the national emergency.[4] Church groups were ripe for the FEPC movement.

NEGRO CHURCH

The church, historically, has been a more integral part of the Negro community than elsewhere. As Mays and Nicholson conclude in their study of the Negro church: "Not finding the opportunity that is given to members of other racial groups in civic and political life, in business enterprises and social agencies, the Negro through the years has turned to the church for self-expression, recognition and

---

3. "The involvement of the religious organizations particularly is an accomplishment of which we have a right to be proud. New doors have been opened to us and passage of the bill assured because we were able to get religious leaders to testify before the House and Senate Committees on behalf of the bill. The difference between the list of witnesses testifying in behalf of our bill as compared with the Anti-Poll-Tax and Anti-Lynch bills is a revelation itself—and a testimonial to the fact that we have developed new and more effective techniques. As a result the chances of passage of the FEPC bill are a thousand times better than the chances of passage of those bills ever were or ever will be."—Letter from Ida Fox to a potential donor, May 19, 1945.

4. "Churches are active. Actively translating Christian ideals into practice is a new trend of many churches. Round table discussions have redefined the Christian's duties in the treatment of minorities. To remove obstacles to the employment of minorities, clergymen of all faiths work with community fair employment councils as, for example, in Detroit."—*Unfinished Business*, p. 10, a pamphlet published by the Metropolitan Detroit Council on Fair Employment Practice, 1944.

leadership."[5] Today it remains a potent force despite the fact that some of the prohibitions against Negro activities have been relaxed within recent years and the church no longer retains its virtual monopoly over Negro life.[6]

However, the Negro church has not been as effective a force in American political life as other churches. The low status of the Negro in our society partially accounts for this fact, but the failings of their churches are even more important as explanations:

> . . . the church's program, except in rare instances, is static, non-progressive, and fails to challenge the loyalty of many of the most critically-minded Negroes; that the vast majority of its pastors are poorly trained academically, and more poorly trained theologically; that more than half of the sermons analyzed are abstract, other-worldly, and imbued with a magical conception of religion; that in the church school less than one-tenth of the teachers are college graduates; that there are too many Negro churches; that the percentage of Negro churches in debt is high; that for the most part the Negro church is little concerned with juvenile delinquency and other social problems in its environment. . . .[7]

The Negro church's occasional forays into politics have stemmed from the aspirations of individual ministers for political careers, in addition to their religious callings; the church itself, as an institution, has rarely attempted to influence public policy.[8] Progressive Negroes,

---

5. Benjamin Elijah Mays and Joseph William Nicholson, *The Negro's Church*, p. 9.

6. According to the *Census of Religious Bodies, 1936*, there were 33 wholly Negro denominations and 25 primarily white bodies reporting Negro membership. Total Negro membership stood at 5,660,618, or 10.1 per cent of the total reported church membership. Negro Baptist Churches made returns for 3,782,464 members and accounted for 66.8 per cent of all Negro church members. Other large returns included: African Methodist Episcopal Church, 493,357; African Methodist Episcopal Zion Church, 414,244; Colored Methodist Episcopal Church, 269,915.

One writer disputes the frequently heard claim that Negroes are more religious than whites by using data in Mays and Nicholson's book based upon the *Census of Religious Bodies, 1926*, which apparently show that 40 per cent of Negroes never attend church at all compared with 42 per cent for the total non-church-going population. Even more significant is the fact that only 46 per cent of Negro men attend which is below the 49 per cent for white men.—Arthur Huff Fauset, *Black Gods of the Metropolis*, p. 97.

7. Mays and Nicholson, *op. cit.*, p. 278. Also see James Weldon Johnson, *Negro Americans, What Now?*, pp. 20-26, for a stinging indictment of the Negro church.

8. See Carter G. Woodson, *The History of the Negro Church*, Chapter XI, "The Call of Politics," in which he describes the political careers of a number of Negro ministers.

consequently, are caustic in their criticism of the conservatism and lack of political awareness of most of their churches and are looking increasingly to racial and interracial action groups for relief from pressing problems.

The urgency of the problem of war employment and the general feeling that the war marked a turning point in the relations between the white and colored races stimulated many Negro church groups to emerge from their isolation from politics and to take the most advanced stand on a legislative issue in their history. The National Council prodded and nursed and cajoled church leaders to act for FEPC with a measure of success.

On April 18 and 19, 1944, Negro clergymen from all denominations representing twenty-seven states gathered in Washington for the National Conference of Christians for Religion, Democracy, and Building a World Community. The Conference was in response to a "mandate issued by the Negro people calling upon the church to present their cause to our Government and its lawmakers."[9] A manifesto containing the following proposal on employment was drafted and was later signed by one thousand Negro pastors:

We urge:
1. A progressive public program for full post-war employment without discrimination on account of race, creed, or color, or national origin. Federal legislation guaranteeing freedom from discrimination in employment because of race, creed, or national origin.
2. An end to the efforts on the part of high Government legislative officials to nullify the effectiveness of the Fair Employment Practice Committee.
3. An adequate appropriation of funds to make permanent the work of the Fair Employment Practice Committee.[10]

The Fraternal Council of Negro Churches in America voted at its June 1944 national convention to send the above resolution to national and state party leaders.

Dr. William H. Jernagin, Chairman of the Executive Board and

9. From testimony by Dr. William H. Jernagin, Fraternal Council of Negro Churches, *Hearings before a Subcommittee of the Committee on Education and Labor, United States Senate, Seventy-Eighth Congress, Second Session, on S. 2048,* August 30, 31, September 6, 7 and 8, 1944, p. 44.
10. *Ibid.*

Director of the Washington Bureau, Fraternal Council of Negro Churches, appeared before the Senate Subcommittee on Education and Labor on August 31, 1944, to testify in behalf of S. 2048, the Chavez-Downey-Wagner-Murray-Capper-Langer bill, for a permanent FEPC. He claimed to speak for the eleven affiliated denominations of the Fraternal Council with a constituency of more than 6,000,000 members when he urged passage of the bill.[11] Before he began his testimony, Jernagin asked permission of Chairman Dennis Chavez to introduce other Negro ministers and laymen of his church. As they rose in a body, Jernagin dramatically asked them to "bow our heads in a moment of silent prayer that this bill will pass."[12]

The Fraternal Council was active again in 1945. In March, Jernagin's bureau wrote Taft charging him with an attempt to split Republican sponsorship of FEPC legislation by introducing his own bill and asking him to withdraw his measure. The Fraternal Council also stimulated a flood of telegrams to the Senate opposing the Taft bill and urging enactment of the bill backed by the National Council for a Permanent FEPC.[13]

The peak in Fraternal Council activity came in the latter part of March 1945 when the Washington Bureau issued a call for Negro ministers to come to Washington to buttonhole their representatives in Congress and to confer with White House aides in the interest of enactment of legislation for a permanent FEPC with enforcement powers. Negro ministers, representing churches, conferences, and conventions covering twenty-one states answered the call. The staff of the National Council for a Permanent FEPC gave the pastors a short course in pressure techniques and then, split into state delegations, the clergymen sallied forth to beard their senators and representatives in their respective dens. Forty-two were interviewed and queried on their position on FEPC. A committee of twelve visited James Barnes, Administrative Assistant to the President, and presented a petition asking the President for a forthright stand on a

11. *Ibid.,* p. 42. The membership claimed seems a bit ambitious in view of the statistics on church membership cited on page 129, footnote 6, even if allowances are made for the passage of eight years since the previous census of churches.
12. *Pittsburgh Courier*, August 31, 1944.
13. *Kansas City Plaindealer*, March 2, 1945.

strong FEPC. Careful notes were taken on all statements. The Fraternal Council was certain that it had contributed its share to victory and had blazed a new trail for the Negro church:

This was the first time in Negro Church History that such a legislative project was initiated by the Church and it represented a distinct departure from traditional ecclesiastical procedure.

The Church leaders who came expressed both delight and satisfaction with the experiment. They were conscious of the new role they played as spokesmen for religion and aside from the great good they were able to render their parishioners they received personal benefits through practical knowledge gained of legislative procedure.

These men had their effect upon the community. They awakened a public consciousness of the new role the Church is destined to play in contemporary social history and the Legislative Bureau, established by the Fraternal Council of Negro Churches in America, became a living reality.

All visiting delegates expressed satisfaction and added zeal for the program and purpose of the WASHINGTON BUREAU. With your financial and moral support this experiment can be repeated a thousand times.[14]

Notwithstanding the "delight and satisfaction" of the amateur lobbyists and the desire of the Washington bureau to justify itself, analysis does not reveal that their efforts, in themselves, brought a single congressman into line. The forty-two congressmen interviewed replied with something less than full candor. In evaluating their responses the clergymen revealed their political naïveté when they recorded some as good prospects for favorable votes who later turned out to be staunch opponents, while several friends of FEPC were listed in the doubtful column.

The Fraternal Council's efforts remained the outstanding contribution of the Negro church. Many ministers permitted the branches of the National Council to stage meetings, hold rallies and take up collections for the movement in their churches but did little to aid the pressure campaign. The general feeling of at least one member of the National Council staff about the part played by the Negro Churches is found in a paragraph from one of her field reports: "Following the business league meeting there is an interracial school of missions at Waveland which Thelma Stevens conducts. I would like to be there

14. *The Capitol Letter*, vol. 1, section 2, April 11, 1945.

so that ——— and the rest of the Church racketeers can not tell her any fancy stories about what they have been doing for FEPC."[15]

Even the Fraternal Council placed a ceiling on its willingness to cooperate with the National Council. On March 13, 1946, the Jernagin group was asked to assist in a money-raising and educational campaign for FEPC without drawing an enthusiastic response. Pressure was applied on Jernagin through his secretary who sized up the situation in a telephone conversation with a National Council staff member as follows:[16]

Pauline Myers called. She indicates that there is further work to be done to get the ministers started here, and is willing to throw herself into the thing to get a campaign actually moving. However, she has run into a major obstacle by way of her Director, who cannot seem to view the thing with enthusiasm, making much of the point that his office itself is in dire need of funds. Pauline takes the position that both problems stand on their own feet, and that raising money for FEPC does not preclude the opportunity for raising money on behalf of the Fraternal Council's Washington office.

She says it would be most helpful if you were to telephone Jernagin telling him how very grateful you are for the amount of cooperation being extended by his office; how helpful his personal appearances have been; but that now we need more than words and appearances. . . .[17]

In summary, while Negro churchmen learned something about political processes through the FEPC movement and made a small contribution to the pressure efforts in its behalf, they were not yet politically emancipated. They were unwilling to take steps to advance the FEPC movement if it meant the assumption of risks or interference with their own church activities.

PROTESTANT CHURCHES AND AUXILIARY ORGANIZATIONS

Although Protestants represent the majority group in the United States and as such are not subjected to discrimination, their progress-

---

15. Douglas, Field Report, July 16, 1945.
16. The National Council found that perhaps the best entree to congressmen, executives, and other important people is through their secretaries. Therefore, efforts were made to cultivate the latters' goodwill. Miss Myers, however, did not have to be sold on FEPC as her interest dated from her early March on Washington Movement days.
17. Memorandum, Beatrice Schalet to Mrs. Hedgeman, March 13, 1946.

ive church groups were generally sympathetic to FEPC on the grounds that application of Christian and democratic principles required the elimination of economic discrimination and the establishment of equality of opportunity. No Protestant church or subsidiary group opposed FEPC; many were vigorous in their support of the principle involved. The interest of some became lost in devious organizational channels or stopped with support of the general principle of FEPC, but the Protestant Church was an asset, if not altogether in a liquid form, to the FEPC movement.

The Federal Council of the Churches of Christ in America, which represents progressive American Protestant thought, is made up of 25 of the leading Protestant denominations claiming a total membership of 25,000,000 churchgoers who worship in 150,000 churches. It is a powerful coordinating body chosen by the governing bodies of the member denominations. In order "to assert the sufficiency of Christianity as a solution of race relations in America," the Federal Council has maintained a Department of Race Relations since 1920 which seeks "to change personality attitudes and behavior patterns among the millions of church members in the affiliated denominations, and through them to change all the people in the local community."[18] It has not confined its activities to the educational sphere, but rather has made use of all available avenues including pressure politics to advance its program.

On June 13, 1941, the Federal Council issued the first of a long list of statements advocating church cooperation in bringing economic discrimination against minorities to an end:

> The executive committee of the Federal Council of the Churches of Christ in America has great concern about the grievous discrimination shown in the exclusion of Negro workers or the workers of other minority groups from defense industries, with a few creditable exceptions, and from opportunities and facilities for training for employment in such industries. We consider this question of such paramount importance that we ask for the largest and fullest cooperation on the part of the churches in order that we may prevent a continuance of this injustice against Negroes and other minorities in defense industries, and that the relations of these workers and employers may be improved.[19]

---

18. *Directory of Agencies in Race Relations*, p. 29.
19. Quoted by Bishop G. Bromley Oxnam, representing the Federal Council at Senate Hearings on S. 2048, *Hearings*, p. 20.

The moral and religious issues involved in discrimination were given full play in the statements. The country was warned that we could win the war but forfeit the peace "unless we weave interracial respect and cooperation into the fabric of our thought and life" because of the growing resentment by colored peoples against white domination. The Federal Council gave wholehearted support to the establishment of the President's Committee in 1941. It was one of the participants in the conference with Chairman Paul McNutt of the War Manpower Commission on April 9, 1943, which led to the revival and strengthening of the President's Committee under Executive Order No. 9346. It was also in the vanguard of the National Council for a Permanent FEPC in urging the passage of permanent legislation in this area. Bishop G. Bromley Oxnam, member of the Federal Council's executive and advisory committees and secretary of the Council of Bishops of the Methodist Church, was consulted by the National Council on FEPC strategy and was present during conferences with national leaders. The prestige brought by the Federal Council's support, as well as its active collaboration, were highly prized by the National Council for a Permanent FEPC.

The United Council of Church Women, formed in 1942 by the union of three groups, is the most important organization of Protestant women in America. The United Council, which claims to have 1200 organized councils, 10,000 groups organized for prayer, and a possible membership of 10,000,000, has taken a broad interest in race relations and seeks to include church women of all racial, cultural, and economic groups in its local councils. Its Division of Social, Industrial, and Race Relations attempts to stimulate local councils to cooperate with other community social welfare and public affairs organizations by analyzing and interpreting national social legislation and by recommending plans for their local activities.

The United Council gave wholehearted support to FEPC through contributions to the National Council, letters and telegrams to Congress and the President, testimony before congressional committees, and analyses of local communities. It was one of the most cooperative and influential supporters of the National Council. And, unlike many so-called cooperating organizations whose support did not go beyond statements from their national offices, the United Council's cooperation extended down to the grass roots level. A number of state councils, including those in Colorado and Oregon, went on record as unequivocally favoring a strong FEPC. The Oregon Council of Church Women distributed 3000 handbills under the title "FEPC is the First Step Toward Peace" and issued instructions to women throughout the state on how to apply pressure on congressmen in behalf of the pending bill.[20]

The New York office of the United Council sent out many appeals to state councils urging pressure on Congress. During the 1946 filibuster, for example, Oregon women were urged:

> Crisis in FEPC calls women in Oregon to appeal Senator Morse use his power to break filibuster. Republican senators must bear this responsibility. Also assure him United Council's firm stand for S 101 as part of our religion. Immediate action essential. Urge many women wire or write.[21]

The Church Woman, national publication of the United Council, carried frequent articles on FEPC. The legislative representative in Washington assisted the National Council in its lobbying activities.

Other Protestant groups also favored permanent FEPC legislation and gave a modicum of support to the legislative struggle. The Religious Society of Friends distributed the National Council's *Manual of Strategy* to its monthly meetings and encouraged its members to write letters and send telegrams to secure passage of the bill. The Friends Committee on National Legislation endorsed the "general principle of such legislation" and promised to "do what we can with our very limited staff to encourage Friends to forward these purposes." The Women's Division of Christian Service of the Board of Missions and Church Extension of the Methodist Church sent letters, in April 1944, to 450 conference leaders of the Woman's Society urging active support of FEPC in response to a National Council request for letters to Congress. Fellowship of Reconciliation leaders, intensely interested in racial justice, endorsed FEPC and wrote letters in its behalf. The Philadelphia Regional Action Committee of "The Protestant," a vigorous and controversial group of Protestant leaders, ran a quarter-

---

20. *Los Angeles Sentinel*, August 16, 1945.
21. Letter from Mrs. Emory Ross to Mrs. Hedgeman, January 24, 1946.

page advertisement in the Philadelphia newspapers, endorsing FEPC and inviting public support. Ministers of liberal denominations, notably Unitarians, permitted their churches to be used by local councils for meetings and delivered sermons on FEPC from their pulpits. Some liberal ministers were officers or members of local councils.

In the South more than a few white Protestant leaders were sympathetic towards FEPC but only infrequently did they challenge the community pattern by following up their views with strong public statements and direct support. When the white Protestant ministers' union of New Orleans was asked by the local council to pass a resolution endorsing the FEPC bills before Congress, the best that the union could do was:

> The Ministerial Union of New Orleans endorses in principle Bills H.R. 2232 and S. 101 now before the U.S. Congress which prohibits discrimination in employment because of race, creed, color, national origin or ancestry. The Ministerial Union does not express an opinion as to all the details in said proposed legislation.[22]

The North Carolina Baptist Convention, holding its 116th annual meeting in Ashville in November 1946, went on record as favoring the elimination of economic discrimination against Negroes and the passage of both state and national legislation to assure fair treatment.[23] Conservative reaction was swift. "Overnight," says Mezerik, "the convention received three thousand indignant telegrams, and the telephone circuits to Ashville were unable to cope with the number of calls for the assembled religious leaders from old familiars who

---

22. Letter from Mary B. Allen, New Orleans Council Secretary, to National Council. May 21, 1945.

23. The same convention voted to support equal rights and facilities for Negroes in the areas of suffrage, hospitalization, and education. The "messengers," as the delegates are called, also unanimously accepted the unprecedented recommendation of their Committee on Social Service and Civic Righteousness to abolish segregation in the church. The Committee's report had argued for the latter step in the following unequivocal language: "If there is an equality of all men by virtue of their relationship to an impartial Creator, and an equality of all believers who share in the redemption of Christ, such equalities must be respected in the body of Christ, which is the church. Therefore, segregation of believers holding to the same tenets of faith, because of color or social status, into racial or class churches is a denial of the New Testament affirmation of the equality of all believers at the foot of the Cross, and alien to the spirit of Christ, the head of the church."—A. G. Mezerik, "Dixie in Black and White," *Nation*, 164 (March 22, 1947), 324-27.

opposed their action."[24] The result was that, by a vote of 253 to 158, a hectic session of the convention rescinded its approval of abolition of segregation in the church and watered down its FEPC resolution from a demand for legislation to one for equal treatment.

The total effect of the Protestant churches' activities was probably best summed up by Joy Falk, legislative chairman of the United Council of Church Women, when she wrote state chairmen in her organization following the 1946 defeat in Congress:

Are church citizens ready to struggle for the christian principles they profess?

February 9, 1946 was a day of reckoning in Congress. After nearly a month of cynical, hatefilled filibuster by a small group of about 18 men, the chance for the United State Senate to make its decision democratically on S. 101 was temporarily lost when cloture was defeated. SOME FEEL THAT CHURCH GROUPS WERE THE DECISIVE FACTOR THAT COULD HAVE CHANGED THE OUTCOME. AND THEY STILL CAN.

The Church worked hard but not hard enough! Not one leading churchman made a special trip to Washington during the filibuster to fight for FEPC. (Union groups did.) Church publicity and statements on the filibuster were lacking, showing a willingness to rest comfortably on previously stated stands.[25]

ROMAN CATHOLIC CHURCH AND AFFILIATED ORGANIZATIONS

The universality and experience of the Roman Catholic Church have given it a broad perspective in dealing with a variety of races. In the United States, Catholics have not succumbed as much to the pattern of racial segregation as other predominantly white churches in compliance with the prejudice of their members. The effect in recent years has been for Negro membership in the Catholic Church to mount. As of January 1, 1940, there were 298,998 colored Catholics in the United States, with more than one-third of them worshipping in mixed congregations.[26]

The hierarchical principle of the Catholic Church has aided in pushing the Church's program of racial equality even in communities

---

24. *Ibid.*, p. 325.
25. "URGENT MEMO—TO STATE PRESIDENTS," February 21, 1946.
26. Reverend John Thomas Gillard, *Colored Catholics in the United States,* November 1941, quoted in *The Negro Handbook,* 1942, p. 102.

where racial feelings run high.[27] When Pope Pius XII, in his Encyclical, *Sertum Laetitiae*, wrote: "We confess that we feel drawn by a strong impulse of charity, under God's guidance, towards your neighbors of the Negro race; we know how their religious and intellectual development calls for, and deserves, special and considerate care. For this reason We pray for God's assistance and wish every blessing to those who are generously devoting themselves to this cause." The American hierarchy interpreted the statement as an order to work for the extension of equality to "our Negro brothers in Christ."[28]

In accordance with the Pope's wishes the Administrative Board of the National Catholic Welfare Conference, at the direction of the archbishops and bishops attending an annual meeting of the Hierarchy in Washington on November 13, 1943, issued a statement "on the essentials of a just peace" in which they stressed the necessity for extending equal justice to all groups of American citizens, saying, in part:

In the Province of God there are among us millions of fellow-citizens of the Negro race. We owe to these fellow-citizens, who have contributed so largely to the development of our country, and for whose welfare history imposes on us a special obligation of justice, to see that they have in fact the rights which are given them in our Constitution. This means not only political equality, but also fair economic and educational opportunities, a just share in public welfare projects, good housing without exploitation, and a full chance for the social development of their race....[29]

---

27. While it is extremely difficult to evaluate how much "grass roots" support there is for the hierarchy's policies, the latter's wishes are law for the Church's membership. The following will illustrate the point: "Ted Le Berthon, Catholic columnist of the *Pittsburgh Courier*, recalls that more than a year ago he took issue against Knights of Columbus Councils guilty of racial 'snobbishness' in excluding Negroes from membership: His specific targets were the Los Angeles councils of the national Catholic organization.

"His challenge drew no response. But, on Christmas Eve last, the Most Rev. John H. Cantwell, Archbishop of Los Angeles, issued an official order calling on all priests of the Archdiocese—many have large Negro congregations—to urge from their pulpits that male parishioners join the Knights of Columbus. That meant *all* men in each parish. It meant that the Knights of Los Angeles had to bow to an authority they could not ignore."—*Interracial Review*, February 2, 1945.

28. Reverend George Higgins, "Catholics and the F.E.P.C. Case," reprinted by the National Council for a Permanent FEPC from the January 1944 issue of *Catholic Action*, monthly publication of the National Catholic Welfare Conference.

29. *Ibid.*

Reasons other than church doctrine also accounted for the hierarchy's support of programs for social justice, including FEPC. In
many parts of the United States, Catholics themselves are victims of
social and economic discrimination. Especially is this true of the
3,000,000 Spanish-speaking Catholics. The hierarchy's fear of the
possible inroads which the Communists may make among discontented
minority groups has spurred Catholic interest in reform programs. So,
for a combination of reasons, the Church has sought to promote racial
equality in the last several decades through such Catholic-sponsored
organizations as the National Catholic Welfare Conference, the Catholic Interracial Council, the National Commission on Interracial
Justice, the Catholic Committee of the South, the National Catholic
Committee on Negro Employment, and others.

The Catholic hierarchy gave good support to the campaign for
permanent FEPC legislation. Without the support of Catholic leadership, reaching the Catholic rank and file would have been a difficult
task; with it, the path was smoothed without extensive field work.
One National Council field representative who stumbled upon this
technique for securing Catholic support wrote the Washington office,
"I'm securing a letter of endorsement on the FEPC from the Catholic
Bishop of this diocese, it eliminates a lot of time and works wonders
with the parish priest. . . ."[30] and "I won't need that Catholic letter
of endorsement as long as the Bishops last in my territory. Bishop
Hielan in Sioux City was perfect."[31] The Catholic press, sociologists,
and educational leaders also publicly supported FEPC.[32]

Statements by Church leaders supporting a strong FEPC were
widely circulated by the National Council for a Permanent FEPC.
Bishop Bernard J. Sheil of Chicago was regarded as a special advocate
of FEPC. Bishop Francis J. Haas of Grand Rapids, former chairman
of the President's Committee, could be counted upon to support the
permanent FEPC legislation at all times.

In the South, Catholic leaders took a more forthright stand on

30. Field Report, Charles Toney, November 8, 1945.
31. *Ibid.*, December 20, 1945.
32. Statement by George K. Hunton, Catholic Interracial Council leader, at the
National Strategy Conference of the National Council for a Permanent FEPC, September 12, 1945.

FEPC than did the ministers of Protestant denominations. From New Orleans, a large Catholic center, the Archbishop sent telegrams to Senators Ellender and Taft in support of FEPC.[33] Archbishop Robert E. Lucey of San Antonio, a large Spanish-American and Negro center, was extremely outspoken in his support of a strong FEPC bill. In 1944 he addressed the following statement to the Senate Subcommittee on Education and Labor concerning the pending FEPC bill, which is all the more remarkable in that it came from the stronghold of opposition to FEPC:

The FEPC, whose life now hangs on the thin thread of an executive order, should be given full statutory recognition with power to enforce its decisions. In no other way can a substantial measure of economic justice be procured for men and women of color. The white problem in our country cannot be solved in any reasonable time without the aid of civil law. Many so-called white men hate and despise their fellow Americans whose skin is dark. It is not the men of color who ignore our Constitution, reject our Declaration of Independence and perpetrate acts of racial bigotry. It is not the Mexican or the Negro who would deprive his fellow citizens of given natural rights. Only the alleged white man does that.

Men of color are pouring out their good red blood on many battle fields today to defend the lives and property of those very racial bigots who thus debase themselves. The FEPC should be made a permanent institution of our country to stand forever as a symbol of human liberty and good government.

On the national level the work of two Catholic organizations for FEPC stood out. The Catholic Interracial Council was represented in the inner councils of the National Council for a Permanent FEPC through the person of George K. Hunton, editor of the *Interracial Review*, who participated in the national drive from its inception. The Catholic Interracial Council was especially notable for the educational work it did among Catholic laymen and college students and for the frequent public stands it took in support of FEPC. Hunton was also helpful in activating other groups with which he had influence. The National Catholic Welfare Conference, the major clearing house for Catholic activities in the United States, was also inti-

33. Letter from Mrs. Anna B. Douglas, New Orleans Council Secretary, to the National Council, February 20, 1945.

mately associated with the National Council for a Permanent FEPC. Several of its officers served on the Washington strategy committee and the Conference cooperated further by sending out telegrams to stimulate support for FEPC and by informing its members on the subject through its publications and bureaus.

Catholics, therefore, because of united planning from above, were able to throw their weight and prestige into the battle to a greater extent than the decentralized and less united Negro and white Protestant churches. On the other hand, there is little evidence to demonstrate that the Catholic rank and file was more active than other denominational groups. All fell short of a maximum effort in behalf of permanent anti-discrimination legislation.

CHAPTER 9   *Organized Labor*

• AMERICAN FEDERATION OF LABOR • CONGRESS
OF INDUSTRIAL ORGANIZATIONS

THE INTERNAL RACIAL POLICIES OF TRADE UNIONS determined the degree of interest which they evinced in the FEPC movement. The labor movement in the United States has had a mixed record on discrimination against the Negro.[1] Racial policies vary from total exclusion of Negroes by some trade unions to complete acceptance by others. Unions motivated by a strong progressive or left-wing philosophy usually have very liberal racial policies. But the bulk of American labor unions take an opportunistic approach toward Negro workers by adapting themselves to local and regional customs and by liberalizing or narrowing their racial policies depending upon the policies of competing unions and the prospects for enlarging membership. Consequently, there were wide variations in the contributions made by organized labor to the FEPC cause.

AMERICAN FEDERATION OF LABOR

The American Federation of Labor denies any race bias and proclaims that "workers must organize and unite under its banner, without regard to race, color, creed, or national origin." At the same time discrimination is widespread within the Federation. At least thirteen of its affiliates exclude Negroes by provisions in their constitutions, rituals, and by tacit consent while seven others limit Negroes to segregated auxiliary status.[2] Because of the autonomous status of its

---

1. The best recent study of trade union discrimination against the Negro worker and the one from which most of this background material is drawn is Herbert R. Northrup, *Organized Labor and the Negro*. Other studies in this area include S. D. Spero and A. Harris, *The Black Worker*; H. R. Cayton and G. S. Mitchell, *Black Workers and the New Unions*; and Chapter IV of Charles S. Johnson, *Patterns of Negro Segregation*.

2. Northrup, *op. cit.*, pp. 3-5.

affiliates under the Federation's constitution, the only way that the AFL can control the racial policies of a member union is to threaten expulsion, which it has never been willing to do. Only the Railroad Brotherhoods can match this record of discrimination.

Why is there division among workers on racial grounds? Unions are subject to the same environmental factors which control all human undertakings. Historically many unions came into being as fraternal and benevolent societies, says Northrup, which made equal treatment of Negroes tantamount to granting them social equality and hence making such groups impossible in many parts of the country.[3] An even more important reason is the extreme "work scarcity" consciousness of skilled craft workers who fear Negro competition for economic reasons.

Following the sizeable Negro migration into northern industry during World War I, the bars against Negroes in the Federation were discussed in convention after convention without any appreciable alteration in the practices of discrimination. Starting with the thirties A. Philip Randolph, as president of the Brotherhood of Sleeping Car Porters, an all-Negro Federation affiliate, waged unending but also unsuccessful war on the color line drawn by many AFL unions.

When the war emergency burst upon the scene with no accompanying relaxation in restrictions on Negro union membership, Randolph attacked the Boilermakers, Shipbuilders, Machinists, Building Trades, and other unions at the 1941 national convention at Seattle for excluding Negroes from airplane plants, shipyards, and defense construction work. Top ranking Federation officials took issue with Randolph. John P. Frey, president of the Metal Trades Department, deplored Randolph's attack and warned that the enemies of labor will take it up, "making our task of organization ten thousand times more difficult than in the past."[4] Other speakers insisted that human nature cannot be changed, that the autonomy of the affiliates could not be disturbed, that "Jim Crow" unions do not signify discrimination, and that Negroes should be grateful for what the AFL has done for them. These arguments failed to deter Randolph. Throughout the war he continued to introduce unsuccessful resolutions at AFL conventions calling for the establishment of a Minorities Committee to

---

3. *Ibid.*, p. 5.
4. *New York Times*, October 15, 1941.

study the problem of discrimination, elimination of "Jim Crow" unions, and support of the President's Committee on Fair Employment Practice, as well as for effective FEPC legislation.

AFL experience with the President's Committee failed to win over some of the international unions to a strong FEPC. A number of AFL affiliates were cited by the Committee and told to "cease and desist" their discriminatory practices which include exclusion of Negroes by custom and tradition;[5] agreements between associations of employers and labor organizations to refuse to hire or upgrade Negroes;[6] refusal by the building trades unions to permit the hiring of Negroes as long as their own white members are unemployed;[7] insistence upon segregated working conditions for Negroes;[8] establishment of auxiliary organizations for Negroes which do not offer equal employment opportunities;[9] and many others. Because the weak President's Committee was not able to secure compliance with its orders, not a single AFL union changed its racial policy. Looking ahead they feared the prospect of a permanent FEPC with strong enforcement powers.

The threat of opposition from the AFL was a matter of great concern for the staff of the National Council for a Permanent FEPC. For months it was rumored that the Federation had lobbied against the appropriation for the President's Committee in the spring of 1944. To avoid similar opposition to the legislation for a permanent FEPC, the National Council sought to convert Federation leadership through Randolph. When the Dawson-Scanlon-LaFollette bill was before the House in 1944, Mrs. Hedgeman wrote Randolph:

> ... our one fear has been of the AF of L situation. Mrs. Norton's office reports to us that John Frey, of the Metal Trades, is opposed to the bill, and expects to blast shortly. It has also been reported that Boris Shishkin and Mr. Hines, the two legislative workers at the AF of L have advised William Green to testify negatively. We have not been able to verify this, but Mr. McLaurin has made contacts with Mr. Green's office and has also made it possible for me to talk to Mr. Fenton, who spoke, I be-

5. *In re Chicago Journeymen Plumbers' Union, Local 130.*
6. *In re Steamfitters' Protective Association.*
7. *In re Chicago Journeymen Plumbers' Union, Local 130.*
8. *In re A.J. Honeycutt & Company.*
9. *In re International Brotherhood of Boilermakers, Iron Shipbuilders, Welders and Helpers of America, Subordinate Lodges 72 and 401.*

lieve, at your meeting in New York, and who, they say, is friendly. Your work on the AF of L situation would be most helpful.[10]

Later reports indicated that the AFL would give little support to the bill. The Associated Negro Press quoted Lewis Hines, Federation lobbyist, as being "in sympathy with the purposes of the bill" but "opposed to that portion of the bill which places unions under the jurisdiction of a commission."[11] It was not surprising, therefore, that the AFL addressed a letter to the Senate committee considering the bill embodying the report of the Federation's executive committee to the 1943 national convention in which the principle of non-discrimination was lauded but opposition to the bill was registered. Several excerpts will indicate the Federation's position at this time:

A small number of our affiliates have not yet joined in the positive efforts of the Federation to assure equality of work opportunity without regard to race or color. The executive council reiterates its belief that discriminatory denial of work opportunity to any person because of race, creed, or color is inconsistent with the principles of industrial democracy and trade union practice which the American Federation of Labor has championed since its inception. We recommend that the officers of the American Federation of Labor be authorized to intensify and extend their efforts to secure complete acceptance of our nondiscrimination policy by all affiliated unions. . . .

The executive council does not believe . . . that imposition of any policy, no matter how salutary, through compulsory Government control of freely constituted associations of workers, accords with the basic right of freedom of association among the American people. While it endorses without reservation the policy of nondiscrimination in employment, the executive council takes strong exception to the compulsory imposition upon unions of this or any other policy interfering with the self-government of labor organizations.[12]

The same month, the AFL was reported to have approached the National Council for a Permanent FEPC, informally offering to withdraw its strong opposition in exchange for an amendment which would "exclude discriminations as may be practiced within the vari-

10. Letter, June 4, 1944.

11. *Monthly Summary of Events and Trends in Race Relations,* July 1944, p. 4.

12. Letter from W. C. Hushing, Chairman, National Legislative Committee, American Federation of Labor, to Chairman Dennis Chavez of the Subcommittee of the Senate Committee on Education and Labor, September 7, 1944, *Hearings,* S. 2048, pp. 194–95.

ous internationals of the federation."[13] No concessions were forth-coming from the National Council which was adamant in its insistence upon a strong FEPC with enforcement powers.

In October 1944 Boris Shishkin, Federation representative on the President's Committee on Fair Employment Practice, warned a Howard University conference on postwar job opportunities for Negroes that labor, meaning the Federation, would oppose any regulation of unions, even to prevent discrimination. Shishkin told the conference that the legislation would open the door to much broader regulation of unions and that labor's spokesmen could not endorse it.[14] Fear of government regulation was again cited in November when the Federation's executive committee lauded the work done to date to eliminate discriminatory employment practices but opposed the provision in the permanent FEPC bill applying to unions which it felt subjected unions to "considerable harrassment" because of their "ambiguous nature."[15]

Nevertheless, there were forces afoot which led to a slow retreat from the Federation's firm opposition to FEPC legislation. The Federation's leadership was forced to give more and more tangible evidence of its willingness to live up to its self-proclaimed policy of non-discrimination as the Congress of Industrial Organizations, its chief rival, set a hot pace in labor circles by its resolutions and statements favoring FEPC. Perhaps more important were the internal pressures exerted by such Federation affiliates as the International Ladies' Garment Workers Union and the Brotherhood of Sleeping Car Porters. These strong FEPC supporters persisted in their efforts until Federation leaders made concession after concession to them.

Before long it was obvious that the Federation was changing its public tune. The December 1944 national convention at New Orleans adopted resolutions favoring FEPC although one advocating criminal penalties for discrimination was defeated. Early in 1945 President William Green promised Randolph that the Federation would not appear "officially" against the bill.[16] Throughout 1945 the Federation's national staff rendered services to the National Council for a Perma-

---

13. *Philadelphia Independent*, September 17, 1944.
14. *PM*, October 29, 1944.
15. *Louisville Defender*, November 25, 1944.
16. *PM*, February 21, 1945.

nent FEPC by asking its regional and state Federation officials to assist the Council's field representatives in gaining entree to local community organizations and their leaders. Boris Shishkin aided the National Council's Washington staff by giving advice on legislative strategy. On June 19, 1945, President Green sent a telegram to the Town Hall meeting on FEPC, urging passage of the pending legislation. Also, at the request of the National Council, he sent the following communication in November 1945 to the officers of state federations of labor, city central bodies, and federal labor unions:

Dear Sirs and Brothers:

   I am writing to request you to communicate with the members of the U.S. Senate from your state urging them to support Senate Bill #101 which provides for a continuation of FEPC legislation. This legislation is designed to prevent discrimination against workers because of race, creed, color or nationality.

   This bill is being resisted by a number of reactionary members of Congress. We must make known to the members of the U.S. Senate the urgent need for the enactment of this legislation. I, therefore, call upon you to quickly communicate with the members of the United States Senate from your respective states, without a moment's delay, appealing to them to give support to Senate Bill #101.

The total contribution of the American Federation of Labor to the FEPC movement was hardly commensurate with the strength of the organization. Yet, in view of the practices of many of its affiliated unions, the fact that the Federation was transformed from an active opponent to at least a passive supporter is some indication of the strength of the idea of fair employment practices in this period and a measuring rod by which to evaluate the efforts of the supporters of permanent FEPC legislation.

CONGRESS OF INDUSTRIAL ORGANIZATIONS

The Congress of Industrial Organizations leads the trade union movement in its willingness to grant equality of treatment to the Negro by deed as well as word. While there are some local exceptions to application of the non-discrimination principle, particularly in the South, no national CIO affiliate excludes Negroes from membership or segregates its Negro members in auxiliary unions with unequal status. National CIO leaders also have taken the lead in advocating fair treatment for Negroes. Northrup sums up the reasons for the CIO's liberal racial policies:

It is not difficult to comprehend why the CIO has pursued its liberal racial policy. Unlike craft unions, which are organized on an exclusive and narrow basis, and which depend upon their control of a few highly skilled and strategically situated jobs to obtain their bargaining power, industrial unions acquire their strength by opening their ranks to all the workers in an industry. The United Mine Workers, the Amalgamated Clothing Workers, and the Ladies' Garment Workers had been organized on an industrial basis for many years prior to 1935 when their leaders founded the CIO. Few, if any, labor unions had better records for fair treatment of Negroes than did these three. Besides, their officers saw the projected campaigns to organize the workers of the iron and steel, the automobile, and the other mass production industries doomed to failure unless the unions in these fields opened their doors to workers of all creeds and colors. Finally, the CIO contains within its ranks most of the left-wing elements in the American labor movement. These groups have always most vociferously opposed racial discrimination in all its forms. For these reasons, then, the CIO has attempted to enroll workers regardless of race, creed, color, or nationality.[17]

On the national level the CIO maintains a National CIO Committee to Abolish Racial Discrimination to effectuate its desire "to bring about the effective organization of the working men and women of America regardless of race, creed, color, or nationality, and to unite them for common action into labor unions for their mutual aid and protection." The Committee headed by a Negro, George L-P Weaver, acts largely as a policy-making and advisory body for the more than one hundred state, county, and city Industrial Union Councils which maintain anti-discrimination committees to handle local cases involving discrimination by unions and to improve internal race relations. The National Committee also seeks to promote racial harmony by organizing local and regional conferences, by distributing literature on the subject, and by cooperating with other national organizations with similar interests.

---

17. *Organized Labor and the Negro*, p. 15. George Mitchell, Southern Director of the CIO Political Action Committee, said in this same connection: "Racial tolerance came to the CIO because of hard necessity. We tried and tried to get wages up and each time we split on the Negro question. . . . A great many people in each southern industrial town would like to see unions disappear. One natural way to do this is to promote race differences."—*Atlanta Journal*, June 25, 1944.

To date eight of the CIO international unions have established their own machinery for combating prejudice and discrimination.[18] The United Packinghouse Workers of America Union has maintained an anti-discrimination committee since March 1945.[19] Race relations in the meat packing industry have been strained since the importation of large numbers of Negroes by the industry following World War I to serve as strikebreakers. UPWA recognized from the start that unless it could unite both races it could not organize the industry. For this reason the Union has sedulously stressed equality of the races in the meat packing industry and in the union's internal machinery. The UPWA emblem shows a black and a white hand united in a handclasp. The union's anti-discrimination committee has a three-fold program:

(1) education, including the showing of films on race relations, speeches by field representatives at all types of meetings, pamphlets, circulation of books and phonograph records, guest speakers, publicity through the union paper; (2) organization, including the promotion of joint Negro and white leadership; systematic attention to and training of the membership in the importance of solidarity; organization of interracial social affairs; local committees on anti-discrimination; and emphasis on unity in connection with the organization of new plants; (3) relation to the public, including working with white and Negro community organizations for such causes as repeal of the poll tax, improved housing, permanent FEPC, removal of discrimination in public places; and independent union campaigns on major issues affecting the CIO in the field of race relations. Specific cases of discrimination are referred to the Committee if adjustments cannot be reached through regular union channels.[20]

The United Auto Workers' Union has also developed a strong program to promote racial equality for its own self-preservation. Following internal disputes and work stoppages in the Chrysler, Packard, and Hudson plants over upgrading and other issues involving Negroes during the war period, the UAW established an active Fair Practices Committee in October 1944, charged chiefly

---

18. *Report of the National CIO Committee to Abolish Discrimination*, November 1946, p. 5.

19. See "Reasons for the United Packinghouse Workers Favoring the Creation by Congress of a Permanent Fair Employment Practice Commission, as Provided in S. 101," a mimeographed statement submitted to the Subcommittee of the Senate Committee on Education and Labor, March 13, 1945.

20. *Directory of Agencies in Race Relations*, pp. 62-63.

with receiving and investigating allegations of violation of the union's anti-discrimination policy. It also collaborates with the union's Education Department in the preparation and distribution of literature designed to eradicate prejudice among UAW members.[21] Finally, the Committee acts as the agent of the union's executive board in matters relating to minority groups and makes recommendations to the board for advancing the anti-discrimination program.

The net effect of the CIO's fear of internal division on the race question, its competition with the AFL for leadership of the labor movement and its general progressive philosophy on such matters, was to make the organization deeply interested in the FEPC movement from its earliest stages. The fact that the CIO had built up a store of experience in politics through its Political Action Committee made it an especially desirable supporter. The National Council for a Permanent FEPC leaned heavily upon it for advice and assistance in bringing pressure to bear upon Congress.

Both the National CIO and its affiliates made contributions. The United Electrical Workers, for example, employed well-known pressure techniques in its efforts to secure an appropriation for the President's Committee in 1944. Its newspaper reported:

> The UE General Office, together with the entire CIO, mobilized the local unions on the issue. And the unions responded vigorously.
>
> In one instance, the unions showed their ability to act clearly and quickly when UE locals in Connecticut showered Senator Danaher (Rep., Conn.), with wires when he attempted to introduce an amendment to the FEPC designed to confuse the entire issue.
>
> Next morning, after the wires had deluged Senator Danaher, he quickly withdrew his amendment. What amendments were slipped into the FEPC are looked upon as of minor importance.[22]

The same organ listed the accomplishments of UE locals in the St. Louis area on this occasion:

> First, every UE local in and around St. Louis was contacted to send telegrams to their Senators and to urge their members to do likewise. All locals contacted pledged immediate action.

---

21. Some of the UAW publications include: *A Bill of Rights for All UAW Members; Order Creating: UAW-CIO Fair Practices Committee; A Manual on Fair Employment Practices; To Unite . . . Regardless; To Stamp Out Discrimination— A Handbook.*

22. *New York UE News,* June 27, 1944.

Second, the district sent telegrams to the eight Senators from Missouri, Indiana, Iowa and Illinois, calling for continuance of FEPC with full budget "urgent to war effort for fullest utilization of our manpower."

Third, St. Louis' leading daily papers, the *Post-Dispatch* and *Star Times* were contacted and asked to run editorials on FEPC, to which both papers agreed.

Fourth, the district contacted the CIO council, urging that all CIO locals be asked to take action.

Fifth, CIO Council secretary promised to call both Senators Truman and Clark on the telephone, requesting that they return to Washington and vote for appropriation.

Sixth, UE contacted the Urban League, Liberal Voters League, League of Women Voters, Inter-Racial Labor Victory Council, National Federation for Constitutional Liberties, Mayor's Committee on Race Relations. All above organizations agreed to send telegrams to Senators and to get their individual members to do likewise. Mayor's Committee has already contacted Senators, and is sending delegate to Washington to appear before House Labor Committee on making FEPC a permanent institution.

Seventh, several members of the clergy were also contacted and agreed to take action.

And finally, District Vice-President William Sentner went to Washington and testified on the necessity of continuing FEPC before the Senate Appropriations Committee.[23]

The United Auto Workers' Fair Practices Committee was active in both the Michigan and national drives for FEPC legislation by canvassing legislators, stimulating telegraph and letter-writing campaigns, and contributing money to the National Council for a Permanent FEPC.[24] The CIO Marine Union, United Rubber Workers, and other affiliates endorsed FEPC at their national conventions. Sidney Hillman's Political Action Committee sent letters to its subscription list urging letters to Senators who had not promised support for FEPC and telegraphed House and Senate leaders frequently to push action on the legislation. The secretary of the Ohio CIO Council wrote all of the CIO locals in Columbus, Ohio, soliciting contributions for the National Council for a Permanent FEPC. Many "action letters" on

23. *Ibid.*, June 24, 1945.
24. Letter from George W. Crockett, Jr., Executive Director, UAW Fair Practices Committee, to Clarence Anderson, Secretary, Metropolitan Detroit Council for a Permanent FEPC.

FEPC were sent out by President Philip Murray to presidents of international unions, industrial union councils, CIO regional directors, and legislative representatives. "Labor USA," the CIO's weekly program over the Columbia Broadcasting System, devoted the program of May 5, 1945, to FEPC; the script was later made available to all CIO unions for local use.

Perhaps the most spectacular lobbying effort in behalf of FEPC and other like issues took place in September and October of 1945 when rank and file CIO members poured into the nation's capital city with petitions containing an estimated 200,000 signatures. The *New York World-Telegram* described the scene as follows:

> The most intensive labor pressure campaign ever seen on Capitol Hill, organized by the CIO and lasting three weeks, left a pattern today for a battering drive next year to unseat Congressmen opposing the CIO program.
>
> CIO delegates from 33 states collared, buttonholed and put on the spot scores of Senators and Representatives. They told the Congressmen how they wanted them to vote. Frequently they warned they would go out to defeat various Congressmen at the polls.
>
> The delegates demanded support for full employment legislation, more liberal employment legislation, more liberal unemployment insurance, a higher minimum wage law, a permanent FEPC and poll tax abolition.
>
> Whether many votes were changed appeared doubtful. CIO officials made no big claims. But looking to the 1946 political campaign, they saw an important gain from the labor blitz here.
>
> The visitors say they learned a lot more about how their government is run. They found that Congressmen, as one official said, are "just human beings" and that they could talk to them. The delegates also learned why and how they must fight to get their program accepted. They know better why certain Congressmen, in the CIO view, must be defeated.[25]

Many congressmen, not being accustomed to the "horny-hand" approach, reacted violently against the bluntness of the mass lobbying technique and threatened to go out of their way to defeat the CIO's program. As a result, the CIO did not again use this technique and it is doubtful whether the FEPC cause was aided one whit by it.

Despite these generally noteworthy activities, the CIO did not make a maximum contribution to the FEPC movement. One difficulty

---

25. October 15, 1945.

lay in the fact that the peak of the drive for national FEPC legislation came at a time when many CIO unions were deadlocked in strikes over wage increases in the immediate postwar period and were, understandably, reluctant to spread their energies too thin. However, the basic problem was the unwillingness of the CIO to repose full confidence in Randolph as the leader of the National Council.

It meant, in the final analysis, that once again the National Council was unable to make the most of the strength of a potential major supporter. The wholehearted support of the CIO was to be sorely missed in the 1946 drive in Congress. Had the CIO supported the National Council fully, sufficient funds might have been available to undertake necessary educational and pressure work and to complete many projects which remained suspended in mid air. This must be listed as another strand in the rope that throttled the FEPC movement in its early stages.

L EFT-WING GROUPS OF COMMUNIST COLORATION
have a general interest in mass reform movements in consonance
with their humanitarian philosophy and their desire to secure a
mass following. They assume the role of guardian and protector of
the underprivileged and oppressed; they direct appeals to all who are
dissatisfied with their lot. In the United States they have sought particularly to woo the labor movement and Negroes on the theory that
labor has a natural kinship with Marxist groups and that Negroes, as
victims of capitalism's "reactionary violence," are especially vulner-
able to promises of equal political and social status and economic
emancipation in the "better world" to come.

Accordingly, strenuous efforts have been expended to reach the
Negro population. Negroes have been elevated to high positions in
the Communist party and affiliated organizations; Negroes involved
in individual cases of discrimination, such as the famous "Scottsboro
boys" in the thirties, have been defended in the courts. Left-wingers
have also supported the anti-poll tax, anti-lynching, and other legislative measures designed to ease the Negroes' lot. Profuse self-praise
has attended all of their activities in this sphere in the hope of attracting a Negro following. It was to be expected that they would take
great interest in the FEPC movement.

On the other hand, many progressive and Socialist organizations
have looked upon the Communists and their supporters with great
skepticism and distrust even when they are in agreement as to the desirability of a specific reform.[1] The motives of the Communists are

---

1. Some progressive groups have accepted all supporters including Communists
on the theory that a united front is needed for the accomplishment of their programs.
The Communists have encouraged this point of view in recent years. See Eugene
Lyons, *The Red Decade, passim.*

• 155 •

suspect; progressives and Socialists have generally felt that the Communists are interested in reform, not as a means to adjust inequalities, but rather as a technique to aid infiltration into progressive movements and to stir up discontent—all with a view to advancing their "blueprint" of a Communist revolution. Consequently, considerable acrimony has punctuated many reform movements, draining badly needed energies into ideological conflicts.

FRICTION OVER FEPC

The FEPC movement suffered its full share from the ideological controversy. Seldom did a month pass without some friction between the leadership of the National Council for a Permanent FEPC and the diverse sympathizers and followers of the Communist party line. Randolph and his circle were hypersensitive to any Communist infiltration into the movement and went out of their way to oppose support from this quarter.

The first scuffle came in November 1943 while the National Council was still a "letterhead" organization. Congressman Vito Marcantonio of New York, an American Labor party leader also regarded by many as a Communist party follower, stole a march on Randolph's organization by introducing a bill for a permanent FEPC in Congress. National Council leadership which was still fumbling about, attempting to draft a bill and seeking congressional sponsors, was urged by its Socialist and other anti-Communist supporters to withhold endorsement of the Marcantonio bill and to spur its own legislative activities. Alfred Baker Lewis, prominent in the Workers Defense League and the NAACP, wrote Randolph:

> I think it is important for you to get the bill for a permanent FEPC introduced in Congress as soon as possible. Marcantonio has apparently jumped the gun again with a bill for this purpose and no doubt the communists will be sending around to all the Negro organizations and the progressive labor ones asking support for Marcantonio. It is always hard to lick something with nothing; so that some of the Negro organizations, even though they have no particular desire to back a communist inspired bill, will be in that position unless there is an alternative bill to support. I speak here from experience, as the committee to support fair employment practices in southwestern Connecticut, to which I am a delegate from the Greenwich N.A.A.C.P. branch, already had the matter of supporting Marcantonio's bill brought before them; and I had considerable

difficulty in getting it, not defeated but merely side-tracked for the time being, in the hope that in the meantime your bill will actually make its appearance in Congress.[2]

Nathaniel M. Minkoff of the Workers Defense League and other similar organizations wrote in the same vein: "Our failure to introduce in Congress the long-discussed measure making the FEPC a permanent institution has once more given our Communist friends an opportunity to 'steal a march' on us. The great 'Mark Anthony' is already a step ahead of us with a bill of his own. May I not suggest that we expedite matters and put our bill into Congress before the C. P. steam-roller gets to work on its own bill." [3]

Randolph's reaction was to urge Thurman Dodson, who was in Washington seeking congressional backers, to move with greater speed. "I consider anything that is initiated by our Comintern friends as the kiss of death," he wrote Dodson.[4] It was not until January 1944 that National Council representatives in Washington succeeded in locating sponsors for their bill and in the meantime the National Council blamed the Communists for placing obstacles in the path of lining up supporters.[5] When the National Council bill was finally introduced, Marcantonio made a public plea for support of all FEPC bills rather than have division over their merits.[6] The national executive board of the National Negro Congress, a Communist-dominated organization, also called for a united front. Edward Strong, its secretary, said, "We can win a permanent FEPC if all three bills are supported. If all three are supported, then one of them will certainly be adopted. Whichever bill is adopted, it can be amended to embody the best features of the other bills." [7] These pleas, sincere or otherwise, were rejected by the National Council; Randolph publicly criticized Marcantonio's bill as weak and "too general" and made no pretense of giving it support.[8]

---

2. Letter, November 5, 1943.
3. Letter to Randolph, November 11, 1943.
4. Letter, November 24, 1943.
5. Letter from B. F. McLaurin to Mrs. Alice Stark, January 13, 1944.
6. *Baltimore Afro-American*, February 19, 1944.
7. *Daily Worker*, February 14, 1944. Strong's reference to three bills included Marcantonio's H.R. 1732, Thomas Scanlon's H.R. 3986, and William L. Dawson's H.R. 4004. Scanlon's bill was shortly thereafter combined with Dawson's.
8. *People's Voice*, January 29, 1944.

From this time forward there was no possibility of unity on FEPC
between these two groups. The struggle took on different guises,
depending upon the immediate circumstances, but the pattern was
nearly always the same: what one group would recommend by way
of strategy or tactics, the other would always reject. Each asserted
that it alone was making an all-out fight and that the other was not
only wrong in its approach but was not even interested in seriously
pushing the issue.

In the summer of 1945 when the President's Committee's budget
for the coming fiscal year was before Congress, the National Council
insisted that there be no let-down in the fight for permanent FEPC
legislation, while the Communists urged that all pressure be directed
to secure an adequate appropriation for the existing committee and
that work for permanent legislation be dropped until the appropriation was assured.

The most serious conflict developed late in 1945 over the National
Council's strategy of pushing for Senate action on the bill first. The
National Council felt that success in the House would be compara-
tively easy to achieve but that southern opposition in the Senate was
the major stumbling block and unless overcome first, the work on
the House of Representatives would go for naught. The left-wingers,
conversely, agreed with the American Jewish Congress and several
other groups which urged the "House first" approach and stressed
the necessity for obtaining signatures on the petition to force the
discharge of the bill from committee, together with the use of the
Calendar Wednesday technique for bringing the bill to the floor.
The National Negro Congress asserted in this connection: "It is well
known that any bill which has passed one house of Congress has the
better chance of passing the other. Hostility in the Senate has been
so marked as to make approval of the House almost a necessity before
passage by the Senate can be expected."[9] In Congress, Marcantonio
and Adam Clayton Powell, Negro church and civic leader from Harlem who was for a time close to the Communist party line, spread the
gospel of the "House first" strategy.

An all-out assault upon the National Council was launched at a

9. *Manuscript*, No. 36, November 19, 1945.

September 25, 1945, conference of eighty-nine organizations under the auspices of the Southern Conference for Human Welfare in New York City. During the luncheon meeting Dr. Max Yergan of the National Negro Congress fired the first gun in what appeared to be a well-planned campaign to take FEPC leadership away from the National Council. The gist of Yergan's remarks was that the permanent FEPC bill had not yet been passed because the campaign had not been properly conducted; what was needed was the establishment of an organization—preferably by the CIO—to involve the masses of the country in an intelligent campaign. The same sentiments were echoed later by representatives of the Independent Committee for the Arts, Sciences and Professions, International Labor Defense, National Lawyers Guild, and other organizations.

This apparently was a build-up for Marcantonio's address in the evening in which he outlined a plan for FEPC victory: House action first through use of the Calendar Wednesday technique and formation of a congressional steering committee to initiate the House campaign and to call a conference of organizations and individuals interested in the fight to mobilize nationwide opinion for the bill. Marcantonio's statement served notice that the split was beyond reconciliation.

During the following days, in the Negro press, in organization meetings, and in minor publications throughout the country there began an open attack upon the National Council, its strategy, and its staff, closely adhering to the lines of attack at the New York conference. Furthermore, according to the National Council, some of the attacks were covert; congressmen and other important people were visited privately in an effort to discredit the Randolph group.[10]

The National Council's supporters unlimbered their heavy guns to make certain that the left-wingers did not succeed in taking leadership away from it. Willard S. Townsend, International President of the CIO United Transport Service Employees of America, charged Marcantonio with insincerity in the following telegram to all of his local unions:

I am amazed at this latest stand taken by the *Daily Worker*, Fellow Travellers and the Communist Party, but I cannot say that I am surprised.

---

10. Unsigned and undated National Council memorandum.

The fact that the Southern Conference for Human Welfare was the host to this trial balloon should give all liberals food for serious thought. The flimsy charge of Marcantonio that failure to use Calendar Wednesday is solely responsible for inability to get HR 2232 to the floor of the House of Representatives is further evidence of the divisive tactics commonly practiced by those whose endorsement is the kiss of death. The use of Calendar Wednesday was fully explored by proponents of the bill and the concensus was that it would involve more time than the petition method. A bill brought to the floor in this manner must be disposed of in that particular day. Mr. Marcantonio is an expert parliamentarian and was well aware of all these implications.

This false accusation stems from the recent change in that particular line and from a desire to join the band wagon at this late hour. Here is another play aimed at attracting the Negro. I am convinced that this is not a sincere show of interest in the enactment of legislation to outlaw discrimination in employment because of race, creed, color or national origin.

The FEPC issue is of such paramount importance, especially now in the reconversion period, that for appeal and as a money raising and unifying medium which can only be compared to the famous Scottsboro case. Surely most of us remember the funds collected in the name of justice which never reached their destination. Let us recognize this jockeying for position in its true light, said Mr. Townsend, and not let us sway from our determination to secure passage of the bill to establish a permanent FEPC commission. As a member of the executive committee of the national council for a permanent FEPC, I call upon you to rally behind that organization and its 52 coordinated national organizations to press for early enactment of HR 2232 and S. 101.[11]

As could be expected, the rivalry between the two factions had its effect upon local work for FEPC. From Boston came this report from the National Council's New England field representative on the difficulties of establishing a non-Communist local council in that city:

. . . we are faced with the problem of the Communists, who control NCPAC; are very powerful in the Negro community—the *Chronicle* is CP; and have used almost every minister in Boston to their purposes including Bishop Hartman. There is absolutely no liberal core of the Reinhold Niebuhr type in Boston. The only non-CP group which knows the score is Dave Niles' crowd, who take their orders from Washington and might be anti-FEPC if that were the Administration line. . . .

The ironical thing is that the most active federal FEPC people are the

---

11. UTSEA, CIO, Press Release, October 5, 1945.

Communists. The person who worked hardest for federal FEPC last year was Mrs. ———, who is suspected of being a fellow traveler. And it is she who everyone, including the liberals, think would be the best secretary of a Boston Council. . . .[12]

The following month, the same representative wrote the Washington office that "harm" had been averted by the selection of a non-Communist secretary and continued: "Preventing federal FEPC from falling into the hands of the Communists was no mean achievement, as they control NCPAC, the Negro press, the Unitarians, and the Methodists, just to name a few."[13] In the end, however, Boston made virtually no contribution to the movement for federal FEPC legislation.

In Fort Worth the Southern field representative was taken to task by an International Longshoremen's and Warehousemen's Union (CIO) representative for not praising Marcantonio, whereupon the former immediately warned the chairman of the local council "of the danger of becoming identified too closely with those people."[14] Rumors of Communist activities also came from East St. Louis, Detroit, Little Rock, and other places. Nowhere did harmonious relations exist between the two groups.

As time passed Communist attacks upon the National Council increased in intensity. When Randolph's group persisted in its "Senate first" strategy in December 1945, the *Daily Worker* lashed out:

> While progressive constituents of reactionary Republican House members are lining up signatures for discharge Petition No. 4, everybody should notice the slick trick which self-styled "friends" of the permanent FEPC are trying to slip over. The National Council for a Permanent FEPC has not only stopped trying to get action on HR-2232; it is trying to get everyone else to stop. The reason it gives is that to continue pressure on the House is useless but that pressure on the Senate might bring favorable results.
>
> That is a plausible lie, dangerous to the whole idea of a permanent FEPC. For if the bill goes to the Senate before having first gone through the House, it will go minus the strength necessary for it to stand up against the murderous attack bound to follow. The reason why it CAN

---

12. Leuchtenburg, Field Report, November 7, 1945.
13. *Ibid.*, December 10, 1945.
14. Douglas, Field Report, July 20, 1945.

be passed in the House is that sentiment and strength for it have already
been built up there. That is why HR-2232 must receive more, instead of
less, support.[15]

Louis Colman, Secretary of International Labor Defense, led an
attack upon the National Council when the Senate filibuster squelched
all FEPC hopes for 1946. After recapitulating the Communist analysis
of the defeat, Colman gloated at the signs of disunity in the National
Council:

> A most encouraging sign is that on both a state and on a national scale,
> organizations and leaders who have up to now followed the misleader-
> ship of DAVID DUBINSKY and A. PHILIP RANDOLPH, both of National Council
> for a Permanent FEPC, show signs of independent action. Some had fol-
> lowed National Council leadership because they were misinformed. Others
> trailed along for political reasons similar to those motivating DUBINSKY and
> his puppets. Many in local areas went along with absolutely incorrect
> policies because they did not realize just how defeatist these were, and
> feared that a fight for correct policies would split pro-FEPC ranks!
> Now many for the first time realize fully the disaster to which the
> DUBINSKY-RANDOLPH policies would lead the fight for FEPC. Others recog-
> nize that the people can't be fooled all the time, and are gingerly shifting
> their positions toward more independence of the National Council.
> It is even within the realm of possibility that DUBINSKY and RANDOLPH
> themselves may see the handwriting on the wall and be forced to follow
> strategy designed to get the bill passed. They can't forever have their cake
> (an unpassed permanent FEPC bill as a permanent base for their political
> operations) and eat it (keep up a reputation as militant fighters for FEPC)
> too.
> With untiring work by sincere supporters of the permanent FEPC bill,
> energetic and aroused public opinion against the "white supremacists"
> north and south and west who block its passage, and wide realization of
> the traps into which the movement can be led by the opportunist mis-
> leadership which has characterized the work of the National Council
> for a Permanent FEPC so far, the bill can really be passed.[16]

The Communists left no stone unturned to put the Randolph group
in a bad light. When the National Council sent large numbers of telegrams during the 1946 legislative battle and urged others to wire
Congress in support of the measure, the Communists accused the

15. December 9, 1945.
16. International Labor Defense Legislative Service, February, 1946.

Council of being a "strike-breaking" organization because Western Union employees were out on strike at this time.[17]

The day that the FEPC bill was precipitately brought to the floor of the Senate in January 1946, a delegation of three hundred, mostly from New York, descended upon the Senate in behalf of the bill. The National Negro Congress and the other participating organizations, mostly left-wing, promptly proceeded to take credit for having forced Senate action despite the fact that the Senate action had been planned by the National Council for a Permanent FEPC for months and had been opposed by the Communists and their friends.

NATIONAL COUNCIL REACTION

Not all of the National Council's opposition to the Communists was due to fear of the "Red bogey." One of the charges which the Council had to fight constantly was that it was a Communist organization; had the Council cooperated closely with the left-wingers it would have appeared to vindicate this viewpoint and would have discouraged many potential supporters from joining hands with the Randolph group. When New York Communist Councilman Benjamin J. Davis, Jr. appeared as principal speaker at a "Mass Rally to Save FEPC" at the Chicago Coliseum under the auspices of the Illinois District Communist party, R. R. Church, Chairman of the Republican American Committee and FEPC supporter, wrote Mrs. Hedgeman:

Confidentially, was this meeting held here last week for Ben Davis, cleared through your Washington office? My only reason for asking you this question, is because you asked me in your letter about the Chicago group, and the mass meetings they were planning here, and since this meeting, which was widely advertised by Communist Party, I have had several important people, who are interested in FEPC, to ask me whether the Davis meeting was arranged for by the National Council in Washington, and whether Davis was on the Council payroll.[18]

Mrs. Hedgeman denied any association with Davis, but because both groups worked for FEPC legislation the ghost was not easily laid.

On the other hand, while the National Council attempted to pacify those who feared the presence of Communists in the Council, it had

17. Letter from Bill Worthy to Mrs. Hedgeman, February 1, 1946.
18. Letter, January 11, 1946.

to assuage the fears of those who resented the Council's anti-Communist policy and preferred that the movement be broadly representative of all FEPC supporters. For example George Crockett, Executive Director of the UAW's anti-discrimination committee, warned Mrs. Hedgeman:

> . . . we look to your organization for leadership in the strategy to be followed in securing FEPC legislation. We shall continue to do this so long as we are convinced that the National Council is genuinely interested in securing the broadest basis of support for this legislation and is not turning down suggestions (from persons) whose political ideology does not accord with the political views of the dominant persons behind the National Council.[19]

In her reply Mrs. Hedgeman was not entirely candid, nor entirely in accord with the facts, when she tried to convey the impression that all interested groups were welcome to join the National Council regardless of their ideological attachments.[20]

The Washington staff, under Mrs. Hedgeman's direction, in time became aware of the dangers involved in waging an anti-Communist crusade while attempting to secure support for passage of the FEPC legislation and sought to avoid further clashes, but Randolph and other top policy leaders could not be silenced. Randolph would make promises to soft-pedal his public attacks and then unloose a blast in his union paper, *The Black Worker*, or in the general press which would make the ideological pot boil even more furiously. The National Council remained stamped with the mark of Cain as far as the Communists were concerned.

Meanwhile the inclination of the Socialists and Communists to wage ideological warfare on the FEPC issue was deplored by those who were interested in a non-partisan approach to passage of the legislation. *Manuscript* reported:

19. Letter, November 30, 1945.
20. Letter, December 3, 1945. In November 1945 Dorothy Funn of the Washington office of the National Negro Congress asked to be placed on the National Council mailing list, precipitating a crisis in the Washington office because it was felt that it would entail admitting the Congress to the Washington strategy committee. Finally, after much discussion, "it was decided to accede to the request in order to avoid public misunderstanding, of our unwillingness to cooperate with other grou s, although they have attacked us. The strategy committee, however, will have to be informed of what we are up against."—Staff Meeting Minutes, November 29, 1945.

Such success as has been enjoyed in the bitter FEPC fights, undoubtedly has been due in part to the rather remarkable cooperation and teamwork of all those who want fair employment practices. Communists, Socialists, Catholic, Jewish and Protestant Church groups; labor organizations, major political parties, and national and local organizations devoted to better citizenship and defending civil and civic rights, have labored together in harmony.

On this account current tendencies of the Communists and Socialists, although present in the fight in relatively small numbers, to use this battle ground to air their personal enmity toward one another, assumes significance. It is noteworthy that FEPC as conceived and presently existing, is neither Communistic nor Socialistic in the accepted sense. It is also noteworthy that calmer heads among the Communists and Socialists frown on this display of lack of harmony.[21]

Pious hopes, however, did not avail. The ideological struggle remained a millstone which slowed and dragged the FEPC movement down.

---

21. *Manuscript*, No. 20, July 30, 1945.

• THE SOUTH: DEFENDERS OF THE FAITH • BUSI-
NESS OPPOSITION • VERMIN OPPOSITION • GEN-
ERAL PUBLIC OPPOSITION

B ECAUSE FEPC WAS A PRECEDENT-SHATTERING
proposal which seemed to assail long-prevailing traditions, social
systems, and economic practices, it was inevitable that efforts to
enact the anti-discrimination principle into federal law would meet
with strong opposition. Yet there is little evidence of a well-
coordinated campaign with a central high command against national
FEPC legislation. The opposition was powerful but piecemeal. The
demands of the war effort were too great to permit opponents to
exert their maximum energies against FEPC. The opposition could
depend upon die-hard opposition in Congress to stop the enactment
of anti-discrimination legislation. Nevertheless, an examination of
both the passive and active opposition to FEPC is worth making as it
reveals something of the difficulties faced by most social welfare
legislation backers in the early period of seeking public support.

THE SOUTH: DEFENDERS OF THE FAITH

In recent years, under the impact of industralization, trade union
penetration, and increasingly enlightened leadership, the old unity
of whites against Negro economic progress in the South has been
softened.[1] However, the unity against social equality for the Negro

---

1. Since 1935 it has been estimated that 1,000,000 white southerners have joined
unions with 100,000 Negroes. In Birmingham, white and Negro United Mine Workers
meet together as equals. Of the Transport Workers Union members in New Orleans
90 per cent are Negroes. Negroes are also found in the Farmers' Union and Farm
Bureau.—"The Deep South Looks Up," *Fortune*, XXVIII, No. 1 (July 1943), 95-100,
218-225. In October 1942, in the midst of war, a group of southern Negroes meeting
at Durham, North Carolina, set forth demands for full civil rights and equal rights in
industry, agriculture, education, social welfare, and military service. In April of the
following year, a group of leading white southerners at Atlanta affirmed the Negro's

race remains the most deep-seated and all-pervasive of the southern *mores*. All measures aimed at the amelioration of the plight of the Negro must still run the "white supremacy" gauntlet.

It was thus that the most embittered opposition to FEPC came from this part of the country where opponents, especially business-men, found it easy to raise the bugaboo of racial equality. Southern officials, almost without exception, described FEPC as an ogre em-powered to destroy the southern way of life and place whites at the mercy of Negroes. Northern interference with the handling of the race problem was bitterly resented throughout the war period. In March 1944 the South Carolina House of Representatives gave vent to its feelings by passing the following resolution:

> We reaffirm our belief in and our allegiance to established white supremacy as now prevailing in the South and we solemnly pledge our lives and our sacred honor to maintaining it. Insofar as racial relations are concerned, we firmly and unequivocally demand that henceforth the damned agitators of the North leave the South alone.[2]

Governor Frank M. Dixon of Alabama rejected a government con-tract to use the cotton mills in the Alabama State Prison for war production because of the non-discrimination clause in the contract. In a letter to the Defense Supplies Corporation he made a typical charge:

> Under cover of this particular clause, the Fair Employment Practice Commission has been operating to break down the principle of segregation of races, to force Negroes and white people to work together, intermingle with each other, and even to bring about the situation where white em-ployes will have to work under Negroes.[3]

The public hearings held by the President's Committee in June 1942 in Birmingham provoked numerous angry and threatening state-ments. Judge Horace C. Wilkinson, an important Alabama political figure, was widely quoted to have said in this connection: "There is

---

right to economic equality: "With so large a proportion of our wage earning popu-lation belonging to the minority race, if we cannot plan for a well-trained, well-employed and prosperous Negro population the economic future of the South is hopeless."—*New York Times*, April 11, 1943.

2. *Washington Post*, March 7, 1944.
3. *New York Times*, July 24, 1942.

need of a League to Maintain White Supremacy . . . the time to act is now. An organization should be formed so strong, so powerful, and so efficient, that this menace to our national security and our local way of life will rapidly disappear."⁴ The *Gadsden* (Alabama) *Times* reported the Birmingham hearings in the following language: "A group of snoopers, two of whom are Negroes, will assemble in Birmingham, June 18, for a three-day session to determine whether the South is doing right by 'Little Sambo.' " Other characterizations of the hearings by southern newspapers included: "group of black-and-tan investigators," "three day inquisition at Birmingham," "halo-wearing missionaries of New Deal Socialism," "Roosevelt racial experts," "an instrument for political and social reform operating under a vicious disguise," and "dat cummittee fer de purtechshun uv Rastus & Sambo."⁵

Southern newspapers frequently went out of their way to misrepresent the objectives of anti-discrimination legislation.⁶ They charged the bill would: (1) nationalize all jobs completely and thoroughly; (2) enable "communists, socialists and all other enemies of freedom" to slip into power in the FEPC bureaus where they would dictate to every American—employer and employee alike; (3) force schools, religious organizations and all other non-profit organizations to hire as FEPC dictates; (4) permit any applicant for a job (even where no opening exists) to force himself on the payroll by appealing to the FEPC; (5) enable shyster lawyers to establish thriving "rackets"

4. *Fortune,* July 1943, p. 223.
5. Quoted by Doxey Wilkerson, "FEPC—The Alphabet of Hope," *New Masses* (October 20, 1942), pp. 4-8.
6. Exceptions included the constructive *Birmingham News* and *Age-Herald, Louisville Courier-Journal, Montgomery Advertiser,* and a sprinkling of other newspapers. Some southern papers overlooked no bets in building up antagonism towards FEPC. The *Lanett* (Alabama) *Valley Times* of July 11, 1945, for example, appealed to textile mill workers to beware: "The cotton mills of the South are founded on 'discrimination in employment.'
"The men and women who were poor, who owned few if any lands, came to the cotton mills, where wives, daughters, sisters and men could work in spinning rooms, weave rooms, card rooms, apart from negro laborers, and could live in village inhabited by white families, separate from a negro quarter.
"The passage of a law by Congress forbidding 'discrimination' in employment would compel the presidents of the companies, operating Monaghan Mills, Johnson Mills, Piedmont, Pelzer, Pacolet, Watts, Orr, Newberry, all other cotton mills, to employ negroes applying for work. Some negroes could 'qualify' as mill workers. . . ."

representing disgruntled employees; (6) force white employees out of jobs; (7) harass employers with purely imaginary or malicious grievances prosecuted through the FEPC; (8) stir up racial strife throughout the country; (9) be unfair to colored people; and (10) force businessmen to make public the details of their private business affairs, thus jeopardizing even secret formulae used in manufacture.

Even among those who were counted as sincere friends of the Negro, there were white southern leaders who publicly opposed FEPC legislation with strong enforcement powers, on the theory that such a law would injure rather than improve race relations. Mark Ethridge, publisher of the *Louisville Courier-Journal* and first chairman of the President's Committee, stated: "No white Southerner can logically challenge the statement that the Negro is entitled, as an American citizen, to full civil rights and to economic opportunity," but northerners "must recognize that there is no power in the world— not even in all the mechanized armies of the earth, Allied and Axis— which could now force the Southern white people to the abandonment of the principle of social segregation. . . ."[7] Others, including the widely-syndicated columnist John Temple Graves and Richmond's Virginius Dabney, affirmed that they were not opposed to an FEPC which relied upon conciliation and persuasion but took exception to compulsory enforcement of the anti-discrimination principle.

Opponents were so successful in their efforts that the FEPC issue was never given a fair hearing in that section. Emotionalism and bombast ruled unchallenged. It was not surprising, therefore, that southern representatives in Congress formed a solid phalanx of opposition to enactment of the legislation advanced by the National Council for a Permanent FEPC. By 1945 the issue became so hot that no congressman from that area could have voted for permanent FEPC legislation and won re-election to public office. Would-be supporters of FEPC took no chances. Senator Lister Hill, a faithful New Deal supporter from Alabama, was so bitterly excoriated by the press in his state for having voted for the 1944 appropriation for the President's Committee that he was never again found in the FEPC column. Senator Claude Pepper of Florida, an extremely vocal friend of the

7. Quoted in *Phylon*, First Quarter, 1943, pp. 82-83.

"common man," failed to support permanent FEPC legislation, despite promises to do so. The intensity of southern opposition together with the possibilities for minority control of our national legislature through the filibuster and other devices are important as reasons for the failure of the legislative drive, at least up to the time of writing.

BUSINESS OPPOSITION

Businessmen, as such, are probably no more prejudiced against fair treatment for minority peoples than the rest of the population. And yet a considerable proportion of the active opposition to the FEPC movement on both the state and national levels came from organizations representing this important group. In explanation of business opposition to FEPC at least several possibilities should be mentioned. First was the ever-present fear of additional government control over business enterprise. With the impact of New Deal regulatory agencies, businessmen became hypersensitive to further intervention by government in the areas regarded as the sacred preserves of ownership and management. The FEPC bill, from their point of view, would have narrowed management's freedom in the choice of employees if they came within the provisions of the proposed legislation. Much of the opposition centered upon this fact.

Secondly, while employers in large establishments have relatively little social contact with their workers, white or Negro, and may have no personal qualms about the introduction of Negroes and other minority peoples into jobs previously closed to them, they often fear the reaction of their white workers and oppose FEPC legislation for this reason. Finally, there were undoubtedly employers who fought FEPC legislation because of personal prejudices against full utilization of minority peoples in their places of business.

The opposition of businessmen to the measure was expressed in no uncertain terms by their organizations and by newspapers representing their point of view. The National Association of State Chambers of Commerce, as well as individual state chambers, was openly fighting both state and federal FEPC legislation.[8] While the National

8. The National Association of State Chambers of Commerce is a separate organization from the United States Chamber of Commerce and does not speak for it although on most matters it can be anticipated that the views of the two groups will

Association was chiefly concerned with state bills, it also made its attitude towards federal legislation known to Congress.[9] A letter from R. B. Skinner, secretary-treasurer of the association, to its members stated the organization's position in April 1945: "It is quite evident that all this hue and cry for legislation covering fair employment practices is the result of a concerted effort by certain radical elements to sow the seeds of discord into our economic and political system, so that they may turn this discord to their own benefit."[10] Without known exception those local chambers of commerce expressing views on the subject went on record as being opposed to federal FEPC legislation with enforcement powers. Fear of arbitrary government action was usually cited as the reason. Typical of many such expressions was that of Ray J. Dunn, Director of the Portsmouth, Virginia, Chamber of Commerce, who called upon local businessmen and industrialists to fight FEPC:

> The bill, known as the FEPC Act, and sponsored by Congresswoman Norton, if passed, would establish a commission with sub-agencies thruout the nation, with power to impose penalties of fines and imprisonment upon employers declared guilty by the commission, or anyone of its sub-agencies, of discrimination in hiring. . . .
>
> Without study, most Americans would heartily endorse such a measure. However, when we scratch the surface we find another angle to

---

coincide. The United States Chamber was singularly silent on FEPC, probably because it followed the strategy of permitting local chambers to lead in the pressure upon Congress rather than because of any affection for FEPC legislation.

9. Business opposition to state FEPC bills was also very strong. In nearly every state the pattern was the same. In New York major opposition came from chambers of commerce, boards of trade, real estate boards, employment agencies, associated industries organizations, and manufacturers' associations.—*Confidential Report on Ives-Quinn Hearings, New York*, undated, p. 3. In Illinois the Chicago Association of Commerce was said to approve the spirit of FEPC but joined with the Associated Employers of Illinois, the Illinois Federation of Retailers and the Illinois Manufacturers' Association in opposing the establishment of an enforcement board.—*Chicago Sun*, May 7, 1945. In Michigan some observers felt that the lobby of the Michigan Manufacturers' Association and the statement to the legislators by the National Economic Council, filed by Merwin K. Hart, terming the FEPC bill a replica of the Communist party "line" of 1935, influenced rejection of the 1945 bill.—*The Committee Reporter*, American Jewish Committee, June 1945, No. 6. In Massachusetts the chief business opposition came from the Associated Industries (the Massachusetts branch of the National Association of Manufacturers), real estate boards, and the Boston Chamber of Commerce.—Henry R. Silberman, "How We Won in Massachusetts," *New Republic*, 115, No. 1 (July 8, 1946), 10-11.

10. *PM*, April 2, 1945.

consider. Such a commission would have unquestioned authority to make sweeping investigations of any concern, subpoena records and place all burden of disproving alleged violations, from any and all sources, upon the employer. Snooping government men would have a continuous field day. . . .[11]

The United States Wholesale Grocers' Association, self-styled "Voice of the Independent Wholesale Grocer," urged wholesale grocers to line up their representatives and senators in "definite opposition" to national FEPC legislation in a bulletin dated June 8, 1945. Said President J. H. McLaurin, "It is up to all employers in this country to throw their united strength against this bill" and proceeded to express doubt that even President Truman is "strong enough" to saddle it on the people.[12]

The Conference of American Small Business Organizations, with headquarters in Chicago, also sought to stimulate active opposition among its members to FEPC legislation.[13] "The bill to legalize business persecution under the guise of anti-race discrimination is now before the Congress," wrote Chairman Frederick A. Virkus to the conference's members. "This is one of the most vicious pieces of legislation ever proposed. If passed, *every* businessman throughout the country will be constantly on the defensive against persecution. With *all* the cards stacked against him."[14]

The Southern States Industrial Council, a propaganda and pressure organization for southern manufacturers, mailed large quantities of letters to all sections of the country claiming that FEPC would produce riots and upheavals in the South if passed.[15] Appealing for funds to help support the Council's efforts to protect the "economic welfare

---

11. *Norfolk Journal and Guide*, July 7, 1945.

12. *Washington Afro-American*, June 30, 1945.

13. The organization's letterhead claims that it "Expresses the Deliberated Opinion of delegates from more than 300 organizations representing over 260 different lines of industry in 48 states, a cross-section of national retail trade, manufacturers, contractors, wholesalers, jobbers, printers and other business associations; a cross-section of state and local chambers of commerce, representing an affiliated membership of over 500,-000 small business concerns."

14. *PM*, June 28, 1945.

15. *Atlanta World*, May 3, 1945. The officers of the Council represent the following corporations among others: Monsanto Chemical Co.; Federal Fibre Mills; Island Creek Coal Co.; Citizens and Southern National Bank; American Zinc, Lead and Smelting Co.; and the Baker-Cammack Hosiery Mills.

and general prosperity of the South," C. C. Gilbert, Secretary, urged pressure to defeat the FEPC legislation:

This letter is addressed to you in person, in order that I may bring to you the most important problem the South has confronted since reconstruction.

There is now pending in the Congress H.R. 2232, commonly designated the Fair Employment Practice Act, the ostensible purpose of which is to insure equality of employment opportunities to all citizens regardless of race, creed or color.

The dangerous features of this measure lie not only in its provisions but in its interpretation and administration. Purporting to establish a nation-wide standard of employment, enough is known of the proponents of the measure and the social and economic ideologies they practice and teach, to justify the charge that this bill is aimed primarily at the South, with the paramount idea that the South shall remain in a condition of economic bondage and that the great industrial progress made by the South in the last two decades must stop.

This measure will not be defeated unless you and others who think as you do bring to all the people a knowledge of what this vicious measure will do, and unless you impress upon your Congressmen and Senators the necessity of fighting the bill with every means at their command. . . .

I urge that you immediately contact the editor of your local paper and the heads of all civic organizations in your community and personally enlist their active participation in this fight.[16]

VERMIN OPPOSITION

Not unexpectedly FEPC legislation drew fire from individuals and groups of anti-democratic persuasion. Opposition from this quarter developed on both the state and national scenes.[17] Lacking general public confidence, these groups were chiefly covert in their attacks upon the anti-discrimination legislation. For the most part, leaflets of the following calibre comprised their ammunition:

20,000 LITTLE BROWN BASTARDS

Twenty Thousand illegitimate babies have been born of Negro American Soldier fathers in England. Quite an example of fair employment

---

16. April 24, 1945.

17. In Illinois, some of the state legislators reported the receipt of a deluge of leaflets from the Hoosier Press of Hammond, Indiana, charging that the Mills bill, then before the 1945 session of the Illinois legislature, was a Jewish conspiracy designed to take jobs away from servicemen and give them to Jews.—*The Committee Reporter*, American Jewish Committee, 2, No. 6 (June 1945), p. 3.

practices. That is what you call FEPC in the flesh. News dispatches reveal that many of the children were born of married women whose husbands were Englishmen in battle. The mothers of these illegitimate half-breeds are now forming an organization hoping that some systematic provision can be made for the unfortunate illegitimates. The mothers say that their returning husbands wouldn't object so strenuously if the children were white, but the little black sheep running in the front yards seem to be more than the returning veterans can endure.

This may seem shocking to some people, but it must be remembered that Eleanor Roosevelt and others of her ilk have been laying the philosophical and ideological foundation for such behavior for many years. . . .[18]

Only one person in this general category appeared before a congressional committee to testify against FEPC legislation. Mrs. Agnes Waters, "unofficial representative of millions of American mothers over this Nation who protest against this bill," appeared before the Senate Subcommittee hearing evidence on S. 2048 on September 7, 1944, and delivered a diatribe against the bill:

I object to this bill on the ground that it sets up and legalizes a Red government in Washington. . . .

I object to it because it is a threat against our national security; that it would violate our constitutional rights and destroy the liberty of both American employer and employee, wrecking American labor interests, American business and industry, American enterprise, individual liberty and initiative, and forcing a Red revolution here in the United States of America. . . .

I am appearing here alone and facing a room full of enemies, except for the presence of God and the spiritual presence of more than 80 percent of the American people who are upholding my hands here today and giving me strength to battle alone against unnumbered foes who pack this committee room. . . .

The majority of these Reds who are asking for this bill are Jews, Negroes, liars, and rats, not Catholics, but atheists; they are foreigners. They never have been assimilated as American citizens. They are listed as enemies of this Republic. . . .[19]

---

18. The only source indicated on the circular was "Post Office Box 2411, Detroit 31, Michigan."

19. *Hearings before a Subcommittee of the Committee on Education and Labor,* United States Senate, Seventy-Eighth Congress, Second Session, on S. 2048, A Bill to Prohibit Discrimination in Employment Because of Race, Creed, Color, National Origin, or Ancestry, August 30, 31, September 6, 7, and 8, 1944, pp. 129-62.

Neither Mrs. Waters nor her friends appear to have had much to do with the defeat of the legislation. The point of view which they expressed was so extreme as to defeat their own purpose. Nevertheless, many of these same slurs, in a more socially acceptable form, were used by more influential opponents of FEPC legislation.

GENERAL PUBLIC OPPOSITION

Past experience with reform movements indicates that the mass of the people are conservative when initially confronted with a proposed reform even when a realistic appraisal of the situation would indicate that change is desirable. The familiar is preferred to the new and uncertain. Strenuous efforts to educate and stimulate people to action are often necessary in order to overcome this inertia.

The FEPC movement suffered perhaps more than most reform drives for lack of general public information and because of the relative novelty of the principle involved. The issue burst upon the scene in 1941 and the drive for permanent legislation got under way in 1944. This gave hardly sufficient time to permit the implications of the proposed legislation to become part of the general public consciousness especially in the midst of the war. Furthermore, the National Council for a Permanent FEPC spent relatively little time in general mass education. This made it easy for the bill's opponents to make wild allegations concerning the extent of its coverage and its likely effect upon business, race relations, and the general public interest with little fear of successful contradiction.

Various public opinion polls taken in 1945 revealed that a sizeable proportion of the white public either had no opinion or no information on FEPC. Assuming that a scientific sample was employed, the *Negro Digest* poll of February 1945 revealed that 58 per cent of all whites queried answered "No" to the question, "Do you know that the President through executive order has prohibited race discrimination in war employment?" [20]

In the same poll, on the question "Should the government guarantee job equality to all races?" widespread indecision among whites was revealed, except in the South. Negroes, as could be anticipated, were almost solidly in agreement on the question:

20. Quoted in the *Philadelphia Tribune*, February 3, 1945.

Whites

North ..... Yes, 32%; No, 30%; Undecided, 38%
West ...... Yes, 38%; No, 31%; Undecided, 31%
South ...... Yes, 3%; No, 87%; Undecided, 10%

Negroes

North ..... Yes, 98%; No, 1%; Undecided, 1%
West ...... Yes, 99%; No, 1%; Undecided, 0%
South ...... Yes, 96%; No, 2%; Undecided, 2%

The Gallup Poll of September 22, 1945, tends to bear out the same point. Thirteen per cent of the whites and Negroes sampled had no opinion on the question, "Do you favor or oppose a law in your state which would require employers to hire a person if he is qualified for the job regardless of his race or color?" The rest of the public was almost evenly divided, 43 per cent in favor and 44 per cent opposed to such state legislation.[21]

The age distribution on the poll reveals a similarity to that of most reform movements: the more youthful, as a rule, were more willing to abolish discrimination in employment, whereas the older age groups preferred to continue on with the status quo. Fifty-five per cent of those from 21-29 were favorable to such legislation and only 34 per cent opposed; 42 per cent favored and 45 per cent opposed in the 30-49 age group; and only 38 per cent of those 50 years of age or older approved, while 48 per cent opposed.

In terms of occupational distribution, the breakdown is equally interesting. The greatest willingness to accept FEPC legislation was found in the group most likely to be affected should the bill become law: 52 per cent of the manual workers approved and only 35 per cent disapproved. Furthermore, the strongest opposition came from farmers who were least likely to have interference with their hiring policies

---

21. By sections, the poll revealed:

New England and Mid-Atlantic States: Yes, 58%; No, 31%; No Op. 11%
East and West Central   Yes, 41%; No, 43%; No Op. 16%
South   Yes, 30%; No, 60%; No Op. 10%
Far West   Yes, 41%; No, 46%; No Op. 13%

In California, the only state which has submitted an FEPC bill to the voters via the initiative, a proposed law was defeated by a margin of 2½ to 1 in the election of November, 1946.

because most employed fewer than the minimum number covered by most state and national bills. The explanation appears to lie partially in the fact that many of the farmers sampled resided in the South and thus reflected a sectional rather than an occupational bias. Generally farmers oppose government interference which is not of direct benefit to themselves. Business and professional peoples opposed by a margin of 48 to 43 per cent and the white collar group also reacted negatively, 51 to 41 per cent.[22]

---

22. The reaction to a second question which seems to the author to have an emotional tinge almost compelling a negative reply: "Would you favor or oppose a state law which would require employes to work alongside persons of any race or color?" was less favorable. Only 34% of those queried nationally replied in the affirmative, 56 per cent opposed and 10 per cent had no opinion. It must be recognized that many of those queried would never be required to work in this fashion, and the question seems to suggest compulsory service.

PART III

The Factor of Communication

CHAPTER 12   *Selling the Public*

• PRESS   • RADIO   • LITERATURE   • MASS MEET-
INGS   • RESOLUTIONS   • SPECIAL EVENTS TECH-
NIQUE   • GENERAL EDUCATIONAL WORK

WINNING A PRESSURE CAMPAIGN INVOLVES SKILL-
ful and careful planning upon several fronts. Especially is this
true when the issue is relatively new and has aroused the active
opposition of powerful forces. In addition to mobilizing immediately
potential supporters, leaders of a campaign for enactment of controversial legislation must carry their fight to the general public.

In the case of the FEPC movement, resources were too limited and
the struggle too swift to permit careful refinement of activities to
stimulate support by the development of specialized appeals. Consequently, this chapter which is devoted to the National Council's
efforts to persuade the country will not, for the most part, differentiate between techniques employed to activate potential supporters
and those designed to secure a friendly response from the general
public.

PRESS

It has become a standard technique for pressure groups to seek favorable newspaper coverage. Despite the inroads made by the radio,
cinema, and other media in recent years, the press has remained the
most important single source of information on public affairs. It is
especially potent in molding public opinion on new issues with which
the public lacks familiarity. Furthermore, a pressure group's budg-
etary problems are eased if it secures the free press coverage which
pursues newsworthy items.

The National Council for a Permanent FEPC sought through various devices to make use of the press of the country in its campaign.[1]

---

1. Experienced publicists subdivide the press into local daily newspapers, weekly
papers, community or neighborhood papers, the labor, Negro and foreign language

Materials were placed in the hands of influential columnists in the hope that they would be given space in the latter's widely syndicated columns. Frequent use was made of press releases and press conferences to spotlight news favorable to the cause. To enhance the prestige of the movement, statements of support by prominent national figures and accounts of testimony before legislative committees by leaders of national organizations who favored the legislation were released. Educational items showing the need for FEPC and clarifying the coverage and procedure of the proposed commission were also made available. Finally, for the information and morale of FEPC supporters, news concerning the work of the National Council and optimistic items on the bill's progress were released through this outlet.

It is commonly recognized that much waste accompanies the use of this technique. The press releases of one group today must compete with those of hundreds of others; only when the editorial policy of a newspaper supports an issue or is not antagonistic to it can the pressure group have any reasonable assurance that its material will be used. As a consequence the pressure group's major task is to make the press receptive to the point of view which it is seeking to promote. In this the National Council had mixed success; Negro papers and the liberal white press were easily brought into camp, but the great bulk of white newspapers and periodicals remained standoffish if not antagonistic.

The Negro press has traditionally lacked objectivity in matters concerning the Negro race.[2] Because of the environment within which they work Negro newspapermen tend to evaluate events almost solely

---

press, newspaper columnists, the wire services, and magazines. Each type of paper, and individual papers within each group, may require different approaches and services.

2. See Frederick G. Detweiler, *The Negro Press in the United States*. According to the Bureau of the Census, the Negro press included 164 active newspapers in 1944. Although 58, or 35.4 per cent, of these publications were accounted for by 20 cities, 34 states and the District of Columbia were represented in the total. Of Negro newspapers 144, making reports for the year ending June 30, 1943, accounted for a combined average net circulation of 1,613,255 per issue. Of the 105 Negro magazines and bulletins reporting in 1943, 79 claimed a combined average net circulation of 1,850,378 per issue. Also, at least 15 news-gathering agencies were operated by Negroes in 1943. Four of these each served 40 or more newspapers with a combined circulation of one-half million or more. One distributed releases to 57 papers with a combined circulation of 947,000.—*Negro Newspapers and Periodicals in the United States: 1943*, Negro Statistical Bulletin No. 1, U. S. Department of Commerce, Bureau of the Census, August, 1944, p. 1.

in terms of their impact upon their race. The desire for advancement of the race breeds a never-ending crusade for issues deemed to benefit Negroes and against those regarded as injurious to them. While little doubt existed concerning the position which the Negro press would assume on FEPC, nevertheless, the National Council had to win support for its legislative strategy in competition with the strategy advocated by other groups already discussed. Furthermore the National Council sought to feed educational material to the Negro papers and to use their columns to activate readers to contribute money and to send communications to Congress urging passage of the pending legislation.

From time to time the National Council sent out specific requests to Negro papers and news-gathering agencies, treating them as active collaborators in the campaign to put FEPC legislation across rather than as objective dispensers of news. For example, in July 1945, members of the National Negro Press Association were asked to consider:

1. Publishing each week beginning now a list of the Representatives in your area who have not signed the discharge petition and asking your readers to visit them and urge them to promise to sign upon their return to Washington? Asking your readers, also, in the same section, to get commitments to the bill from their Senators and Representatives, and commitments for cloture from their Senators?

2. Printing the following, in little fillers throughout your paper: "Has your representative signed the FEPC petition?" "Is your Senator committed to vote for cloture for FEPC?"

3. Publishing editorials from time to time, based on the results of interviews with local political leadership and area Representatives and Senators, on the Bill, Petition and Cloture?

4. Making a special effort to give publicity to the community activities of the Local Councils for Permanent FEPC where they exist in the area of your coverage?[3]

The response of the Negro papers and news-gathering services to this and similar appeals was usually good. Big city papers such as the *Chicago Defender*, *Pittsburgh Courier*, *Baltimore Afro-American*, *Los Angeles Sentinel*, and others, while sometimes critical of National Council leadership, gave the FEPC issue primacy over all others in their news coverage.

---

3. Letter from Mrs. Anna Arnold Hedgeman, July 27, 1945.

Beyond this the Negro press functioned as a pressure group in generating public and congressional support for the legislation. *Manuscript* reported that the Negro Newspaper Publishers Association threw its weight behind FEPC and urged support of those congressmen, regardless of party affiliation, who pledged their support to the pending bill.[4] Claude A. Barnett wrote letters in the name of the Associated Negro Press to twenty congressmen from Indiana and Illinois asking for signatures on the House discharge petition to permit the FEPC bill to reach the floor for a vote.[5] In California, Leon H. Washington, Jr., publisher of the *Los Angeles Sentinel*, sought to exert pressure upon Chairman Robert E. Hannegan of the Democratic National Committee by threatening withdrawal of support in future elections:

The California Negro Newspaper Publishers Association with a membership of 12 Negro newspapers printed throughout the state with a circulation of over 150,000 has requested that I as president secure a statement from you concerning the information received here that the National Democratic Committee is using little and practically no effort in securing the passage of permanent FEPC bill. Your action in this matter will affect the support of our Association in the 1948 election, Congressional, Senatorial and Presidential.[6]

Negro newspapermen in Washington could always be depended upon to send home enthusiastic accounts of the FEPC fight. Harry McAlpin, Mrs. Venice Spraggs, Joe Shepherd, and other reporters for large newspapers and syndicates followed the FEPC fight avidly and filled their dispatches with details unavailable in most white newspapers. On at least one occasion the sympathies of the Negro reporters in Washington caused them to venture unsuccessfully into the field of lobbying to forestall a President's Committee hearing which they felt would antagonize southern representatives and thus endanger the permanent FEPC bill. Later the *Chicago Defender* rapped their knuckles with the following comments:

Those long-faced frightened Negro reporters in Washington, who predicted a dire fate for the Permanent FEPC bill if and when the com-

---

4. April 16, 1945.
5. August 22, 1945.
6. January 1, 1946.

mittee holds the Capital Transit Company hearings must be rather put out these days.

The probe of the stubborn D.C. transportation outfit, which insists that only white men can operate street cars and buses, has come and gone. Nothing cataclysmic has occurred as yet to threaten the permanent FEPC measure any more than it has in the past.

That little bloc of Negro newsmen in Washington, who abandoned their typewriters for the nonce to stick their noses into lobbying and attempted to sidetrack the probe, should take wisdom from the misdirection of their predictions regarding the effect of the hearing.

Much as they would like to make the news, their job still remains solely to report it.

It is to be hoped that in the future they leave politics to the professionals. In their little venture on the FEPC probe, they have shown themselves strictly amateurs.[7]

Some of the Negro papers and reporters, especially the leftish *New York Peoples' Voice* and Ralph Matthews of the *Baltimore Afro-American*, sided with the critics of the National Council and attacked both Randolph and Mrs. Hedgeman for their failure to work more closely with other organizations and criticized the National Council's legislative strategy. After the Senate defeat in 1946, criticism of the National Council reached a new high. On the issue itself, however, there was virtually no division among the Negro papers.

In contrast with the excellent coverage of most northern Negro newspapers, the southern Negro press was not nearly so effective in informing its readers on FEPC developments and did little to interest them in an active pressure campaign. The *mores* of the South probably had something to do with it, but the generally poor quality of the southern Negro press was perhaps the chief reason for its failure to keep up with its northern counterpart. Mrs. Douglas, the National Council's southern field representative, complained in this connection:

As I go along, I've been noticing that the local weekly papers (Negro) have very little about FEPC (just what McAlpin sends out, and all of them don't use that). We're getting publicity in the *Courier* and the *Defender* and the *Afro*, which is excellent where they go but when you leave Carolina you leave the *Afro*, and the local papers are the ones that shape the thinking of the local people and stimulate them to action. For example, in New Orleans we never bothered about space in the *Courier*,

7. February 3, 1945.

but used the local *Weekly*. Most of these local papers know nothing about the bill or the Council, so we don't get the kind of publicity we need.[8]

Jackson Valtair, active in Texas FEPC work, echoed these sentiments when he made the following point in explaining the lethargic campaign in many Texan cities:

[There is] poor support for the National Council program on the part of the Negro Press, at least that section of it which is most read locally, the Informer chain. We have found it very difficult to secure adequate news coverage on our local council activities. In two instances, although the rabid *Dallas News* carried stories on local council programs, the Negro Press didn't even mention them. Many of our releases have been misplaced or lost. As a final illustration, the *Dallas Express* carried its first and only account of the Washington Conference. The *Express* account was sketchy and inaccurate. It did not print our local release on the conference at all.[9]

The non-Negro minority press was also in the FEPC column because of the applicability of the legislation to its readers, but the degree of coverage and the intensity of interest varied considerably from group to group. Catholic newspapers and periodicals with an estimated circulation of 8,000,000, together with more than 150 Jewish newspapers and periodicals, gave the most frequent and favorable attention to the movement in their columns. On the other hand, the nationality press took but a limited interest in FEPC. Spanish-American newspapers, for example, while favorable to FEPC in principle, almost completely ignored the issue in their columns. The National Council's failure to evolve a special minority press campaign was costly in this area.

The general white press was even more difficult to convince. A handful of large northern metropolitan dailies such as the *New York Post*, *PM*, and the *Chicago Sun* supported the FEPC movement vigorously and gave ample coverage to the work being carried on in its behalf. An additional number of northern papers gave editorial support to the efforts to defeat the 1946 Senate filibuster, not because all favored the proposed legislation, but rather because of general anti-

8. Douglas, Field Report, May 20, 1945.
9. Letter, September 22, 1945.

pathy to the use of the filibuster device by a minority of the Senate to halt the work of that body.[10]

For the most part, however, the northern press took little cognizance of the pressure movement until the spectacular legislative battles hurtled FEPC into national prominence. Virtually no inroads were made into the "slick" magazine field which provides leisure reading for millions of Americans. On the local community level the white press customarily relegated announcements of local council activities to the least desirable space or, more frequently, refused to print them at all.[11] Most editors regarded FEPC as merely another Negro movement and, therefore, of limited news interest.

Because newspapers are also business enterprises, it was inevitable that some would oppose FEPC as a restraint upon the freedom of an employer to choose his workers without government interference.[12] Editorials on this theme appeared in many parts of the country. For example, the *Fort Wayne News-Sentinel* pursued this approach vigorously:

There is a bill before the House of Representatives which, if it ever becomes law, will do more to create racial hatred in this country than anything that has happened since the days of Negro slavery. . . . If the bill were to pass, the bureau would be telling every employer that he had to employ one-fifth or one-fourth of his workers from the ranks of colored persons.

It presumably could also tell him that he would have to hire a certain number of Chinese, and a certain number of Filipinos. The probable outcome of this sort of thing is easy to imagine. Furthermore, there have

---

10. On the other hand, some self-proclaimed newspaper friends of the legislation, such as the *Washington Post*, took the National Council and others to task for making a prolonged fight in the Senate while many bills of "more urgent nature" were awaiting action early in 1946.

11. Most local publicity came through the Negro press, handbills, newsletters, and similar outlets. Co-Chairman C. L. Sharpe of the Cleveland Council described the local situation as follows: "I wish to assure you that despite the lethargy and outright antagonism of the three daily newspapers in Cleveland toward the FEPC we are attempting by word of mouth, by letters, postal cards, mobile public address service, notice to churches and the organizations, both white and Negro to build a good meeting for us on the 29th of January."—Letter, January 10, 1946.

12. "The extent of favorable newspaper publicity given to certain interest groups is, of course, conditioned by the fact that the newspaper itself is a commercial enterprise and frequently, therefore, has a stake in legislation."—Belle Zeller, *Pressure Politics in New York*, p. 233.

been reports from some of the keener observers in Washington that the social planners, if the FEPC bill were to become law, would use it to enforce the employment of a specified ratio of Communists.[13]

Virtually no inroads were made into the southern white press. The racial pattern of the area was too inflexible to yield to any movement advocating the establishment of racial equality by law. Here and there, large city papers assumed a semi-friendly but cautious attitude towards FEPC; for the most part, the southern press was vituperative in its attack against the entire movement.[14] The National Council was strategically wise in its decision to ignore the South in its campaign; for it would have been impossible for a single group to have made sufficient inroads against so fixed a set of *mores* to have warranted the expenditure of energies badly needed elsewhere.

RADIO

Radio, in its relatively short life, has become one of the most eagerly sought after media of social communication in America.[15] At the same time it is expensive to use; only the more affluent interest groups can have frequent recourse to it. Groups with slender purses must depend chiefly upon the willingness of broadcasting companies and local stations to make free time available if they cannot inveigle regular sponsors into devoting programs to subjects of interest to them.

The Federal Communications Act of 1934, the rules and regulations, and the body of rulings and decisions in particular proceedings of the Federal Communications Commission, establish the right of legally qualified candidates for public office to have equal broadcasting opportunities with all other candidates on commercial or sustain-

---

13. March 3, 1945.
14. The New Orleans Council was delighted when it got an item printed in a leading newspaper and reported to the Washington office: "The enclosed clipping is from *The Times-Picayune* of May 15, and is a belated report of the endorsement of the New Orleans Committee on Race Relations. It is notable only because it is almost impossible to get news of interracial matters inserted. It was on the page devoted to radio news and comics and therefore very satisfactorily located."—Letter from Mary B. Allen, Secretary, May 21, 1945. The Fort Worth Council sought to overcome the newspaper blockade by placing literature in homes and offices for distribution.—Letter, May 31, 1945.
15. In terms of opportunities for publicity, radio may be subdivided into local stations, networks, and commentators; the various program channels range from such outlets as newscasts and forums to youth, farm, and women's programs.

ing time.[16] Access by impecunious pressure groups to the air, however, is not well-protected by the above act, rules and administrative decisions. Each radio station is required to set aside a certain proportion of its time for free, sustaining, non-commercial programs as a community service. Yet even this requirement does not guarantee radio time for all interested groups; the station manager is permitted considerable discretion in allocating sustaining time because of the large number of requests. Only when the manager permits one side, but refuses the other, time to present their views and opinions does ground exist for complaints to the FCC. Many managers play it safe by refusing to give hearings to either side on a controversial issue.

The National Council for a Permanent FEPC had infrequent direct access to radio. It was almost entirely dependent upon the limited largesse of the networks and local stations. On several occasions national networks were persuaded to carry discussions of FEPC as part of their public service program with Randolph, Mrs. Hedgeman, Congressman Charles M. LaFollette, and other proponents of FEPC as participants. Most of the discussions took the form of debates or forums with an effort on the part of the broadcasting company to give a balanced picture on the issue. Nevertheless, it gave the National Council the opportunity to air its views to a broader public than was ordinarily available to it.

Cooperating organizations also set aside some of their radio programs for FEPC discussions. The CIO devoted one of its "Labor USA" programs on May 5, 1945, to this subject which was carried by WJZ and the Columbia Broadcasting System. In 1945 a series of Protestant-Catholic-Jewish discussions of FEPC stressing the need for enactment of permanent legislation was staged over WQXR, New York, under the auspices of the National Conference of Christians and Jews. In the same year the New York Metropolitan Council on FEPC sponsored a series of twenty-four broadcasts over WEVD aimed at educating the public on FEPC and stimulating support for national, state, and local agencies working for fair employment practices.

Local adjuncts of the National Council also made limited use of the radio in their work. One of their jobs was to cajole local stations

---

16. See, for example, FCC Rules and Regulations, Part 3 and WDSU Case (Docket No. 6740) as reported in F.C.C. News Release, September 5, 1945, No. 84582.

into airing occasional national FEPC broadcasts. The results of their efforts were mixed; correspondence from local councils reveals that radio stations in New York, Minneapolis, Wichita, Buffalo, and other northern cities were fairly cooperative. On the other hand very few southern stations carried the broadcasts. Even some of the northern stations, fearing the controversial aspects of FEPC, refused to comply with local council requests on the ground that they had failed to carry previous broadcasts against FEPC and deemed it unfair to present only the favorable side.[17]

Efforts to obtain time for local FEPC broadcasts met with scattered successes.[18] In Buffalo a local station gave time for spot announcements advertising a play sponsored by the local council to raise money for the FEPC movement.[19] WWJ, Detroit's NBC affiliate, carried a five minute speech by Senator Wayne Morse (Rep. Ore.) on April 21, 1946, to open the city's "FEPC Week" and the local council's fund-raising drive. The East St. Louis Council was able to obtain coverage of part of a local mass meeting by local station WTMV.[20]

To assist the local affiliates to make the best use of whatever radio

---

17. A study of techniques used by pressure groups to gain access to the so-called free press, radio, and other avenues of communication would be very revealing of how difficult the task of reaching the public has become for the average reform movement.

"When your wire came on the Broadcast with LaFollette I called the Station that carries the American network and they told me they were not planning on carrying the Broadcast so I started hunting around to get a lead to the Manager and finally late Thursday afternoon Gloster Current located Judge Watts who agreed to do the job for us, he called back and said he had; we had 45 minutes to make the deadline on the Friday papers so some of us got some Reporters on the phone and they agreed to release a notice for us. I listened to WXYZ from ten to twelve P.M. and your broadcast did not come through so I called the Program Manager Saturday morn and he told me the person that had told Judge Watts they would carry the Program had no authority to do so and furthermore there had been a previous Broadcast against FEPC which they had not carried so they did not think it was a good policy for them to carry the Broadcast for FEPC. We straightened ourselves out with the Reporters but otherwise we messed the job up for you."—Letter from Laura Davidovich, Secretary, Detroit Council for a Permanent FEPC to Mrs. Hedgeman, August 3, 1945.

18. "*Persistence Pays Off.* Keep in constant contact with your radio stations and try to interest them in any speakers you may have. If they get to know you well, eventually, you may be able to spot an occasional program, speech, or, at the least, some radio announcements on FEPC. If you have good acting talent in your community, you might be able to interest your radio station in a short series of programs dramatizing evils resulting from unfair employment practices. Your National Council will be glad to add ideas along these lines, if you request them, and allow sufficient time."—*Manual of Strategy,* p. 11.

19. April 1, 1946.

20. June 1, 1945.

time they could secure, the National Council prepared a few scripts
and recordings. For example, when Congresswoman Helen Gahagan
Douglas (Dem. Calif.) debated the desirability of permanent national
FEPC legislation with newspaperwoman Mrs. George Mero, who was
opposed to FEPC, on the Esther Tufty program over the American
Broadcasting Company on October 31, 1945, the National Council
made a recording of the debate which was made available to local
councils and interested organizations at cost. A fifteen minute script
entitled "The Right to Work" was prepared by the National Council
and was also available upon request. On one or more occasions, spot
announcements were written for local councils.[21]

In the end, radio was of little importance in the National Council's
campaign. This area was neglected because the Washington office
lacked specialists in the radio field who could obtain free sustaining
time and who could prepare scripts which would help to sell the
issue. The broadcasts which did go out were too infrequent to make
much impression upon the general public.[22] Only in a few cases where
the local supporters were able to purchase time or get a generous
sponsor to surrender some of his time was it possible to do much by
way of urging public pressure upon Congress over the air.[23]

LITERATURE

Pamphlets, leaflets, and posters are important in a pressure campaign where new political ideas are advanced and, more particularly,

---

21. Also Washington and network commentators were sent data on FEPC and
letters urging favorable comments on the issue.

22. Only in New York State during the fight for state FEPC is there any record
of a well-conducted radio campaign: "Many of the upper State stations have already
done quite a bit of work on the discrimination question, particularly those in the
vicinity of the capital where the fight was waged in favor of the legislation.

"This includes the stations of WABY, Albany, WTRY, Troy, and WGY and
WSNY, Schenectady. There has been a regular series of broadcasts over the Albany
airlanes during the past season which will be resumed in the fall. Many of the programs included representatives from the three major faiths and various Negro speakers.
Most recent airing to the discrimination question was given over the Union College's
"Town Meeting" over WGY during its final program of the season, when race issues
were brought to the light of day."—*Pittsburgh Courier*, July 21, 1945.

23. During the crisis involving the appropriation for the President's Committee in
June 1945, for example, the Detroit Metropolitan Council sponsored three 150 word
spot announcements each evening over Station WJLB, calling upon listeners to wire
some specific person in Congress or with influence on the national scene.—Letter from
Executive Secretary Charles Anderson to Mrs. Hedgeman, July 5, 1945.

where strong political action is advocated.[24] The reluctance of the general press to give favorable coverage to most campaigns aiming at reform of the existing order makes the use of special literature indispensable as a means of reaching the public. Furthermore, special literature accomplishes ends which the press and radio do not: it has the advantages of concentration and partiality. The pamphlet or leaflet devotes itself, if properly prepared, to the presentation of a single issue and is therefore likely to make a more lasting impression than a newspaper item read along with many others. Pamphlets and leaflets make no attempt to be objective but aim rather to put across a given point of view and to promote action. The press and radio can seldom be used so advantageously.

Effective use of literature is an art involving knowledge of: 1) the subject and how to express it simply, interestingly, and convincingly; 2) the intended audience; and 3) the technique and expense of publication and distribution. For these reasons, it is highly desirable that the responsibility for the preparation of literature be in the hands of a specialist.

The movement for a permanent FEPC was not noteworthy for the excellence of its literature. In fact the movement made rather poor use of this medium of social communication. Only a few original pamphlets and leaflets were prepared and distributed by the National Council. At least two of the leaflets had as their major objectives the solicitation of funds and support from the general public. The first sought to explain the work of the President's Committee and how the National Council was seeking to make the Committee permanent.[25] The other was devoted to recounting the history of the FEPC movement, ending with February 1945, on the note that funds and letters to Congress were necessary to win the battle for the bill sponsored by the National Council.[26]

The final major item of original literature was a pamphlet, first mimeographed and finally printed in 1946, entitled *Answer the Critics*, containing arguments most frequently used for and against

---

24. The following general discussion of literature is based upon the *Manual of Practical Political Action*, National Citizens Political Action Committee, edited by Lewis C. Frank, Jr. and Ralph E. Shikes, 1946, pp. 11-17.
25. *A Permanent FEPC—Let's Work Together*, 1944.
26. *A Permanent Fair Employment Practice Commission*, 1945.

federal permanent FEPC legislation. It sought to answer such questions as: 1) Can the public welfare be fully served without an FEPC law? 2) What is its effect on business? 3) Is it a good public investment? 4) What about administration and enforcement? and 5) What about constitutionality? Typical sections of the pamphlet contain such pro and con arguments as:

AGAINST—Prejudice is an attitude, and attitudes cannot be changed by law any more than the Prohibition Law changed the drinking attitudes of the *nation.*

FOR—This law has nothing to do with prejudice itself; it merely seeks to prevent the manifestations of prejudice of one person from inflicting themselves upon the economic life of another, within the limits of federal jurisdiction in employment. FEPC is related to prejudice only as laws forbidding driving while drunk are related to driving.[27]

AGAINST—The mere existence of FEPC would encourage every unsuccessful candidate for a job to presume discrimination, and to harass and involve business and unions in unjustifiable and costly litigation with FEPC.

FOR—Absence of discrimination is equally easy to prove. Trained investigators can screen out and dismiss groundless charges without formal proceedings, and sometimes even without contact with the persons accused. Herein lies one of the greatest advantages of having an administrative agency on hand to protect management as well as employees. The wartime FEPC dismissed as groundless two-thirds of all complaints filed with it.[28]

Much of the literature distributed by the Washington office was not original with it but was reprinted from other sources. Favorable columns by Thomas L. Stokes, Dorothy Norman, and Lowell Mellett and editorials from the *Washington Post* and other newspapers were reprinted and distributed. Considerable use was made of such magazine articles as: "Prejudice: Our Postwar Battle" from *Look,*[29] "Whites and Blacks *Can* Work Together" from the *Reader's Digest;*[30] "Catholics and the FEPC Case" from *Catholic Action;*[31] "The Negro, His Future in America" from the *New Republic;*[32] and "Our Con-

27. p. 1.
28. p. 9.
29. May 1, 1945.
30. By William Hard, March 1944.
31. By Reverend George Higgins, January 1944.
32. Special supplement, October 18, 1943.

flicting Racial Policies" from *Harper's Magazine*.[33] Frequent recourse was made to reprints from the *Congressional Record* containing speeches and articles favorable to FEPC. Not a few of these speeches were written by National Council staff members and placed in the hands of friendly congressmen. Articles were planted in the *Record* to make up for the lack of publicity outlets in the press and radio.[34] Even technical law articles were reprinted by the National Council and distributed where it was felt they would do the most good.[35]

Finally, some of the more effective literature was supplied by other organizations interested in the passage of FEPC legislation. Excellent posters were prepared by the Anti-Defamation League of B'nai B'rith. The Workers Defense League published a pamphlet by Winifred Raushenbush entitled *Jobs Without Creed or Color*; the Postwar World Council, James Rorty's pamphlet, *Brother Jim Crow*; the American Jewish Congress, several pamphlets by Rabbi J. X. Cohen, including *Who Discriminates and How?*; the Council for Democracy, *On the Color Line*; and many other groups also published leaflets and pamphlets.

While there was no quantitative lack of literature, its effectiveness was not great. Most of the pamphlets fell into the same general mold of appeals to fair play and presentation of the costs of discrimination to minorities and to the country at large which, while good themes, do not exhaust the possibilities of propaganda appeals. Most of the literature was too verbose, sacrificing simplicity for coverage. Very little was done to differentiate the appeals so that farmers, businessmen, professional men, veterans, and others would feel that FEPC would be advantageous to them. Even the channels of distribution were limited so that much of the literature fell into the hands of those who needed little convincing on the subject of FEPC legislation.

---

33. By Will W. Alexander, January 1945.

34. Representative Mary T. Norton's (Dem. N.J.) speech on April 27, 1945, "Questions and Answers About Permanent Fair Employment Practice Commission," was an important item of National Council literature. Typical of planted articles was Senator David I. Walsh's (Dem. Mass.) "FEPC: A Challenge to Democracy," actually a reprint of an article by the same name written by Father Richard J. Roche, published originally in *America*, April 14, 1945.

35. Bruce A. Hunt, "The Proposed Fair Employment Practice Act: Facts and Fallacies," reprinted from *Virginia Law Review*, 32, No. 1 (December 1945), 1-38. Abraham Wilson, "The Proposed Legislative Death Knell of Private Discriminatory Employment Practices," reprinted from *Virginia Law Review*, 31, No. 4 (September 1945), 798-811.

MASS MEETINGS

The mass meeting is a traditional device used by protest groups to build *esprit de corps*, to raise money, and to focus public attention upon their demands. While the effectiveness of mass meetings is disputed in some circles, protest movements continue to repose considerable confidence in their efficacy. The mass meeting has many dangers as well as potential advantages. Unless headline speakers are used or a good show put on they tend to reach only those people who are already sold and while the supporters may thus be stirred to greater effort, they may also be left discouraged. A small turnout at a meeting that was planned for a large attendance may have that result. A big meeting must be big to be successful. In addition, if it is big it must also be good—with a well-handled program. If skeptics do come they must be won over—at least part way. They must not be permitted to become even more skeptical.

The National Council for a Permanent FEPC promoted a large number of these meetings.[36] In this the hand of Randolph, thoroughly convinced of the desirability of mass rallies, is evident. The rallies, staged by nearly all of the local councils, conformed to a general pattern. The aim was to direct the entire program towards the promotion of FEPC legislation. All speeches were planned to have a direct bearing upon the purpose of the meeting. One or more outside speakers, not infrequently National Council leaders or sympathetic congress-

36. "MASS MEETINGS ARE IN GREAT DEMAND. . . . The people are impatient to demonstrate their will for enactment for a Permanent Fair Employment Practice Commission. . . . *They know* they must mass together their combined voices. Make this possible for your community by LAYING PLANS FOR MASS MEETINGS NOW—TO OCCUR IN JANUARY BY THE 25TH (to coincide with Senatorial pressure campaign) . . . . January may seem far away now—but it is closer than you think! Remember that speakers have crowded schedules and many advance speaking dates. Remember that Christmas shopping and holiday plans absorb a great deal of time. Remember that once you set a date ahead for a meeting, you give your group a goal towards which to work for success.

"REVIEW THE 'MANUAL OF STRATEGY,' pgs. 7-11 SET YOUR DATE AND ADVISE NATIONAL OFFICE ENGAGE THE LARGEST PUBLIC HALL YOU CAN . . . THROW OUT YOUR LINES TO PRESS AND RADIO . . . MAKE THE CALL FOR WIDEST CROSS-SECTION. . . .

"Aim for the broadest base of people representative of your community. Consult the list of cooperating organizations that appear on pgs. 18-19 of the Manual. Make sure your meeting is all American—Jewish, Negro, Catholic, Protestant, Spanish-American, Oriental-American, labor, civic, Chambers of Commerce, women's organizations and trade union in character in its fullest sense."—"News From Washington," National Council release, November 20, 1945.

men, were usually featured. Even the entertainment, often of high calibre, was often arranged to promote the over-all objective of the meeting.[37] Negro choirs sang such songs about FEPC as:

> Some say we fight a losing cause
> But God's plan they can't see
> For He has power above all laws
> And likes FEPC.[38]

The speakers nearly always found homogeneous audiences which needed no selling on the issue but wished to be reassured that legislative victory was forthcoming. Feelings were often intense; references to Senator Bilbo and other enemies of FEPC were sufficient to set off a series of boos and catcalls. The serious intent of those in attendance at a Minneapolis rally stirred Brenda Ueland, a local columnist, to write:

Deeply moved by a meeting at the Wesley Temple on Friday, the night of the ten-below-zero wind. Felt a triangular lump in the throat. I will never forget it just as I never forgot the woman suffrage meetings of my childhood—the same pathos, the same dignity, the same world-neglect offered to nobly dignified people.[39]

No rally was complete without a collection being taken up for the National Council. Most of the rallies raised several hundreds of dollars chiefly in small contributions; occasionally the cost of staging the demonstration exceeded the collections.

The National Council sought to stage rallies in every large community, timed to coincide with the peak of the legislative campaigns. While many of these rallies were held and were attended by crowds ranging from a few hundred in some communities upwards to 20,000 in New York and Chicago, there is little reason to believe that they influenced the legislators one way or the other, yet they did serve to raise the morale of FEPC supporters.

RESOLUTIONS

A technique frequently employed by the National Council was to have resolutions favoring FEPC introduced at the national and state

---

37. At one New York rally, Canada Lee, Helen Hayes, Orson Welles, and the Frieda Louise Andrews choir of 1,000 women's voices appeared in addition to a number of lesser known performers.

38. Ralph G. Martin, "FEPC Rally," *New Republic* (March 18, 1946), p. 380.

39. *Minneapolis Times*, February 16, 1946.

conventions of a wide variety of organizations. This technique served two purposes: it helped make potential supporters aware of the FEPC issue and, where successful, put organizations on record as favoring the proposed legislation which could be used to demonstrate its popularity to Congress. Field representatives were provided with lists of convention dates and were asked by the Washington office to attend as many meetings as possible. Sympathetic delegates were ferreted out and provided with resolutions already drafted by the staff members of the National Council. The response to these resolutions was mixed; church and labor organizations, already sympathetic, generally passed the resolutions while other groups were far less interested.

SPECIAL EVENTS TECHNIQUE

The special events technique was also employed. Local councils in East St. Louis, Detroit, Philadelphia, and other cities promoted "FEPC Sundays" on which ministers were asked to preach special sermons on FEPC and to take up collections for the pressure movement. In Philadelphia an "FEPC Week" was staged:

The week's program started on a Saturday. In Philadelphia there are three large civic leagues. All three were asked to sponsor and direct a Tag Day, using the starting day of the week (Saturday). All details of planning, obtaining volunteers, placement of tag collections etc. were thus put into the hands of one specific group.

The second day, Sunday, was made the responsibility of the Philadelphia Federation of Churches. The Federation's Executive Director contacted all the ministers in Philadelphia, and asked them to give a short talk on FEPC and to take up special collections when possible.

Monday was turned over to the CIO and AFL. They distributed literature and sold buttons through their locals that were meeting during the week.

Tuesday was given to the organized Women's Clubs and organizations and they held a series of church suppers, card parties, etc.

Wednesday was Fraternal Day, and the Elks staged evening parades in separate sections of Philadelphia.

Thursday was Education Day. The Youth Council of Fellowship House in cooperation with the AVC Speakers Bureau and the organized teachers' groups secured the permission from the Board of Education to give short talks on FEPC in all of the high schools in the city.

Friday, the YWCA took on the sponsorship of a large public meeting as the final episode of the week.[40]

---

40. Field Report, undated, Milo Manley, who directed FEPC Week in Philadelphia.

In some cities, it was possible to stimulate public officials to use the prestige of their offices to advance the FEPC cause. In New York and Chicago the local councils were able to get their mayors to proclaim "Fair Employment Practice Days" for their cities. The mayor of Detroit was prevailed upon to promulgate an "FEPC Week." The Board of Aldermen of St. Louis passed a resolution approving S. 101. In Stamford, Connecticut, the mayor was induced to write the governor in behalf of a state FEPC law. However, these scattered examples of official approval were not representative of the reactions of the vast number of public officials who were yet to be convinced of the desirability of FEPC or of the strength of its supporters.

GENERAL EDUCATIONAL WORK

Educational work, in the customary sense of the term, was not highly developed. Debates, forums, and workshops were contrived in the larger cities. The Birmingham Council held educational meetings throughout the city and the Lycoming County, Pennsylvania Council established a twenty-member speakers' panel for the same purpose. Nearly all of the councils distributed the literature sent them by the Washington office. Beyond this there was a minimum of popular educational activity. Education suffered because the National Council stressed political action in the hope that a quick legislative victory could be won. The results of the campaign through the summer of 1948 made manifest the need for more mass education on such a new issue as FEPC.

CHAPTER 13 *Political Communication*

• REPUBLICAN LEADERSHIP AND FEPC •DEMO-
CRATIC PARTY AND FEPC • 1944 PRESIDENTIAL
CAMPAIGN • WHITE HOUSE • USE OF NEGRO
REPUBLICANS • LINING UP INDIVIDUAL CON-
GRESSMEN • LOCAL PRESSURES • USE OF LOCAL
BOSSES

R EPRESENTATIVE GOVERNMENT DEPENDS FOR ITS
proper functioning upon adequate opportunities for individuals
and groups to communicate their political aspirations to their
representatives in office. Nearly all groups find it expedient to express
their views to the legislative and executive branches in the hope of
securing government assistance in furthering group objectives and
of forestalling opposition efforts to thwart or injure their progress.
With the increasing complexity of modern life and the multiplication
of group interests, competition for access to the ears of those who
determine public policy has been mounting. The techniques for com-
municating with legislators and executives have, through trial and
error, become fairly standardized. Successful use of these techniques
depends, in part, upon the employer's skill in selecting approaches
which will meet the needs of the immediate situation, his comprehen-
sion of the total environment within which public officials work and
his ability to convince the officials through both rational and emotional
pleas. In large measure, however, the power relationship of the group
to the individual official and the party organizations is more important
in making for success or failure of a pressure effort; if the group can
lay claim to a sizeable bloc of votes and has funds available for
political purposes, representatives in government can usually be impressed with the validity of the case which the group presents.

The FEPC movement, not unlike most reform drives, could offer
little by way of campaign funds or direct campaign assistance to the

men who would decide the fate of FEPC legislation.[1] Lacking these strengths, positive results could be achieved only if individual congressmen and party leaders could be convinced of the desirability of the legislation from the standpoint of national interest or, even more efficacious in the arena of practical politics, by the manipulation of a threat of an "FEPC vote" which could be marshalled either for or against a candidate depending upon his stand on FEPC legislation.

Consequently, FEPC leaders sought to exploit the alleged fluidity

---

1. Requests were made of the National Council for funds or campaign assistance by Senators Tunnell (Dem. Del.), Guffey (Dem. Pa.), Chavez (Dem. N.M.) and Representative LaFollette (Rep. Ind.) in the 1946 election campaigns. But the National Council failed to satisfy any of these requests fully. While assistance was rendered to LaFollette it proved insufficient to overcome the Indiana Republican organization's opposition to LaFollette's senatorial aspirations. The following excerpts from a memorandum from a National Council legislative representative to Mrs. Hedgeman reveal something of the give and take involved in lobbying work: "While on the Hill, yesterday, Mr. Conant, who is Senator Tunnell's secretary, buttonholed me downstairs to ask if he could have a few words with me.

"He said that Senator Tunnell is now trying to come to a decision as to whether he should run again. As you know, Tunnell comes up for re-election in November and is compelled to run the gamut of the Dupont Machine in Delaware. He is now a first-termer, having won the 1940 election by a bare 4,500 votes.

"Conant said the Senator has asked him to analyze what the potentialities of his campaign might be. Apparently, the Senator is unwilling to run if he feels the cards are stacked too strongly against him and defeat is certain. Conant wanted to know what our program was in terms of the approaching elections.

"I told him exactly how we operated—that we were a strictly non-partisan org.; that we had not as yet formed any political policy where candidates are concerned. I also pointed out the efforts we make to get word to constituents as to the role and the vote of the individual Senators, through such avenues as our own mailing lists, community meetings, church groups, etc. I said I thought this would have some effect but could not possibly estimate its extent.

"Conant pointed out that there were many liberal orgs. who took a rather complacent attitude toward his excellent voting record but that such an attitude alone does not get out the vote on election day. He made it very clear that he was not looking for financial support but that he was hopeful of some concerted efforts to arouse the Negro minority in Delaware to the necessity of Tunnell's return to the Senate.

"I told Mr. Conant that we were appreciative of all that Senator Tunnell had done to help both in committee and on the floor, and that we realized it was his strong stand which helped break Buck's [Republican Senator from Delaware] resistance toward cloture. . . . I asked Conant if he thought that Tunnell would now be ready to enter a greater period of activity on the floor, such as public speaking before groups, inserting such speeches as Schwellenbach's in the *Record*, and so on. I stressed this as a necessity since superficially speaking Tunnell and Buck are now tied in the sense that each has voted for cloture. Conant indicated that he was fairly certain the Senator would undertake the role outlined."—Memorandum from Mrs. Beatrice Schalet to Mrs. Hedgeman.

of the Negro vote which was said to be wavering in its fidelity to the New Deal standard as a result of anti-Negro discrimination in the armed services and war industries. In large part, the work of the National Council on the legislative front centered upon convincing the Democratic party that it would lose the minority vote unless it took the leadership in securing the enactment of permanent FEPC legislation; at the same time, urging the Republicans to seize the initiative and reap the harvest of a grateful minority vote which would go to the party responsible for government safeguards on equal employment opportunities. This chapter is devoted to an analysis of the campaign to win the support of party leaders and individual congressmen conducted by the National Council for a Permanent FEPC and other interested individuals and groups.

REPUBLICAN LEADERSHIP AND FEPC

Republican party leaders were indeed eager to use the issue to coax minority groups over to their column in the presidential election of 1944 and again in the congressional race of 1946. Furthermore, they considered the FEPC bills to be an excellent device to divide northern and southern Democrats in Congress and thus prevent control of the legislative branch by the Roosevelt faction of the party.

But counterbalancing the above factors were others which moderated Republican leadership's enthusiasm for FEPC legislation. Foremost was the reluctance of Republican congressional leaders to antagonize the southern Democratic bloc in Congress, for the majority of Republicans were working hand in hand with southern Democrats in the period between 1942 and 1946 to thwart the legislative programs of both Presidents Roosevelt and Truman and were not sufficiently impressed with the extent of popular demand for FEPC legislation to risk giving full support to a measure which was anathema to southern congressmen.[2] Secondly, even if Republican congressional leaders could be persuaded that the Negro vote was worth endangering the inter-party working arrangement, rank and file Republicans in the national legislature, with notable exceptions, did not react favorably

2. See "The News Letter" of the Anti-Defamation League of B'nai B'rith, June, 1945; also News Release, National Council for a Permanent FEPC, II, No. 1, January 20, 1945.

to the FEPC measures. They were critical of the "New Deal" character of FEPC; they opposed the "communistic" implications involved in interfering with an employer's hiring policies and viewed with alarm the establishment of another "bureaucratic" agency.[3] Finally, many Republican congressmen were dubious whether support of FEPC would be sufficient to wean Negroes away from the New Deal.[4]

Wishing to take advantage of the vote-getting possibilities of FEPC and yet not antagonize southern Democrats and recalcitrant rank and file Republican congressmen, Republican leaders in Congress evolved a complicated and shifting strategy to meet the pressures upon their party. The principle of FEPC was endorsed by them, but specific provisions in the bill, especially the parts dealing with administrative procedure in the proposed quasi-judicial agency, were assailed by leading Republicans. Senator Taft of Ohio for a time advanced a bill of his own which would have set up an FEPC without enforcement powers.[5] Minority Leader Martin refused to apply pressures

---

3. A newspaper account of a House Republican caucus on FEPC would seem to bear out this observation: "Ninety per cent of the Republican congressmen are opposed to a permanent Fair Employment Practice Act, it was estimated today. This estimate was made by Rep. Harold Knutson (Rep. Minn.) after a caucus of Republican members of the House yesterday. Mr. Knutson is chairman of his party's steering committee in the House. Representative Charles M. LaFollette of Indiana had pleaded with his colleagues for permanent FEPC support. His supporters were few. Most of the members sat on their hands as he concluded his speech. At that point, Rep. John Taber (Rep. N.Y.) ran down the aisle to the speaker's microphone. There was loud applause. But Mr. Taber ignored the LaFollette plea. Instead he talked about cutbacks in appropriations. . . . Mr. LaFollette pointed out that the permanent FEPC was part of the party platform in its last presidential campaign. It was enacted into law in New York under Governor Dewey, the GOP presidential nominee.

"After Mr. Taber talked, the LaFollette stand was challenged. Rep. Ross Rizley of Oklahoma, struck out against it with gestures. He called it 'unconstitutional' and other things. His speech brought both favorable questions and applause. Later Rep. Mott of Oregon condemned a permanent FEPC in even more emphatic terms. He labelled it 'communistic.' The anti-FEPC stand seemed to have large majority support among the Republicans. Judged by the applause, the Knutson 90 per cent estimate seemed about right."—Daniel M. Kidney, Scripps-Howard staff writer, *Washington Daily News,* September 15, 1945.

4. Even when Republican House leader Joseph W. Martin, Jr. was finally lured into the FEPC camp in 1946, with the November congressional elections in the offing, he reported: "Our greatest difficulty is that in districts where the colored vote predominates, only Democrats have been elected, and that has made it difficult to arouse the enthusiasm you would normally expect among the Republicans."—Letter, Martin to Curtis H. Waterman of Boston, May 15, 1946.

5. S. 459, introduced into the first session of the Seventy-Ninth Congress.

upon individual Republicans to support the House measure, explaining to one group of FEPC supporters in 1945, when H.R. 2232 was lodged in the Rules Committee which refused to report it out, that he could not lead the drive to force the bill out to the floor "without specific authorization" from the Republican House Conference.[6] As the campaign unfolded, it became apparent that the Republican leaders further sought to make certain that the bill would come to the floor first in the Senate where they hoped that a southern Democratic filibuster would make a House vote unnecessary, thus sparing many Republicans from having to vote against their convictions for fear of the reaction of minority voters back home. If southern Democrats in the Senate killed the bill, Republicans could use this as an issue in the 1946 and 1948 campaigns against the Democrats.

Positive Republican support of the measure in the House did not come until it was obvious that the National Council had decided in December 1945 to aim for Senate action first. This decision made possible the following House Republican announcement: "We believe that equality of opportunity should be available to all, regardless of race, creed, or beginning. Every individual should be afforded an opportunity to prosper according to his talents, his ability and his diligence subject only to a like right for his neighbor."[7] When queried as to whether this meant that House Republicans would act on the bill after the first of the year, minority leader Martin replied, "I think that it is quite possible that the legislation will be acted upon in Febru-

---

6. At this meeting Martin also indicated that he felt that the party's 1944 pledge had been wiped out by the defeat at the polls in November.—*PM*, June 26, 1945.

7. According to the National Council's legislative representative in the House, Ida Fox, the circumstances which preceded this commitment involved: "First, there had been the cumulative pressure of rank and file Republicans. Second, there had been an unfavorable reaction to the failure of the Republican National Committee Chicago Meeting to take positive action on FEPC. Third, there had been the break of organized labor and the minorities with the President; for the first time since President Roosevelt was elected, the Administration began to feel it no longer had the labor and minority vote in its pocket; and for the first time the Republicans began to feel perhaps there was a chance they could win at least the Negro and Jewish vote. Fourth was the fact that on November 23 we had initiated our campaign for immediate Senate action. Every member of the House is up for re-election this year, and if the Republicans are to achieve their goal of control of the House, they will have to hold their own and capture about 30 seats from Democrats in urban areas who have signed."—Minutes of the Executive Committee, January 3, 1946.

ary or the first of March. That is giving it a little leeway."[8] Even this
commitment was not sufficient. By June 1946 only 73 of the 190
Republicans in the House had signed the discharge petition.[9] The
combination of defeat in the Senate in February 1946 and the lack
of party cohesion on the issue prevented fulfillment of Martin's
promise.

DEMOCRATIC PARTY AND FEPC

The schism in the Democratic party, apparent as early as 1938, was
largely a split between "New Dealers" and conservatives over the role
of the national government in the economic and social life of the
country. In its geographical aspect it also proved to be a split between
northern Democrats representing the liberal branch of the party and
southern Democrats who, with outstanding exceptions, opposed the
Roosevelt leadership of the party. In the 1940's, despite nominal
Democratic control of Congress, southern Democrats found far more
in common with the conservatives of the Republican party than they
did with their northern brethren and cooperated across party lines to
block New Deal measures.

The FEPC issue burst upon the scene in the midst of this party
split and served to widen the breach. Because of its objectives it was
to be expected that it would arouse the fierce antagonism of the southern delegations in Congress which did not have to answer to Negro
voters.[10] On the other hand, Democrats from the North, in most cases

---

8. Memorandum on telephone conversation between Martin and Ida Fox of the
National Council, January 1946.

9. Since there is no official announcement of the names of petition signers, this
number is based upon an unofficial list gathered by friendly congressmen for the
National Council.

10. Despite the fact that Democratic control of Congress depended upon holding
the low income minority vote in large northern cities, during the 1946 filibuster
southern senators expressed their hope that Negroes would go back to the Republican party:

Eastland (Dem. Miss.): "Does not the Senator from Louisiana think that the
Negro voter makes a grave mistake in voting the Democratic ticket?"

Overton (Dem. La.): "I certainly think so. I think that for a short term of political
advantage the Negro made a very bad bargain. I think the Negro ought to have stood
by, and I think the Negro today ought to stand by, the great party which has been
the Negro's friend since the day of the Emancipation Proclamation by Abraham
Lincoln up to the present time. I believe the Negro made a mistake when he yielded
his friendship for the party which had stood by him through thick and thin in return
for the aid which has been given to him during the last few years."—*Congressional
Record*, January 17, 1946, 79th Congress, Second Session, p. 92.

representing large metropolitan communities where the minority vote was important, found support of FEPC advisable.[11]

Democratic leaders in Congress found themselves in a difficult position. While they recognized the need for pacifying Negro demands, they feared to further antagonize the South. The result was that they straddled and ignored the issue wherever possible. In 1945 FEPC was omitted from the Democratic legislative program. In the same year party leaders effected a compromise on the appropriation for the temporary President's Committee which was satisfactory to no one but temporarily removed the issue as an intra-party irritant.[12] When pressure for congressional action upon the permanent FEPC measure began to mount in late 1945, Democratic leaders sought to effect the reverse of Republican strategy—it was their hope that the bill would come up first in the House of Representatives, thus forcing the Republicans to take a stand. If a number of Republican representatives voted with the southern Democrats the bill could be killed without going to the Senate where threatened use of the filibuster would focus public attention upon the Democratic party as being responsible for defeat of FEPC.

However, when a coalition of liberal Republicans and Democrats signified their willingness to lead an all-out fight in the Senate in January 1946, the National Council gave its approval to a "Senate first" campaign which fell in with Republican strategy. The anticipated filibuster did eventuate and succeeded in preventing a vote on FEPC when the attempt to secure cloture failed by a vote of 48 to 36, 8 fewer than the requisite two-thirds. Of those favoring cloture, 22 were northern Democrats, 25 were Republicans and 1 was a Progressive. Paired in favor of the bill were 2 Democrats and 4 Republicans; 1 absent Democrat was recorded as favoring cloture. Of the 36 negative votes, 19 came from southern Democrats, 9 from northern Democrats and 8 from Republicans. By this time the party situation was so confused that it could be said that neither party wished to see FEPC legislation on the books and that both shared the responsibility for its defeat.[13]

---

11. Approximately 105 of the 125 odd northern Democrats in the House signed Petition No. 4 to discharge the FEPC bill from the Rules Committee in the Seventy-Ninth Congress.

12. See Chapter I, *supra*.

13. ". . . filibusters have been broken without invoking the cloture rule. The

1944 PRESIDENTIAL CAMPAIGN

A familiar technique used to secure passage of desired legislation is to demand definite commitments from parties and candidates during the course of election campaigns in exchange for promise of support. While a commitment does not assure enactment of a proposal, it makes negative action more difficult. Hence the scramble by pressure groups for favorable platform planks and open support by candidates. Parties and candidates, on their side, are tempted to promise the sky in the hope of winning the election, even though they are aware of a day of reckoning.

As the 1944 Presidential campaign opened, Negro leaders sought to impress both major parties with the fact that the Negro voter no longer "belonged" to either party but:

. . . will judge political parties, as well as candidates, by their words and deeds as to whether they show a determination to work for full citizenship status for thirteen million American Negroes and to better the lot of all disadvantaged peoples. Political parties and candidates that seek the votes of Negroes must be committed to the wholehearted prosecution of the war to total victory, must agree to the elimination of the poll tax by Act of Congress, the passage of anti-lynching legislation, the unsegregated integration of Negroes into the armed forces, the establishment of a permanent Federal Committee on Fair Employment Practices, and a foreign policy of international cooperation that promotes economic and political security for all peoples.

The votes of Negroes cannot be purchased by distributing money to and through party hacks. They cannot be won by pointing to jobs given a few individual Negroes. . . . Negroes are no longer persuaded by meaningless generalities in party platforms which are promptly forgotten on election day.[14]

---

friends of FEPC made only half-hearted attempts to break this one. The struggle against the filibuster seemed to many political observers a sham, if not a fraud. The supporters of the FEPC on both sides of the aisle conducted the fight in a Marquis of Queensbury atmosphere. Every courtesy was extended to the opposition and no effort put forth to make their task more difficult. To many, the struggle of the FEPC bloc seemed almost like a political chore, a disagreeable duty to be got over with as soon as possible. A flabby majority could not expect to beat down a determined filibuster.—Will Maslow, "FEPC—A Case History in Parliamentary Maneuver," *University of Chicago Law Review*, 13, No. 4 (June 1946), 440-41.

14. Quarter page advertisement appearing in the *Pittsburgh Courier*, July 1, 1944, signed by officers of Negro church, fraternal, labor, civic, and educational organizations "with a total membership of more than 6,500,000."

The national conventions of the two major parties became the first objective of the pro-FEPC forces.[15] Seeking platform recognition for Negroes at the Republican convention were Walter White, Walter Hardin of the United Mine Workers, Maynard E. Jackson of Dallas, Texas, Randolph, and National Committeeman Robert Church of Tennessee.[16] The general theme of the Negro appeal to the platform committee was that "the colored vote holds the balance of power in a close election in seventeen States having a total of 281 electoral votes" and that the Republicans could win this bloc by taking a forthright stand on Negro demands.[17] Republican convention leaders recognized the importance of the Negro vote to the party's future by adopting a rather strong Negro plank, promising to work for a constitutional amendment to outlaw the poll tax, passage of anti-lynching, and FEPC legislation.[18]

The Democratic National Convention was thereby placed on the spot. If a strong minority plank were adopted, some of the southern delegations threatened rebellion against the national party organization.[19] If such a plank were not adopted, the Negro vote might return to its traditional moorings in the Republican party. Senator Edwin C. Johnson of Colorado grumbled that the Republicans had had no particular interest in minority groups before their convention but that they "deliberately added a permanent FEPC to their platform to embarrass the Democrats. The plank is purely mischievous."[20]

---

15. "Political platforms usually reflect the demands of those groups which political leaders deem so powerful that it is imprudent to ignore their wishes. Often platform drafters are confronted by the necessity of making a choice between diametrically opposed interests, and the outcome may be an equivocal or vague platform pronouncement. As an organized group gradually convinces the public of the desirability of its cause, the successive party declarations may become firmer, with both parties progressing toward complete acceptance of the view of the organized groups at about the same rate."—V. O. Key, *Politics Parties and Pressure Groups*, p. 210.

16. Other Negroes at the convention: Milton P. Webster, David Grant, B. F. McLaurin, Thurman Dodson, Dean Andrew Ransome, Eugene Davidson, Dr. Morris N. Ervin, Mrs. U. Grant Bailey, Mrs. Helane Wilson, Earl B. Dickerson, Reverend J. A. Winters, Reverend Archibald J. Corey, Jr., Charles Wesley Burton, Morris Lewis, and A. N. Cartman.—*Loc. cit.*

17. *Baltimore Afro-American*, July 1, 1944.

18. "We pledge the establishment by federal legislation of a permanent FEPC."

19. The Texas, South Carolina, and Mississippi state organizations threatened to choose their own slates for the electoral college if the convention adopted a racial equality plank.—*Mobile Register*, July 3, 1944.

20. *Loc. cit.*

While permanent FEPC legislation had strong backers in the New Deal-Wallace faction of the party, the tide had turned by 1944 in the direction of greater conservative southern control of the party which made adoption by the convention of a forthright FEPC plank virtually impossible in the face of southern threats to boycott the party if the platform even hinted at racial equality. The result was, said the *Nation*, a plank on racial and religious minorities with a "Southern drawl."[21] The plank expressed the airy sentiment that these minorities have "the right to live, develop, and vote equally with all citizens and share the rights that are guaranteed by our Constitution. Congress should exert its full constitutional powers to protect these rights."[22]

Negro reaction was swift and negative. Said Walter White:

To call the section on the Negro a plank is a misnomer. It is best characterized as a splinter. Badgered by professional bigots from the South and dictated to by Northern political machines more interested in votes than principle, the Democratic mountain labored and brought forth a mouse of evasion by merely asserting that rights guaranteed under the constitution exist and that Congress "should exert its full constitutional powers to protect those rights." When the 14th Amendment was ratified in 1868 it said better what the Democratic platform of 1944 asserts.

While the 1944 presidential campaign was unfolding, hearings by the House Committee on Labor were suspended on August 24. It later developed that both parties had agreed to hold up the bill until after the November election because neither wished to go on record on the issue at this time. National Council representatives sought to reach the White House for weeks in an effort to get President Roosevelt to issue a statement which could be used to bring about resumption of hearings and to make FEPC an issue in the 1944 election.[23] Finally Negro leaders Tobias, White, and Bethune were given an opportunity to confront the President in a White House conference during the course of which the President pledged his support by pointing out that he had "invented FEPC."[24] This constituted the first public indication given by Mr. Roosevelt that he supported a permanent FEPC.

21. 159 (July 29, 1944) p. 114.
22. *Official Proceedings of the Democratic National Convention*, Chicago, Illinois, July 19th to July 21st, inclusive, 1944, pp. 94-95.
23. Interview with Mrs. Hedgeman.
24. *Chicago Defender*, October 7, 1944.

As the campaign moved into high gear presidential and vice-presidential candidates wooed the Negro vote in campaign speeches. In a major address at Chicago on October 28, Mr. Roosevelt declared: "The work of that committee [FEPC] and the results obtained more than justify its creation. . . . I believe that the Congress of the United States should by law make the committee permanent." Vice-presidential candidate Harry S. Truman, running with Mr. Roosevelt, was obliged to defend himself against charges that he was prejudiced against Negroes:

My attention has been drawn to statements attributed to me by a Socialist Party agent and published last week in a few Negro newspapers supporting the Dewey-Bricker ticket.
Without qualification, I brand these alleged statements as false, a deliberate fraud on the Negro people. The purpose of the fraud is clear— to win a few badly needed votes for the hopeless Republican cause. But I know the Negro people and am confident that the fraud will not succeed.
I am a liberal, as proved time and again by my record in the Senate, and I dare anyone to challenge these facts.
I am for a permanent FEPC.
I am for a Federal law abolishing the poll tax.
I am for a Federal anti-lynching law.[25]

Governor Thomas E. Dewey of New York, the Republican candidate for president, also suffered from charges that he was not interested in the welfare of the Negro population. Opponents maintained that Mr. Dewey had delayed favorable action upon FEPC legislation in New York State by appointing commissions to study discrimination in the state, despite the readiness of the legislature to prohibit the discrimination which everyone knew existed.[26] It was

---

25. *Kansas City Plaindealer*, October 27, 1944.
26. "Now that the election campaign is in its final weeks, Governor Dewey's campaign managers out on the prowl to corral the all-important Negro vote are circulating a one-page list of job appointments made by the New York governor in the hope of convincing colored people that the word Dewey is synonymous with jobs. . . .
"What is Dewey's record on this score? Now don't turn crimson, governor!
"Yes, we're talking about the New York State Commission on Discrimination in Employment.
"This is the body that Dewey named to study job discrimination. The commission took its job seriously, came back with two suggested bills to do something about employment bias. Dewey's legislative leaders sidetracked and tabled the measures. Dewey tried to cover up by having a special legislative committee named to 'study' the situation and report back next year.

alleged that Dewey sought to capture the southern "lily-white" Republican delegations to the National Convention before he committed himself on the issue.[27]

Dewey's record in New York caused Negro Republican leaders to urge him to take a forthright stand on FEPC which he finally did in a radio address on October 20.[28] When asked by the *Baltimore Afro-American* to clarify his position on equal opportunities for Negroes, in view of conflicting reports on his views, Dewey backed the Republican platform plank to the hilt:

The custom of hiring colored workers last and of letting them go first because of the color of their skin and without regard to their diligence or abilities is an evil practice which strikes fundamentally at our goal of equal opportunity. This denial of justice and equal opportunity must be stopped.

The platform of my party in these words, pledges a cure for this grave evil: "We pledge the establishment by federal legislation of a permanent FEPC." I unreservedly accept this party promise and have repeatedly pledged its performance.

I consider this commitment most important. It removes artificial barriers to full employment, and hence is imperative. If we are to undercut the prejudice, the bitterness, the discrimination and the segregation to which our colored American citizens have been subjected, we must have an America in which there are jobs and opportunity for everyone, no matter what his color, his creed, or his national origin. . . . My administration will have only one prejudice. It will be prejudiced against injustice."[29]

Nevertheless, before the campaign ended Mr. Dewey was accused by Henry Wallace of "double talk" on the subject of FEPC. According to Wallace, full texts of Dewey's Seattle speech, as carried by the *Memphis Press-Scimitar* and the *St. Petersburg Times*, showed that Dewey had listed the FEPC as one of the bureaus which had "smothered our labor relations." On the other hand, charged Wallace, northern newspapers had carried the statement: "We shall establish the FEPC as a permanent function authorized by law."[30]

"Eight members of the commission resigned in protest. Dewey named another commission to start a 'study' all over again. This outfit has done exactly nothing to date."—Editorial in the *Chicago Defender*, October 21, 1944.

27. *PM*, June 16, 1944 and interview with Mrs. Hedgeman.
28. *Chicago Defender*, October 28, 1944.
29. *Baltimore Afro-American*, October 28, 1944.
30. Apparently what had happened was that "after releasing advance copies of his speech to newspapermen, Dewey inserted a passage declaring he would establish the

The results of the 1944 election do not appear to bear out the widely circulated assertion that the Negro vote was about to desert the Democratic column because of the increasing southern white domination over the party. In keeping with the general trend of the country, Negro support for the Democratic party declined, though the magic appeal of the Roosevelt name for low income and minority voters was sufficient to hold the majority of Negro voters in line.[31]

WHITE HOUSE

Lacking united party support on either side of the aisle in Congress, FEPC supporters frequently turned to the White House for executive leadership to break the numerous log-jams which beset their measure. The President, it was felt, possessed sufficient power and prestige as party leader to be influential with those Democrats who usually voted for social welfare legislation and could perhaps be persuaded to appeal over the heads of congressional opponents to the public for support, after the fashion of the early New Deal days.

President Roosevelt, notwithstanding his claim to FEPC paternity, was difficult to move to action once the issue met with highly vocal opposition by southern representatives in Congress. From his own words, it appears that he regarded this period as one of "Dr. Win-the-War" rather than of "Dr. New Deal" and preferred that no social reform issue be permitted to interfere with prosecution of the war; from his reluctance to intervene in behalf of the legislation it can be deduced that he feared to further antagonize dissident Democrats whose votes were needed to secure enactment of laws and ratification of treaties desired by him. Thus it was that the only public commitment by Roosevelt on permanent FEPC legislation came during the course of the bitterly contested 1944 campaign.

The avenues to the President during the war were of necessity limited. Only after his White House assistants had screened demands

FEPC now operating under executive order as 'a permanent function authorized by law.'"—*Topeka Capitol*, September 19, 1944. If the newspapers carried only the advance release they would not contain the latter reference. However, both the Memphis and St. Petersburg papers contradicted Wallace by claiming that they had carried the supplementary statement on their front pages.—*Rockford* (Illinois) *Register-Republic*, October 30, 1944.

31. Henry Lee Moon, "How the Negroes Voted," *Nation*, 159 (November 25, 1944), 640-41.

for executive action thoroughly and were convinced that top-level action was indicated was it possible for a domestic issue to reach the chief executive in those pressing days. For the most part, National Council representatives found it easier to have friendly congressmen raise the issue with the President than to obtain a personal audience. However, on occasion, FEPC supporters sought to convince the President of the desperate character of Negro morale by having outstanding Negro leaders meet with him in the White House. One such meeting was held in September 1944 and a second was planned in the spring of 1945 when Roosevelt's sudden death intervened. Mrs. Roosevelt, whose sympathies for FEPC were strong, was prominent as a "go-between" in getting information to and from the President and in assisting in arranging meetings with him.[32]

President Harry S. Truman is generally not regarded as strong a "New Dealer" as his predecessor. Yet upon becoming the nation's chief executive, his record on permanent FEPC legislation was superior to that of Roosevelt, perhaps out of zeal to demonstrate his faithful adherence to liberal Democratic principles. On the other hand, even as a senator from Missouri, he had supported the anti-poll tax bills in 1942 and 1944 and had voted in favor of appropriations for the President's Committee on Fair Employment Practice. As vice-president he expressed himself as being in favor of a permanent FEPC with strong enforcement powers.[33]

Upon becoming President in April 1945, Truman continued in his forthright support of FEPC legislation. In conferences with Walter White and Negro newspapermen in May, he indicated that the House of Representatives was the stumbling block and that if FEPC supporters could force the bill through the lower chamber, he could get it through the Senate.[34] On June 6, 1945, Truman addressed a strong letter to Chairman Adolph J. Sabath (Dem. Ill.) of the House Rules

---

32. Memoranda on telephone conversations with Mrs. Roosevelt are found in the National Council's files. This indication of Mrs. Roosevelt's active role in her husband's administration is confirmed by Frances Perkins' recollections in *The Roosevelt I Knew.*

33. The commitment was made during a meeting with a large interracial delegation from Minnesota.—*Little Rock* (Arkansas) *Gazette,* February 28, 1945.

34. *Manuscript,* No. 11, May 28, 1945, and letter from James E. Cook, Co-Chairman of the St. Louis Council to Mrs. Hedgeman, June 5, 1945. It will be observed that the President's suggestion was in keeping with the Democrats' "House first" strategy.

Committee calling for a rule to permit the appropriation for the President's Committee to reach the floor for debate and a vote, in which he took a stand in favor of permanent FEPC legislation:

The war is not over. In fact, a bitter and deadly conflict lies ahead of us. To abandon at this time the fundamental principle upon which the Fair Employment Practice Committee was established is unthinkable.

Even if the war were over, or nearly over, the question of fair employment practices during the reconversion period and thereafter would be of paramount importance. Discrimination in the matter of employment against properly qualified persons because of their race, creed, or color is not only un-American in nature, but will lead eventually to industrial strife and unrest. It has a tendency to create substandard conditions of living for a large part of our population. The principle and policy of fair employment practice should be established permanently as a part of our national law.

On June 19, 1945, Truman telegraphed support to a "Save the FEPC" rally held in New York at Town Hall and extended greetings on June 25 to a crowd of 20,000 attending a "Negro Freedom Rally" in New York, gathered, according to Truman's statement, "to reaffirm their faith in the policies and principles of my lamented predecessor, firm in the conviction that the FEPC which he brought into being, is an instrument to promote national unity."

The climax of Truman's support came on September 6, 1945, when he sent a twenty-one point legislative program for reconversion to a peace-time economy to Congress in which he demanded enactment of a permanent FEPC.[35] The message was hailed by much of the press for its spirit and comprehensiveness although there was general agreement that FEPC was the most difficult to achieve of the twenty-one points.[36] Southern newspapers as a group expressed the opinion that FEPC must be defeated even if the entire program be jeopardized. Editorialized the *Dothan* (Alabama) *Eagle:*

. . . it will jeopardize passage of many phases of his postwar planning program certain phases of which the whole country needs and which it must have if we are going to find anything like smooth sailing in the next few years.

---

35. *Chicago Sunday Bee,* September 16, 1945.
36. Thomas L. Stokes, *New York World-Telegram,* September 7, 1945.

But now the lines have been drawn again. There will be less hesitancy, we believe, to fight the FEPC and retard the program than there was to fight the FEPC and delay vital war appropriations as happened only a few months ago when the FEPC [President's Committee] was finally given a "liquidating" fund which was so large that the agency could remain alive for a long time.

The South wants and needs a lot of things that the President's recommendations to Congress can bring, but it doesn't want them so much that it will bow to establishment of FEPC as a permanent agency.[37]

Throughout this period indications increased that the "era of good feeling" in Congress ushered in with Truman's elevation to the presidency was beginning to pass. Liberals objected to his conservative appointments to high positions and his apparent lack of implementation of his self-proclaimed support of FEPC and other issues; conservatives frowned upon his flirtation with such "radical doctrines" as FEPC.[38] By the fall of 1945 the old coalition of southern Democrats and Republicans against the executive was again in evidence and operating successfully to thwart the President's leadership.

From this time forward, Truman's aggressive support of permanent FEPC legislation declined; holding the party together became a major concern for him as it had been for President Roosevelt. He was criticized increasingly by FEPC proponents for failing to clarify the role of the President's Committee in the reconversion period and for not continuing his early courageous leadership for permanent legislation on the subject.[39] In the end the lack of a working majority in Congress served to limit President Truman's influence over passage of the legislation as it had his predecessor's.

USE OF NEGRO REPUBLICANS

If a pressure group has strong supporters within a party organization who can be depended upon to work in its behalf, the task of winning party support may be simplified. There has been a group of Negro leaders in the Republican party since the Reconstruction Era who

37. September 7, 1945.
38. *Chicago Sun,* July 8, 1945.
39. *Chicago Defender,* September 29, 1945; *New York Amsterdam News,* September 29, 1945; *Manuscript,* No. 35, November 12, 1945; *Manuscript,* No. 37, November 26, 1945; *Manuscript,* No. 40, December 17, 1945; and *Republican News,* December 1945.

consider Republican politics to be their chief preoccupation. Most are leaders of "black and tan" organizations from southern states where the Republican party is weak; others come from northern urban communities where there is a high concentration of Negro voters. The National Council sought to make use of these Negro leaders by appealing to them upon racial grounds to use their influence to further party support of FEPC. Nearly all responded to this plea by performing such tasks as were requested of them by FEPC leaders.

Interviews with Republican leaders were arranged for National Council workers by influential Negro Republicans which helped to give the National Council more bargaining power in these discussions.[40] Also, at the request of the National Council, Negro Republicans dispatched letters and telegrams to party leaders urging support of FEPC legislation and warning that the Negro vote was teetering in the balance. During the battle over cloture in the Senate in January, 1946, Attorney T. Gillis Nutter of Charleston, West Virginia, wrote Senator Chapman Revercomb (Rep. W. Va.):

. . . As you know, I am an uncompromising Republican and I know if you vote against CLOTURE, it is going to rebound against the Republican Party in the next election in this state. Senator Kilgore's very friendly reaction to all measures in which the Negro is interested has been a telling blow against the Republican Party in West Virginia—Negroes feeling that they do not have to be concerned as to how he will vote, as they know, he will react favorably. If you fail to sign petition, it means that we are going to have a big job on our hands at the next election to overcome the disastrous effect, and your refusal will be particularly disastrous when you come for reelection. The Republicans will not be able to carry this state in the next election unless they shall be able to get a large percentage of the Negro vote.[41]

Many Negro Republicans became increasingly concerned as 1945 wore on and their party failed to take the initiative in the FEPC battle. Meeting in New York in August 1945, the Republican American

---

40. For example, Judge Francis Rivers of New York secured an appointment for National Council representatives with ex-Senator John A. Danaher, Legislative Coordinator of the Republican National Committee; National Committeeman Robert Church of Tennessee arranged interviews with other Republican leaders including Senator Robert A. Taft of Ohio. Church was, by far, the most helpful of all the Negro Republicans. Roderick Stephens, Bronx, New York, retail fuel merchant, was very cooperative in making use of his acquaintance with prominent New York Republicans, including Dewey and Brownell, to advance the FEPC cause.

41. January 30, 1946.

Committee, an all-Negro organization headed by National Committeeman Robert Church, passed resolutions calling for immediate passage
of the FEPC bill, implementation of the Atlantic Charter especially as
it applies to Haiti, Liberia, and Ethiopia, and a pledge toward the
"four freedoms."[42] Church later followed up this action by writing
Dewey, National Chairman Herbert Brownell, and the members of
the Republican House Legislative Committee, urging Republican action on FEPC without notable results.[43]

If the experience with FEPC is a typical example, it must be concluded that Negro Republicans have relatively little influence over
top party leadership. Only when party leaders find minority demands
compatible with general party objectives do Negro Republicans carry
weight. Thus, in the case of FEPC, Negro Republicans performed
many useful jobs for the National Council, but their actual achievements in moving party leaders to favorable action on the issue were
not great.

LINING UP INDIVIDUAL CONGRESSMEN

In lining up congressional support for FEPC legislation, National
Council representatives did not distinguish themselves by inventing
new techniques or even by making maximum use of old ones. Nevertheless, some analysis of the successes and failures of the FEPC proponents in dealing with individual congressmen is necessary to indicate how reform pressure groups operate and how our congressmen
react to proposals for social and economic reform.

The first task of any pressure group in dealing with a legislative
body is to separate the "sheep" from the "goats" to narrow the area
of concentration and then to make "sheep" of as many "goats" as possible. To determine the positions of representatives and senators on
FEPC the staff of the National Council engaged in various activities.
First, use was made of poll letters. In October 1944 candidates for
Congress were polled by mail to ascertain whether they would support FEPC legislation. However, because candidates for public office
are notorious for their love for humanity, few indicated opposition to
FEPC.[44] A similar letter was sent out on March 13, 1945, to members

---

42. *Manuscript*, No. 31, October 15, 1945 and *New York Times*, August 26, 1945.
43. October 5, 1945.
44. Some observers regard these pre-election questionnaires as becoming increasingly important: ". . . it is a common practice for pressure groups to question can-

of the House to determine whether they would vote for FEPC in the event that the Rules Committee permitted it to come to the floor.

Far more important were the interviews conducted by National Council legislative representatives and other interested friends with individual congressmen and, on a few occasions, with state delegations in Congress. The telephone was also used extensively to communicate with congressmen and their secretaries. Information from all sources was carefully tabulated and placed upon file cards which were kept up to date throughout the legislative campaigns. These cards also revealed "points of influence," such as church membership or local supporters, who might be used to bring reluctant congressmen into the FEPC column.

If in interviews congressmen proved to be friendly, the National Council representative usually followed the strategy of being frank and of explaining the legislative situation. Sometimes sympathetic congressmen were asked to join in sponsoring the bill; more frequently they were asked to assist by influencing their friends in Congress to support the legislation. In return for support the lobbyists promised to let minority groups in their district know of the congressman's stand.

If a congressman appeared to be undecided, the legislative representatives would offer to explain the bill carefully and to supply literature to clarify doubtful points. These borderline congressmen were carefully sized-up to determine which arguments and which local or national pressures would be most influential in swinging them in favor of the legislation. If the congressman proved unfriendly, it was necessary to determine whether further educational or pressure work was worth undertaking. Congressmen from the Deep South were early crossed off the books as being very unlikely prospects for successful lobbying activities.

LOCAL PRESSURES

At crucial points in the legislative history of the National Council's bill, local supporters were called upon to exert full pressure upon

didates before election with reference to their views on matters of interest to these groups, their replies serving as guides to the members in voting for public officers. These pre-election pledges are becoming more important, as attested by their increased number, the promptness with which legislators respond to them, and the wider publicity which they attract."—Belle Zeller, *Pressure Politics in New York*, p. 237.

their representatives.[45] Nearly every local branch of the National Council sent letters and telegrams to Congress, party leaders, and the President urging action on FEPC. In Easton, Pennsylvania, the Maids and Matrons Club formed itself into a letter-writing committee.[46] More than ninety telegrams were sent to Congress by the Jackson (Mississippi) Council during the crisis over FEPC appropriations in July 1945.[47] Similarly, the Buffalo Council deluged Senator Mead with telephone calls to force more active support of FEPC.[48] Senators Byrd and Chavez received fifty-six telegrams from the Roanoke Council during the 1946 filibuster.[49] Petitions and resolutions were also sent in large numbers.[50]

The National Council furnished its local supporters with information on the positions of their representatives and senators and indicated what special action was necessary to win each one over. For example, after the unsuccessful Senate battle of 1946, analyses for each

45. "When a vote is to be taken, and the moment comes to turn on the elections, it is inspiring to watch a big lobby in operation. Constituents arrive by train, air and motor car. Sometimes they walk, or ride in buggies, or even on high-wheeled bicycles. Telegrams pour in like autumn leaves. Strong men stagger down Senate corridors under bursting sacks of mail. Editorials blossom in the local papers, duly canned for the occasion in crisp, short sentences. The wires and airwaves crackle with radio speeches and long-distance phone calls.

"Young Voters' Leagues, political clubs, Independent Citizens' Committees swing into action, apparently with utter spontaneity. Movie queens, sob sisters, local celebrities get in front of flashlights. The wretched legislator is made dizzy by these activities. A big uprising, he concludes; a Great Big Public Uprising!

"The agent lies low while the uprising is on. Some professionals advise getting out of Washington altogether.

"A modern lobby would be unthinkable without modern technology, specifically telephone, telegraph, radio, rotogravure press and telephoto. The words often fall in the nostalgic cadences of Jeffersonian agriculture, but the technical devices which transmit these cadences are strictly up to date."—Stuart Chase, *Democracy Under Pressure*, pp. 27-28. Chase stresses too much the naïveté of the legislators who in reality become, before very long, blasé about popular demonstrations.

46. NAACP bulletin, "The Outcry," November, 1945, Easton, Pennsylvania.

47. Letter from S. W. Miller, President of the Jackson Council, July 29, 1945.

48. Letter from Mrs. Elizabeth M. Lockett, Secretary of the Buffalo Council, July 3, 1945.

49. Letter from Rev. William J. Simmons, Chairman of the Roanoke Council, July 3, 1945.

50. The New Orleans Council secured endorsement of the resolution it circulated from many groups including the New Orleans CIO Council, the Texas Synod of the Evangelical and Reformed Church (serving Mississippi, Louisiana, Texas and New Mexico), and the New Orleans Committee on Race Relations which included representatives of the local Chamber of Commerce.

state were prepared to show how their senators might be persuaded to use their influence to bring the bill to the floor again that year. Part of the Ohio analysis reads:

Your Senators are answerable to you. How did they vote? Did they confine themselves merely to voting for cloture without challenging the tactics used by the filibustering Southern bloc? Did they take part in the filibuster, or support the filibusterers? Were they on hand for the vote?

Here are the outstanding facts of your Senators' roles with a few suggestions for action in preparation for the next attempt to enact FEPC legislation:

OHIO

Senator JAMES W. HUFFMAN (Democrat)—*Voted for Cloture*
(Senator Huffman has indicated that he is for the bill as well as cloture. However, he did not give any apparent support to the legislation during the 18 days it was on the Senate floor.)
Recommendation: Write Senator Huffman expressing appreciation for his cloture vote. Urge him to undertake an active role in bringing the bill back to the Senate floor and in supporting it after it reaches the floor. Senator Huffman is up for re-election this year. It is important to determine the position of other candidates for the Senate seat, both in the primary and in the general election.

Senator ROBERT A. TAFT (Republican)—*Voted for Cloture*
(Although Senator Taft has openly indicated his opposition to S. 101, he did defend cloture on the Senate floor during the filibuster. He also challenged, together with Senator Barkley, the McKellar ruling blocking the application of cloture to the reading of the Journal.)
Recommendation: Senator Taft should receive letters indicating appreciation of his stand on cloture. In addition, he should be urged to reconsider his position on the legislation in order that the problem of employment discrimination might be met. Ask him to use his influence to bring the bill back to the floor again this session before the problem gets out of hand, and to do what he can toward organizing Republican support behind the bill when it does get back on the floor.

Organization of local delegations to converge upon Washington to secure commitments from individual representatives and senators and to break filibusters and committee log-jams was a major interest of the National Council. The Washington office issued instructions on how to set up a delegation representing a large variety of community groups, when to come to Washington, how to secure publicity for the trip, arrangement of appointments with congressmen, how best to present the case for FEPC during the conference, and other miscellaneous information.[51] Some of the well-planned delegations were successful in securing commitments from their representatives. The Minnesota delegation in 1945 obtained commitments from Senators Ball and Shipstead. Following a visit on February 2, 1945, by a large interracial delegation from Cincinnati, Senator Robert A. Taft's home, the Ohio Senator stopped pushing his own bill, and although he did not support the National Council's measure, he was not counted as a major foe of FEPC legislation thereafter.[52] In other cases worldly-wise congressmen refused to be impressed by what they regarded to be "manufactured" delegations. Taken all in all the results of the work of the delegations when properly planned seems to indicate that the technique is influential to a considerable degree.

USE OF LOCAL BOSSES

An interesting use of the boss of Jersey City, Mayor Frank Hague, to line up an important Democrat was made by the National Council at the beginning of the first session of the 79th Congress in 1945. When it appeared that Rep. Mary T. Norton (Dem. N.J.) was going to back an FEPC bill which differed on some points from the bill sponsored by the National Council, Mrs. Hedgeman communicated with Louis E. Saunders, a prominent Negro attorney in Jersey City, and asked him to get Mayor Hague to exert pressure upon Mrs. Norton to drop her bill and support the National Council's measure. Saunders and other Negro leaders telegraphed Hague:

In behalf of a committee of Colored citizens of the State of New Jersey which is affiliated with the National Council for a Permanent FEPC which

---

51. "Instructions How to Organize Delegations for the Senate Filibuster Period," undated.

52. "I wanted to tell you that despite the fact that Senator Taft voted against S.101 on May 24, it is our feeling here that the favorable action of all the other Republican members of the Committee was in great degree due to your efforts. The emphatic and immediate opposition registered from Ohio to Taft's 'toothless' proposal led him, we feel sure, to abandon any attempt to make his a 'Republican' bill.

"This is a great example to me, at least, of how effective constituents can be when they take the trouble to find out what their legislators are doing and express themselves accordingly.

"My hat is off to the people of the State of Ohio!"—Letter from Mrs. Beatrice B. Schalet, May 31, 1945. See also "Transcript of Conference of Ohio Delegation with Sen. Robert Taft—February 2, 1945."

our great President has publicly promised to make permanent in one of his radio addresses. This bill of vital importance to Colored citizens. Must have Mrs. Norton sponsor the bill and every Democratic member from the State of New Jersey endorse same. Endorsement of this bill by New Jersey Democrats will add substantially to the strength of the Democratic Party throughout the state of New Jersey and the entire Nation.[53]

The speed with which Mayor Hague accomplished this objective reveals much as to why bosses receive strong support in many communities.[54] The following day Hague replied:

Your telegram received requesting me to have Congresswoman Mrs. Mary Norton introduce FEPC bill. I have contacted the Congresswoman and she has agreed to introduce the bill immediately when Congress convenes and to support it. The Democratic Party in New Jersey is solidly behind it. The Democratic Party is honored to be of service in the effort to secure equal justice for your people.[55]

Despite the use of these techniques, sufficient pressure was not generated in the 79th Congress to secure enactment of the desired FEPC legislation. The battle just completed in the 80th Congress was similarly unavailing.

---

53. December 30, 1944.

54. "Few organized groups are so ignorant of practical politics as to fail to appreciate the role and influence of that 'invisible' yet all too visible agency of government: the American political boss. Exceptional indeed is the pressure group which would hesitate to approach the political leaders responsible for the nomination and election of the men and women who sit in our State Legislature. This has been universally recognized as one of the most practical and realistic ways of obtaining results. The 'boss' in American politics is thus widely courted by individuals and groups with the noblest, as well as the most ignoble, purposes."—Belle Zeller, *op. cit.*, p. 238.

55. Telegram to Mr. Fred Martin, December 31, 1944.

CHAPTER **14** *Retrospect and Prospects*

THE STORY OF THE NATIONAL COUNCIL FOR A
Permanent FEPC's efforts to secure the passage of national legislation to eliminate discrimination in employment by bringing pressures to bear upon Congress from a wide variety of groups serves to
illustrate what Professor E. E. Schattschneider has called the "law of
imperfect political mobilization of interests." While the armchair
political strategist assumes that basic harmony and agreement upon
fundamental policies and strategy prevail within organized pressure
groups, analysis leads us to conclude that rarely is this the case in
real life.

Reform movements, no less than the powerful economic pressure
drives, fail to exert maximum influence in politics because of internal
shortcomings and divisions, as well as the counter activities of opposing groups. The National Council was certainly no exception to this
general rule. Notwithstanding widespread interest in the FEPC cause,
catalyzed by wartime experience with discrimination and the President's Committee's efforts to check it, efforts to secure favorable
congressional action have thus far been unavailing.

The reasons for this failure, as recounted in this study, are complex.
Internal difficulties revolving about A. Philip Randolph, the Chairman,
are central in any explanation of the lack of success at the time of
writing. Starting first with the National Council's staff, confidence
in Randolph's generalship was not great, with consequent adverse
effect upon staff morale. Also Randolph's preoccupation with a multitude of activities deprived the movement of the day-to-day leadership
so essential in a swiftly moving campaign. Furthermore, his disinclina-
tion to share planning responsibilities, his ideological intransigence,
and his general personality qualities alienated many groups and individuals who should, by reason of their interests, have been in the fore-
ground of the battle.

The National Council also suffered from the inexperience of its staff which had to learn the ropes of pressure politics as it went along, sometimes to the detriment of the issue. The staff must share with Randolph much of the responsibility for the failure to involve existing reform groups more fully in the campaign and for the limited and poor quality of the propaganda appeals. Lack of adequate finances explains part, but not all, of these shortcomings.

To its credit is the imaginative effort to stir up strong local support for the issue through use of the local council device. The effort was a drain upon the limited resources of the National Council, yet the educational value of the local council experience, especially in the South, will smooth the path for future attempts to secure local support for this issue and others of the same type. The theory of reaching congressmen through their own constituents is thoroughly sound although the execution of the idea must, for success, be better planned and better financed than was that of the National Council.

The reasons for the Randolph organization's lack of funds are also somewhat involved. The nature of the issue certainly served to limit contributions from many donors who had contributed large amounts to reform causes in the past but who were convinced of neither the feasibility nor the desirability of such a measure. Yet even more important were the failures of the National Council to evolve a campaign plan which could win the confidence of would-be supporters and the organizational rivalries engendered by some of the short-sighted policies of the FEPC coordinating group. In short the National Council was faced with a dilemma: it needed money to carry out its program and, at the same time, money failed to flow in because of wide dissatisfaction with the organization's program and leadership.

Part II of this study has been written with the thought that one can gain more insight into the field of reform politics by analyzing the impact of a single issue upon a wide cross-section of organizations and social groups than by making a detailed structural study of individual organizations. Nothing lays bare the strengths and weaknesses of organized groups better than the dynamics of a legislative campaign in which special demands are made upon organizations professing interest in the issue involved. Only in the heat of battle can the "letter-head" aspirations of the hundreds of reform pressure groups be tested.

The FEPC movement affords an unusual opportunity to view reform politics in action; few social action groups could ignore the moral implications of this drive to secure economic justice for so large a segment of our population; few were not asked to aid the legislative drive within the limits of their organizational abilities. Upon their performances can they be judged.

Negro organizations, notwithstanding the very considerable contributions of some of the groups discussed, fell short of making a contribution to the movement which was commensurate with their organizational strength and their vital stake in the issue. Rivalry for leadership among Negroes, organizational and ideological struggles, general lack of faith in the National Council for a Permanent FEPC, and distrust of its motives split and debilitated Negro strength. Some small solace can be found in the fact that important Negro groups have rarely been successfully united and activated in political movements requiring extended planning and work. Still FEPC offered a better than average opportunity for united action which was not capitalized upon.

Other groups defending minority rights proved no more effective than Negro organizations. Many of the Jewish, as well as civil libertarian, groups revealed a "billboard" psychology which holds that "fair play" exhortations in the form of advertisements, lectures, pamphlets, and the like will be sufficient to safeguard minority interests. In the case of some groups, this attitude is the result of timidity, in others the tax exempt character of their operating funds prevents sizeable expenditures for politics, and in still others an outmoded conception of how attitudes are formed and changed and how minority rights are best advanced is responsible.

Obviously, the task of activating such organizations politically can only be accomplished by the most skillful of pressure politicians. The National Council's preoccupation with the Negro phase of FEPC, and other shortcomings already discussed, prevented it from succeeding in this delicate undertaking. Contributions of modest sums of money made up the most tangible evidence of interest and support of FEPC by many of these groups.

Despite the churches' awakening interest in interracial activity, they have much to learn yet about working together in common causes. Institutional and doctrinal differences have divided the churches in politics as well as in religion. In addition there is evidence of a broad gap between the church leaders who support measures aimed at ameliorating conditions for racial and other minorities and the lay churchgoers who, for the better part, have yet to be fully convinced of the merits of such programs. Churches, like other organizations, must reach their own members before they can expect to reach the makers of public policy.

The record of labor organizations on FEPC can be interpreted largely in terms of self-interest, sometimes but not always intelligent. The split in the American labor movement, in a sense, worked to the FEPC issue's advantage. Without the competing presence of the CIO, it is doubtful whether the AFL's position could have been changed from an extremely unfriendly one to one which was at least publicly non-antagonistic. Competition for both moral leadership of the labor movement and increased membership proved salutary. In the end the great tragedy of the labor aspect of the movement was the failure to fully involve the resources of the CIO in the campaign. In less than a decade and a half the CIO has emerged as the leader of liberal forces in America; its progressive leadership and sizeable resources have given it a pre-eminent role whenever it has joined with other groups in a common cause. Yet, as described in the chapter on organized labor, the CIO contributed no more money or energy than did many lesser organizations.

The conflict with the Communists and their sympathizers is a familiar story in liberal movements. Those who are not acquainted with the details of the ideological battle may see little reason for the intense antagonism between groups which can agree on so many immediate reforms which they would like accomplished. Differences of opinions as to proper ends and means bulk so large that many reform movements have been irreparably split by them. The leaders of the National Council were old hands at ideological controversy; it was as natural as breathing for them to vigorously oppose any and all Communist efforts to share in the FEPC movement. To say that the two groups should have worked together better is to ignore basic motivations beyond easy control; one can merely observe that the FEPC movement suffered because of the conflict.

The outstanding feature of the opposition to FEPC during the period studied was its lack of formal organization. No group comparable to the National Council arose to fight the efforts to secure FEPC legislation. Nevertheless, this did not mean that opposition was absent. Public apathy, ignorance of the implications of the issue, fear of upsetting existing social statuses, and fear of further government regulation of business were great handicaps in putting FEPC legislation across. Especially was this true when these feelings were manipulated by die-hard congressmen, aided by the filibuster device in the Senate and the all-powerful Rules Committee in the House.

Finally, study of the FEPC movement reveals a dangerous inflexibility in the public opinion industry which makes it increasingly difficult for the causes of "little men" to gain a general public hearing. Except for the specialized press, which has a limited circulation, the doors of radio and the general press are almost closed to those who promote minority causes unless they have the resources to pay their own way. The result is that minority movements must make use of less effective techniques, such as the mass meeting and the "throwaway," to reach the public. The question of whether to impose controls upon the press and radio to secure a fair hearing for causes which may be unpopular with the operators of media of communication is not new, but a detailed examination of the experiences of one such minority group serves to dramatize the necessity for a solution of the problem if the status quo is not to crystallize and afford minorities no opportunity to become majorities, contrary to democratic theory.

No examination of the FEPC question would be complete without some reference to the merits of the proposed measure. Can a federal FEPC actually accomplish the things which its proponents maintain? The best bases for judgment are the experiences with the wartime President's Committee on Fair Employment Practice and the FEPC's in states where strong legislation has been enacted.

What was the President's Committee able to accomplish in its lifetime? It is not possible to make a precise evaluation because of the presence of immeasurable factors such as the war itself and the accompanying tight labor market; still comparison of statistics on the employment of Negroes before and after the application of the nondiscrimination principle is indicative of some success. During the life of the President's Committee discrimination in the federal government service declined substantially. In the District of Columbia, Negroes constituted only 8.4 per cent of the total number of government employees in 1938, while by 1942 the proportion had risen to 17 per cent. A survey undertaken by the Committee in 1944 revealed that Negroes made up roughly 12 per cent of all persons in the federal service as contrasted with 9.8 per cent in 1938.[1] Even more significant is the fact that in 1938 about 40 per cent of the Negro government employees were classified as "custodial," while by 1944 the figure had dropped to approximately 23 per cent.

In industrial employment Negroes constituted fewer than 3 per cent of all war workers in early 1942. By late 1944 the proportion of non-white workers had risen to 8.3 per cent.[2] A study by the President's Committee of firms which had been charged with discrimination, to determine whether they were complying with "cease and desist" orders, revealed a larger percentage of non-whites employed by them in January 1944 than when the complaints had been made. Thirty-one companies involved in four public hearings before the issuance of Executive Order 9346 employed only 1.5 per cent non-whites at the time of their hearings, but by the winter of 1943-44 non-whites comprised 5.1 per cent of all employees in these companies.[3] These compliance studies further disclosed that in five out of eight industries examined, the companies under surveillance for previous discrimination showed greater proportionate increases in non-white employment than did other firms in the same industries.

Since the experience with the President's Committee, more than a half-dozen states have enacted FEPC legislation, ranging from laws with strong enforcement powers, as in New York, Massachusetts, Connecticut, and New Jersey, to those giving state officials authority merely to investigate charges of discrimination, as in Indiana and Wisconsin. Minneapolis, Milwaukee, and Chicago now have FEPC ordinances and other cities are giving consideration to adoption of similar provisions.

1. J. A. Davis, C. L. Golightly, and I. W. Hemphill, "The Wartime Employment of Negroes in the Federal Government," Committee on Fair Employment Practice, January 1945 (mimeographed), pp. 21-25.

2. *First Report*, p. 65.

3. *Ibid.*, pp. 66, 70-1. Chapter VII of this report contains other examples of the Committee's effectiveness.

In the states having laws with "teeth" the record has been good. The much-feared controls over the employer's freedom to select his own workers have not produced the dangerous situations predicted by opponents. Employers have not had to hire incompetents or crackpots, nor have they had to dismiss white employees to make room for Negroes. The fact that no decision from any state commission had been appealed to the courts at the time of writing is a tribute to their skill in negotiating satisfactory adjustments of complaints at the conference level. Nearly all of the commissions have placed much emphasis upon educating employers rather than upon prosecuting them. While discrimination in these states is far from eradicated, it is possible to say that some inroads are being made into the economic manifestations of prejudice.

It is foolhardy to prognosticate the future of federal FEPC legislation. Some steps have been taken to improve the prospects for victory. The bill pushed in the second session of the 80th Congress sought to meet some of the more specific criticisms directed at its predecessors by limiting coverage to employers of fifty or more workers, by providing more adequate procedures for appeals from the commission's decisions, and by calling for an extensive educational program as part of the commission's work. This may help to satisfy those whose failure to support the bill in earlier years was due to criticism of the form of the bill rather than of the issue itself. Also the National Council has been reorganized with Elmer Henderson as executive secretary and efforts have been made to include representatives of major reform organizations in top planning for the campaign.

The moral right of minorities to fair treatment is being brought home repeatedly by such declarations as the Atlantic Charter, resolutions by the International Labor Organization and the Economic and Social Council of the United Nations, and in November 1947 by the report of the President's Committee on Civil Rights. The political expediency of fair treatment for minorities is indicated by experience with recent uprisings of colonial peoples and the fates of European countries professing but not practicing democracy. In the end, however, adequate planning and machinery for political pressure will be more important than moral claims in securing the passage of a federal FEPC.

Bibliography

Bibliography

BOOKS

Baker, Paul E. *Negro-White Adjustment, An Investigation and Analysis of Methods in the Interracial Movement in the United States.* New York: Association Press, 1934. Pp. 267.

Bentley, Arthur F. *The Process of Government.* Chicago: The University of Chicago Press, 1908. Pp. 501.

Brazeal, Brailsford R. *The Brotherhood of Sleeping Car Porters.* New York: Harper & Bros., 1946. Pp. 258.

Cayton, H. R. and Mitchell, G. S. *Black Workers and the New Unions.* Chapel Hill: University of North Carolina Press, 1939. Pp. 473.

Chase, Stuart. *Democracy Under Pressure.* New York: The Twentieth Century Fund, 1945. Pp. 142.

Crawford, Kenneth G. *The Pressure Boys.* New York: Julian Messner, Inc., 1939. Pp. 308.

Detweiler, Frederick G. *The Negro Press in the United States.* Chicago: The University of Chicago Press, 1922. Pp. 274.

Drake, St. Clair and Cayton, Horace. *Black Metropolis.* New York: Harcourt, Brace & Co., 1945. Pp. 809.

Fauset, Arthur Huff. *Black Gods of the Metropolis.* Philadelphia: University of Pennsylvania Press, 1944. Pp. 126.

Greene, L. J. and Woodson, C. G. *The Negro Wage Earner.* Washington: The Association for the Study of Negro Life and History, Inc., 1930. Pp. 388.

Herring, E. Pendleton. *Group Representation Before Congress.* Baltimore: The Johns Hopkins Press, 1929. Pp. 304.

Johnson, Charles S. and associates. *To Stem This Tide.* Boston: The Pilgrim Press, 1943. Pp. 142.

———. *Patterns of Negro Segregation.* New York: Harper & Brothers Publishers, 1943. Pp. 332.

Johnson, James Weldon. *Negro Americans, What Now?* New York: The Viking Press, 1934. Pp. 103.

Karpf, Maurice J. *Jewish Community Organization in the United States.* New York: The Bloch Publishing Company, 1938. Pp. 234.

Key, V. O. Jr. *Politics Parties and Pressure Groups.* New York: Thomas Y. Crowell Company, 1942. Pp. 814.

Linfield, Harry S. *The Communal Organization of the Jews in the United States, 1927.* New York: The American Jewish Committee, 1930. Pp. 191.

Logan, Edward B., ed. *The American Political Scene.* New York: Harper & Brothers Publishers, 1936. Pp. 264.

Logan, Rayford W., ed. *What the Negro Wants.* Chapel Hill: The University of North Carolina Press, 1944. Pp. 352.

Lyons, Eugene. *The Red Decade.* New York: The Bobbs-Merrill Company, 1941. Pp. 423.

Mays, Benjamin Elijah and Nicholson, Joseph William. *The Negro's Church.* New York: The Institute of Social and Religious Research, 1933. Pp. 321.

McKean, Dayton David. *Pressures on the Legislature of New Jersey.* New York: Columbia University Press, 1938. Pp. 251.

Northrup, Herbert R. *Organized Labor and the Negro.* New York: Harper & Brothers Publishers, 1944. Pp. 312.

Odegard, Peter H. *Pressure Politics, The Story of the Anti-Saloon League.* New York: Columbia University Press, 1928. Pp. 299.

———. *The American Public Mind.* New York: Columbia University Press, 1930. Pp. 308.

Perkins, Frances. *The Roosevelt I Knew.* New York: The Viking Press, 1946. Pp. 408.

Pierce, James E. *The National Association for the Advancement of Colored People—A Study in Social Pressure.* Unpublished M.A. thesis, The Ohio State University, 1933. Pp. 198.

Spero, S. D. and Harris, A. *The Black Worker.* New York: Columbia University Press, 1931. Pp. 509.

Sterner, Richard. *The Negro's Share.* New York: Harper & Brothers Publishers, 1943. Pp. 433.

Weaver, Robert C. *Negro Labor.* New York: Harcourt, Brace and Company, 1946. Pp. 329.

Woodson, Carter Godwin. *The History of the Negro Church.* Washington, D. C.: The Associated Publishers, 1921. Pp. 330.
Zeller, Belle. *Pressure Politics in New York.* New York: Prentice-Hall, Inc., 1937. Pp. 310.

PERIODICAL ARTICLES

Alexander, Will W. "Our Conflicting Racial Policies," *Harper's Magazine,* 190 (January, 1945), 172-79.
"Arms and the Manpower," *Fortune,* XXV (April, 1942), 73-75, 182-86.
Beecher, John. "8802 Blues," *New Republic,* 108 (February 22, 1943), 248-50.
———. "Meat-Axing Manpower," *New Republic,* 108 (March 29, 1943), 406-8.
Brown, Earl. "American Negroes and the War," *Harper's Magazine,* 184 (April, 1942), 545-52.
Curti, Merle. "The Changing Pattern of Certain Humanitarian Organizations," *The Annals of the American Academy of Political and Social Science,* 179 (May, 1935), 59-67.
Daniels, Jonathan. "A Native at Large," *Nation,* 152 (February 8, 1941), 158.
"Deep South Looks Up, The," *Fortune,* XXVIII (July, 1943), 95-100, 218-25.
Granger, Lester B. "A Hopeful Sign in Race Relations," *Survey Graphic,* XXXIII (November, 1944), 455-6, 476-7, 479.
"Half a Million Workers," *Fortune,* XXIII (March, 1941), 96-98, 163-66.
Hard, William. "Whites and Blacks Can Work Together," *Reader's Digest,* 44 (March, 1944), 17-22.
Harris, Edward A. "The Negro Faces November," *New Republic,* 111 (August 28, 1944), 241-43.
Henningburg, Alphonse. "Adult Education and the National Urban League," *Journal of Negro Education,* XIV (Summer Number, 1945), 396-402.
Huddle, Frank P. "Fair Practice in Employment," *Editorial Research Reports,* 1 (January 18, 1946), 1-51.
Hunt, Brace A. "The Proposed Fair Employment Practice Act: Facts and Fallacies," *Virginia Law Review,* 32 (December, 1945), 1-38.
"Jobs and Workers," *Survey,* LXXIX (November, 1943), 309-10.
Johnson, Guy B. "Negro Racial Movements and Leadership," *American Journal of Sociology,* XLIII (July, 1937), 57-71.
Kallen, Horace M. "National Solidarity and the Jewish Minority," *The*

Annals of the American Academy of Political and Social Science, 223 (September, 1942), 17-28.

Liveright, A. A. "The Community and Race Relations," *The Annals of the American Academy of Political and Social Science*, 244 (March, 1946), 106-116.

Martin, Ralph G. "FEPC Rally," *New Republic*, 114 (March 18, 1946), 379-81.

Maslow, Will. "FEPC—A Case History in Parliamentary Maneuver," *University of Chicago Law Review*, 13 (June, 1946), 407-44.

———. "The Law and Race Relations," *The Annals of the American Academy of Political and Social Sciences*, 244 (March, 1946), 75-81.

McWilliams, Carey. "Race Discrimination—And the Law," *Science & Society*, IX (Winter, 1945), 1-24.

Mezerik, A. G. "Dixie in Black and White," *Nation*, 164 (March 22, 1947), 324-27.

Moon, Henry Lee. "How the Negroes Voted," *Nation*, 159 (November 25, 1944), 640-41.

Morison, James. "White Only," *New Masses*, XXXVII (December 31, 1940), 15.

"Municipal Interracial Councils," *The American City*, LIX (August, 1944), 74.

"Negro, His Future in America, The," *New Republic*, Special Supplement (October 18, 1943), 535-50.

"Negro's War, The," *Fortune*, XXV (June, 1942), 77-80, 157-64.

Northrup, Herbert R. "Let's Look at Labor, V. Union, Restricted Clientele," *Nation*, 157 (August 14, 1943), 178-80.

Ottley, Roi. "Negro Morale," *New Republic*, 195 (November 10, 1941), 613-15.

Silberman, Henry R. "How We Won in Massachusetts," *New Republic*, 115 (July 8, 1946), 10-11.

Trent, Jr., W. J. "Federal Sanctions Directed Against Racial Discrimination," *Phylon*, III (Second Quarter, 1942), 171-82.

Weaver, Robert C. "An Experiment in Negro Labor," *Opportunity*, 14 (October, 1936), 295-8.

———. "Detroit and Negro Skill," *Phylon*, IV (Second Quarter, 1943), 131-43.

———. "Racial Policy in Public Housing," *Phylon*, 1 (Second Quarter, 1940), 149-61.

Wechsler, James A. "Pigeonhole for Negro Equality," *Nation*, 156 (January 23, 1943), 121-22.

White, Alvin E. "Four Freedoms (Jim Crow)," *Nation*, February 21, 1942, 154 (February 21, 1942), 213-14.

Wilkerson, Doxey. "FEPC—The Alphabet of Hope," *New Masses*, XLV (October 20, 1942), 4-8.

Williams, Charles. "Harlem at War," *Nation*, 156 (January 16, 1943), 86-88.

Wilson, Abraham. "The Proposed Legislative Death Knell of Private Discriminatory Employment Practices," *Virginia Law Review*, 31 (September, 1945), 798-811.

U. S. GOVERNMENT RELEASES, REPORTS, MONOGRAPHS, ETC.

Congressional Record, 1944-47.

Economic Power and Political Pressure, Monograph No. 26, Investigation of Concentration of Economic Power, Temporary National Economic Committee, 76th Congress, 3d Session. Washington: U. S. Government Printing Office, 1941. Pp. 222.

Federal Register, 1941-45.

Hearings Before a Subcommittee of the Committee on Education and Labor, United States Senate, Seventy-Eighth Congress, Second Session, on S. 2048, August 30, 31, September 6, 7, and 8, 1944. Pp. 231.

Hearings Before a Subcommittee of the Committee on Education and Labor, United States Senate, Seventy-Ninth Congress, First Session, on S. 101 and S. 459, March 12, 13 and 14, 1945. Pp. 189.

Labor Supply and Demand in Selected Defense Occupations Through the Period May-November 1941, Bureau of Employment Security, U. S. Social Security Board, September 1941.

Negro Newspapers and Periodicals in the United States: 1943, Negro Statistical Bulletin No. 1, U. S. Dept. of Commerce, Bureau of the Census, August, 1944.

President's Committee on Fair Employment Practice, *Releases*.

President's Committee on Fair Employment Practice, *Report of—Confidential*, May 1943. Pp. 93.

President's Committee on Fair Employment Practice, *First Report, July 1943-December 1944*, 1945. Pp. 152.

YEARBOOKS, DIRECTORIES, ETC.

American Jewish Year Book, 1944.

American Year Book, 1943, 1944, 1945.

Directory of Agencies in Race Relations, Chicago, Julius Rosenwald Fund, 1945. Pp. 124.
Negro Handbook—1942.
Official Proceedings of the Democratic National Convention, Chicago, July 19th to 21st, 1944. Pp. 399.
Statistical Abstract of the United States, 1944-45.

PAMPHLETS

Cohen, J. X. *Helping to End Economic Discrimination, Second Report on Jewish Non-Employment,* presented to the adjourned session of the American Jewish Congress, Washington, D. C., November 28, 1937 and reprinted by the American Jewish Congress, New York. Pp. 15.
—— *Who Discriminates—And How?,* American Jewish Congress, undated. Pp. 31.
Duffy, John F., Jr., *State Organization for Fair Employment Practices,* Legislative Problems Number One, Bureau of Public Administration, University of California, December, 1944. Pp. 25.
Raushenbush, Winifred, *Jobs Without Creed or Color,* Workers Defense League, 1945. Pp. 32.
United Automobile Workers, *A Bill of Rights for All UAW Members.*
—— *Order Creating: UAW-CIO Fair Practices Committee.*
—— *A Manual on Fair Employment Practices.*
—— *To Unite. . . . Regardless.*
—— *To Stamp Out Discrimination—A Handbook.*

NEWS LETTERS, ORGANIZATIONAL

PERIODICALS, ETC.

Capitol Letter, Fraternal Council of Negro Churches.
Catholic Action, Monthly publication of the National Catholic Welfare Conference.
Committee Reporter, American Jewish Committee.
Common Ground, Common Council for American Unity.
Information Service, Federal Council of the Churches of Christ in America.
International Labor Defense Legislative Service.
Interracial Review, Monthly publication of the Catholic Interracial Council.
Manuscript, Washington news letter specializing in Negro news.
Monthly Summary of Events and Trends in Race Relations, publication of the Social Science Institute of Fisk University.

News Letter, American Council on Race Relations.
News Letter, Anti-Defamation League of B'nai B'rith.
Southern Patriot, Southern Conference for Human Welfare.

REPORTS, MANUALS AND SPECIAL STUDIES

American Council on Race Relations Programs Under Way. Chicago: American Council on Race Relations, (mimeographed) August 22, 1946.
Confidential Report on Ives-Quinn Hearings, New York. Chicago: American Council on Race Relations, (mimeographed), undated.
Davis, J. A., Golightly, C. L., and Hemphill, I. W. "The Wartime Employment of Negroes in the Federal Government." Washington: President's Committee on Fair Employment Practice, (mimeographed) January, 1945.
Findings and Principal Addresses. Hampton, Virginia: The Hampton Institute Conference on the Participation of the Negro in National Defense, November 25-26, 1940.
From War to Peace—American Liberties, Annual Report of the American Civil Liberties Union, July, 1946.
In Support of Fair Employment Practice, A History of Four Years of Activities of the Metropolitan Detroit Fair Employment Practice Council, January 1942-December 1945. Detroit: Metropolitan Detroit Fair Employment Practice Council, 1945.
Liberty on the Home Front in the Fourth Year of War, Annual Report of the American Civil Liberties Union, July, 1945.
Manual for Official Committees. Chicago: American Council on Race Relations, 1945.
Manual of Practical Political Action. New York: National Citizens Political Action Committee, edited by Frank, Jr., Lewis C. and Shikes, Ralph E., 1946.
March on Washington Movement. Proceedings of Conference Held in Detroit, September 26-7, 1942.
Negro Platform Workers. Chicago: American Council on Race Relations.
"Reasons for the United Packinghouse Workers Favoring the Creation by Congress of a Permanent Fair Employment Practice Commission, as Provided in S. 101," a mimeographed statement submitted by the United Packinghouse Workers to the Subcommittee of the Senate Committee on Education and Labor, March 13, 1945.
Report of the National CIO Committee to Abolish Discrimination, November, 1946.

State FEPC—What the People Say, American Council on Race Relations, 1945.

"Statement of Objectives," New York Metropolitan Council on Fair Employment Practice," November 23, 1945.

Unfinished Business, A Fair Employment Practice Handbook. Detroit: Metropolitan Detroit Council on Fair Employment Practice, January 12, 1944.

ENCYCLOPAEDIA ARTICLES

Harris, Abram L. and Spero, Sterling D. "Negro Problem," *Encyclopaedia of the Social Sciences,* XI, 335-55.

Schmidt, Richard, "Leadership," *Encyclopaedia of the Social Sciences,* IX, 282-86.

NEWSPAPERS

Atlanta Journal
Atlanta World
Baltimore Afro-American
Birmingham News
Chicago Sun
Chicago Sunday Bee
Daily Worker
Dothan (Alabama) *Eagle*
Fort Wayne (Indiana) *News-Sentinel*
Kansas City Plaindealer
Little Rock (Arkansas) *Gazette*
Los Angeles Sentinel
Louisville Courier-Journal
Louisville Defender
Minneapolis Times
Mobile Register

Montgomery (Alabama) *Advertiser*
New York Amsterdam News
New York Times
New York UE News
New York World-Telegram
Norfolk (Virginia) *Journal and Guide*
Pasadena (California) *Independent*
People's Voice
Philadelphia Independent
Philadelphia Tribune
Pittsburgh Courier
PM
Rockford (Illinois) *Register-Republic*
Washington Afro-American
Washington Daily News
Washington Post

Index

www.ingramcontent.com/pod-product-compliance
Lightning Source LLC
Chambersburg PA
CBHW020342270326
41926CB00007B/282